Lecture Notes in Computer Science 14623

Founding Editors

Gerhard Goos
Juris Hartmanis

W0235098

The series Lecture Notes in Computer Science (LNCS), including its subseries Lecture Notes in Artificial Intelligence (LNAI) and Lecture Notes in Bioinformatics (LNBI), has established itself as a medium for the publication of new developments in computer science and information technology research, teaching, and education.

LNCS enjoys close cooperation with the computer science R & D community, the series counts many renowned academics among its volume editors and paper authors, and collaborates with prestigious societies. Its mission is to serve this international community by providing an invaluable service, mainly focused on the publication of conference and workshop proceedings and postproceedings. LNCS commenced publication in 1973.

Yaqi Wang · Xiaodiao Chen · Dahong Qian ·
Fan Ye · Shuai Wang · Hongyuan Zhang
Editors

Semi-supervised Tooth Segmentation

First MICCAI Challenge, SemiToothSeg 2023
Held in Conjunction with MICCAI 2023
Vancouver, BC, Canada, October 8, 2023
Proceedings

 Springer

Editors
Yaqi Wang (iD)
Communication University of Zhejiang
Hangzhou, China

Xiaodiao Chen
Hangzhou Dianzi University
Hangzhou, China

Dahong Qian
Shanghai Jiao Tong University
Shanghai, China

Fan Ye
Hangzhou Dianzi University
Hangzhou, China

Shuai Wang
Hangzhou Dianzi University
Hangzhou, China

Hongyuan Zhang (iD)
Shenzhen University
Shenzhen, China

ISSN 0302-9743   ISSN 1611-3349 (electronic)
Lecture Notes in Computer Science
ISBN 978-3-031-72395-7   ISBN 978-3-031-72396-4 (eBook)
https://doi.org/10.1007/978-3-031-72396-4

Preface

This volume contains the proceedings of the international challenge on Semi-supervised Teeth Segmentation (STS 2023), held in conjunction with the International Conference on Medical Image Computing and Computer Assisted Intervention (MICCAI) in 2023. By "proceedings", we mean to say that this volume contains the papers written by participants in the STS challenge to describe their solutions for automatic teeth segmentation using the official training dataset released for this purpose.

Panoramic X-ray image and dental cone-beam computed tomography (CBCT) examination are the efficient ways for dentists to determine invisible caries, impacted teeth and supernumerary teeth among children. However, identifying teeth from panoramic X-ray images or dental CBCT scans and further manually annotating the teeth is time-consuming and labor-intensive. Thus, we usually cannot obtain a huge number of labeled cases. As a potential alternative, semi-supervised learning can explore useful information from unlabeled cases.

This challenge aimed to promote the development of teeth segmentation in panoramic X-ray images and dental CBCT scans. Specifically, the challenge consisted of two rounds: the preliminary and the final. In the preliminary round, 2,000 panoramic X-rays and 212 CBCT scans were provided as training data, with 500 panoramic X-rays and 10 CBCT scans for evaluation. In the final round, a total of 3,000 dental panoramic X-ray images and 312 CBCT volumes were provided as training data, with 1,000 dental panoramic X-ray images and 50 CBCT volumes provided as the test set. The segmentation algorithm was expected to accurately segment teeth regions using deep learning approaches. Besides, the segmentation inference results were evaluated using Dice Similarity Coefficient (DSC), Intersection over Union (IoU), and Hausdorff Distance (HD). All metrics were used to compute the ranking.

Finally, 434 teams participated in the preliminary stage across both tracks, of which 64 teams advanced to the finals. Participants in the final also submitted their methodology papers on the OpenReview platform. Each paper received three to five single-blind reviews. Based on the initial reviews and the authors' revisions and responses, we accepted 16 papers. These proceedings provide the state-of-the-art methods for semi-supervised teeth segmentation. We thank all the participants, reviewers, and program committee whose incredible work made this possible.

November 2023

Yaqi Wang
Xiaodiao Chen
Dahong Qian
Fan Ye
Shuai Wang
Hongyuan Zhang

Organization

Program Committee Chairs

Yaqi Wang   Communication University of Zhejiang, China
Xiaodiao Chen   Hangzhou Dianzi University, Hangzhou, China
Dahong Qian   Shanghai Jiao Tong University, China
Shuai Wang   Hangzhou Dianzi University, China
Fan Ye   Hangzhou Dianzi University, China
Hongyuan Zhang   Shenzhen University, China

Program Committee

Yunxiang Li   University of Texas Southwestern Medical Center, USA
Patrice Monkam   Northeastern University, China
Taolin Qin   Brown University, USA

Organization

Program Committee Chairs

Contents

Convolutional Neural Network-Based Multi-scale Semantic Segmentation for Two-Dimensional Panoramic X-Rays of Teeth

Qixuan Wang[1]($\boxtimes$)(ib), Yangzheng Zhao[2], and Zhuofan Zhang[3]

[1] China Academy of Information and Communications Technology,
Beijing 100191, China
wqx_2008@163.com
[2] School and Hospital of Stomatology, Shanxi Medical University,
Taiyuan, Shanxi, China
[3] School of Computer Science and Statistics, Trinity College Dublin,
Dublin 2, D02 PN40 Dublin, Ireland

Abstract. In this study, we propose a semantic segmentation framework based on convolutional neural networks (CNNs) aimed at segmenting teeth in 2D panoramic radiographs. To enhance the model's performance, we adopt a data augmentation strategy based on the combination of Mosaic and multi-scale image scaling, which significantly enriches the training set samples. Additionally, we propose a post-processing strategy based on the model's prediction probability map to address the issue of inaccurate points predicted by the model. The proposed framework is tested and evaluated on 2D panoramic radiographs, including 1000 unlabeled radiographs. The Dice coefficient, Intersection over Union (IoU), and $1 - H(d)$ achieve 0.9341, 0.9814, and 0.0244, respectively, resulting in a total score of 0.9607, ranking fifth on the leaderboard. This demonstrates the superiority of the proposed framework in tooth segmentation of 2D panoramic radiographs.

Keywords: Tooth segmentation · Panoramic x-ray · MICCAI challenge

1 Introduction

The importance of maintaining optimal oral health and preserving natural teeth has become increasingly evident in contemporary society [7]. Meanwhile, healthy teeth significantly enhance the quality of life [8]. Oral health is closely linked to overall health. The World Health Organization has recognized it as one of the ten fundamental criteria for human health.

Dental caries, periodontitis, and tooth loss represent common dental diseases that individuals may experience. Dental caries, in particular, is the most prevalent oral disease [1]. It manifests as cavities in the teeth caused by the erosion of tooth

Y. Wang et al. (Eds.): STS 2023, LNCS 14623, pp. 1–13, 2025.
https://doi.org/10.1007/978-3-031-72396-4_1

enamel due to plaque [6, 27]. In advanced stages, dental caries can result in nerve damage, leading to increased sensitivity to thermal stimuli and severe pain.

It is crucial to underscore that cavity-induced damage is irreversible and may lead to tooth loss if not timely addressed. Therefore, early detection and treatment of dental caries are imperative to prevent irreversible harm and maintain optimal oral health [5].

When encountering a patient with dental caries or other oral conditions, a dentist's foremost goal is to promptly assess the disease's severity and choose the most suitable treatment tailored to the patient's specific needs. Early intervention is crucial for reducing patient discomfort and averting additional oral health deterioration. While the severity of these conditions may differ, medical imaging techniques afford dentists a precise and comprehensive view of the patient's oral health status.

By examining medical images of teeth, dentists can determine the proximity of roots to nerves, assess the risks of tooth extraction, verify the accuracy of root canal treatments [2], identify any remaining roots in gaps of extracted teeth, and ascertain the correct placement of implants, among other evaluations. Beyond traditional medical imaging methods such as CT and X-rays, intraoral cameras and optical coherence tomography have become essential in contemporary dentistry. These technologies facilitate real-time imaging of intraoral surfaces and tissues, enabling early detection of dental issues and tracking the progress of treatments. These imaging techniques provide detailed views of specific oral cavity areas, offering extensive information about the condition of teeth, gums, and adjacent tissues.

However, in areas with constrained medical capabilities, dentists' proficiency in interpreting medical images is limited. Consequently, there is a pressing necessity for a viable approach to aid dentists in the interpretation and analysis of oral medical imagery.

In recent years, computer-aided diagnosis based on artificial intelligence has developed rapidly, and deep learning models have been widely used in medical image segmentation [14, 24, 25]. Artificial intelligence methods have shown better performance in automatic dental segmentation. Since 2012, deep convolutional neural networks (CNNs) have been used for the segmentation of anatomical structures. For instance, mask region-based CNNs (e.g., Mask R-CNN [9]) provide a powerful framework for predicting the segmentation masks for each region of interest, enabling object detection, segmentation, and classification. In tooth segmentation, Silva et al. [20] first tried the Mask R-CNN for automatic tooth segmentation on panoramic radiography. However, their results did not accurately detect the tooth structure. In contrast, Wirtz et al. [21] obtained ground truth by manually annotating individual tooth morphology on 10 panoramic images, and their results outperformed those of Silva et al. [20]. There are also several works exploring tooth segmentation based on U-Net [12, 18] or fully convolutional networks (FCN) [11, 19] . However, with the rapid development of deep learning, these works have not experimented with the most recent models, potentially leading to limited segmentation accuracy. Additionally, due to the diversity of tooth morphology, these studies do not adequately consider the effect of different morphologies on the segmentation performance of the models.

In this paper, we propose a multi-scale segmentation method based on CNNs to solve the tooth segmentation task based on 2D panoramic images (STS challenge) in the MICCAI 2023 Challenges. Our main contributions can be summarized as follows:

- We employ UperNet [22] as the architecture for the segmentation network and replace the backbone network with ConvNeXt-XL [16], which demonstrates improved segmentation results compared to other baseline models.
- To address the issue of teeth with varying shapes and sizes, we propose a training strategy based on multi-scale learning. This strategy enhances the model's robustness by allowing it to learn features at different scales. The effectiveness of this method is verified through ablation experiments.
- To further enhance the model's prediction performance, we propose a post-processing method based on the model's prediction probability map. Through pixel-by-pixel analysis, we adjust the pixel values of points with prediction probabilities lower than the set threshold to 0 (i.e., the background). This method significantly improves the accuracy of the predicted results.

2   Method

2.1   Preprocessing

In order to perform cross-validation, for the primary and final labeled data, we implemented the same 5-fold division strategy based on scikit-learn [17], where one fold of data is used as the validation set for each training, and the remaining four folds are used as the training set for model training. After obtaining five training results, the division with the optimal result was taken, and the training images of this fold were rotated by 180° and added to the training set. Notably, unlabeled images were not used in our method.

2.2   Proposed Method

Model Architecture. We used UperNet [22] to solve this semantic segmentation task. The model structure is shown in Fig. 1. The idea of UperNet is mainly derived from Feature Pyramid Network (FPN) [15], considering that different objects and scenes often require different levels of features.The FPN algorithm can take advantage of the characteristics of each level of the deep convolutional network, and then give full consideration to the semantic information of each level, which is conducive to improving the network performance. In addition, due to the superiority of ConvNeXt on image segmentation tasks in recent years [16], we replaced the backbone network with ConvNeXt-XL, whose four-stage outputs were fed into the feature pyramid of the superhead, where the fourth stage had to go through the Pyramid Pooling Module (PPM) to fuse the multi-scale features extracted by ConvNeXt. Additionally, we sent the feature mapping output from the third stage into the auxiliary head FCN for deep supervision to optimize feature extraction and gradient propagation.

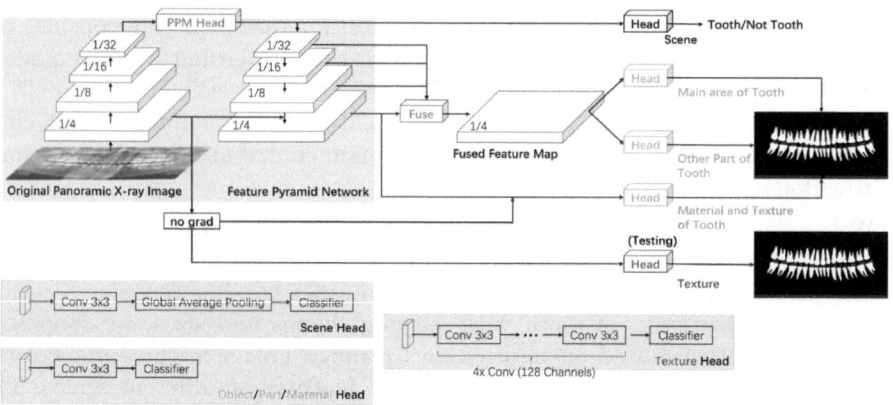

Fig. 1. The model architecture of our proposed method, which is based on UperNet.

Loss Function. We used a cross-entropy loss function to supervise the training process:

$$L = -\sum_{c=1}^{M} y_c log(p_c) \tag{1}$$

where M denotes the number of categories and y_c is a one-hot vector with only 0 and 1 elements. If the category is the same as that of the sample, it takes 1, otherwise it takes 0. p_c denotes the probability of predicting that the sample belongs to category c. however, when only the foreground and background need to be segmented and the number of foreground pixels is smaller than the number of background pixels, the loss function with $y = 0$ component of the loss function becomes dominant, making the model heavily biased towards the background and leading to poor segmentation. Therefore, we adopt a cross-entropy loss function with category weights:

$$L = -\sum_{c=1}^{M} w_c y_c log(p_c) \tag{2}$$

where $w_{background}$ was set to 0.8 and w_{tooth} was set to 1.0, which worked best in our experiments.

2.3 Post-processing

In the post-processing stage, firstly, we used test time augmentation. Specifically, for each of the images, we first scaled it with $[0.125, 0.25, 0.5, 0.75, 1.0, 1.25, 1.5, 1.75, 2.0]$ respectively. We then performed vertical flip and horizontal flip once for all the scaled images. Next, we aggregated the inference results of the flips at each scale and finally aggregated the inference results of all scales for this image to get the inference result of that image.

Algorithm 1. Proposed post-processing algorithm

Input: *Raw predicted probability map* M; *Raw predicted segmentation mask* m;
Output: *Refined predicted segmentation mask* m';
 1: **for all** $i = 0, 1, \cdots, 319$ **do**
 2:     **for all** $j = 0, 1, \cdots, 639$ **do**
 3:       $p_{i,j} = max(M[i,j][0], M[i,j][1])$;
 4:       **if** $p_{i,j} < 0.6$ **then**
 5:         $m[i,j] = 0$;
 6:       **end if**
 7:     **end for**
 8: **end for**
 9: $m' = m$;
10: **return** m'.

Second, we proposed a post-processing method based on predicted probability maps. During the inference stage, each image had a prediction probability matrix of size $(2, 320, 640)$, meaning that each pixel point had two probabilities for belonging to the dental region and not belonging to the dental region, with the sum of the probabilities being 1. We defined the points where the model is "unconfident" as pixel points where the maximum value of the model's prediction probability is less than 0.6. Upon examining all the predictions, we observed that most of the "unconfident" points were located in the border region of the tooth. Therefore, our post-processing method involved iterating through all the pixel points in the probability matrix for each image. If the maximum value of the predicted probability of a point was less than 0.6 (i.e., a "non-confident" point), we changed the pixel value of that point to 0 (i.e., the background), while keeping the remaining points as predicted. This approach also improved the final prediction. The reason for setting the threshold at 0.6 is that, for a predictive probability matrix, each pixel point has two probabilities of belonging to the tooth region and not belonging to the tooth region with a sum of 1. Therefore, if the maximum of the two probabilities of a point is less than 0.6, this means the difference in two probabilities is less than 0.2, and we consider that the model has a high level of uncertainty about this point. The algorithm flow is as follows:

3 Experiments

3.1 Dataset

Medical image segmentation relies heavily on the quality and diversity of datasets, which ensures the correctness of deep learning model training. In view of these challenges, we express our gratitude to the organizers who provided the finely labeled datasets [28] in this competition, which has significantly advanced deep learning in the field of oral medicine, particularly in the development of X-ray image segmentation. This dataset consists entirely of dental panoramic X-ray images, all of which are 640×320 pixels in size and have a density resolution of 16-bit grayscale. The size of the teeth in the images depends not only on

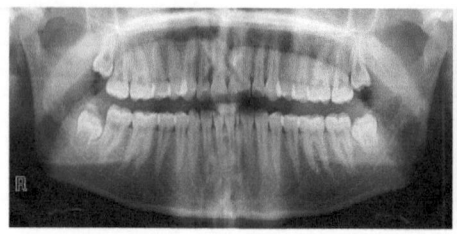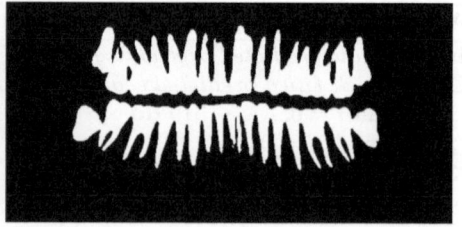

Fig. 2. Example of a panoramic dental x-ray image and labeling in this dataset. The white areas in the labeled images are teeth.

Table 1. Distribution of datasets at different stages.

Stage	Preliminary			Final		
	Train	Validation	Test	Train	Validation	Test
5-fold (first training)	1600	400	500	720	180	1000
best fold (retraining)	3200	400	500	1440	180	1000

the image size but also on the imaging position of the patient. Labeled images of tooth regions were generated by manually labeling all tooth regions as shown in Fig. 2.

The competition dataset was divided into two parts: the preliminary dataset and final dataset. The preliminary dataset consists of 2500 dental panoramic images, of which 2000 contain pixel-level annotations (i.e., training set) and the remaining 500 contain no annotations (i.e., test set). The final dataset consists of 4000 panoramic images of teeth, of which 900 contain pixel-level annotations (i.e., training set), 2100 have no pixel-level annotations (i.e., unlabeled dataset), and the remaining 1000 are the test set. The detailed data distribution is shown in Table 1.

3.2   Evaluation Metrics

The Dice coefficient, Intersection over Union (IoU) and 2D Hausdorff Distance (HD) were used to measure the segmentation effect in this competition.

Dice coefficient is an ensemble similarity measure function which is usually used to calculate the similarity of two samples and takes values in the range of [0,1]:

$$Dice = \frac{2 \times |A \cap B|}{|A| + |B|} \tag{3}$$

where $|A \cap B|$ is the intersection between A and B, and the $|A|$ and $|B|$ sub-tables denote the number of elements of A and B, where the coefficient of the numerator is 2 because of the presence of the denominator that double counts the common elements between A and B.

IoU is used to describe the degree of overlap between the labeled region and the predicted region and takes values in the range of [0,1]:

$$IoU = \frac{(A \cap B)}{(A \cup B)} \tag{4}$$

The 2D Hausdorff distance is the minimum distance between two shapes or curves obtained by the Hausdorff transform:

$$H(d) = min(|x_1 - x_2| + |y_1 - y_2|) \tag{5}$$

where (x_1, y_1) and (x_2, y_2) denote the coordinates of the two pixel points, and $|x_1 - x_2|$ and $|y_1 - y_2|$ denote the distance on the corresponding axes. This formula represents the sum of the absolute distances between two pixel points on the horizontal and vertical axes in a two-dimensional medical image, i.e., the Hausdorff distance at the pixel level.

For scoring purposes, the competition uniformly normalized the Hausdorff distance to a value between 0 and 1. The final weighted average of the three metrics was taken and the specific scoring formula was:

$$score = 0.4 \times Dice + 0.3 \times IoU + 0.3 \times (1 - H(d)) \tag{6}$$

3.3   Implementation Details

Environment Settings. Code writing, training, and inference were performed on the CentOS 7 operating system. The CPU used is an Intel(R) Xeon(R) Gold 6240 CPU at 2.60 GHz, 2.59 GHz. 32GB of RAM is available. The system is equipped with five NVIDIA Tesla T4 16G GPUs.The CUDA version installed on the system is 11.2.The programming language used for development is Python 3.7.The deep learning frameworks used include PyTorch 1.10.1, torchvision 0.11.2.

Training Protocols. Given the small size of the datasets, we focused our data augmentations on increasing data diversity. Specifically, firstly, given that most of the teeth showed vertical growth, we rotated all training set images offline by 180°C and saved them, greatly expanding the number of training sets. Second, we introduced Mosaic data augmentation, which randomly crops the input four images with 50% probability, and then stitches them into one image as input. Considering the different sizes and lengths of teeth, we also introduce multi-scale scaling training, rescaling the input image size keeping the aspect ratio as one of $[40 \times 80, 80 \times 160, 160 \times 320, 320 \times 640, 480 \times 960, 512 \times 1024, 640 \times 1280]$. This greatly expanded the diversity of the datasets and made the model robustness enhanced. Notably, unlabeled images were not used in our experiments.

Other training protocols: In the training phase, we introduced a pixel-based online hard sample mining strategy, where pixel-valued points with confidence scores below 0.9 were used for training and at least 100,000 pixel-valued points

Table 2. Training protocols.

Network initialization	ImageNet
Batch size	2
Total iterations	80000
Optimizer	AdamW with betas (0.9, 0.999)
Initial learning rate (lr)	8e-5
Weight decay	5e-2
Lr decay schedule	LinearLR (0–1500 iteration); PolyLR (1500–80000 iteration)
Training time	10.5 h
Loss function	Weighted Cross Entropy Loss

Table 3. Performance of the proposed segmentation model on the validation set.

Method	Validation Set		
	Dice(%)	IoU(%)	HD(mm)
Our Model	94.98 ± 1.72	94.03 ± 2.58	0.0231 ± 0.0175

are retained during training. We used the weights trained on ImageNet to initialize the model parameters. The batch size for training was set to 2, and the initial learning rate was 8e-5. The optimizer was AdamW, betas were set to (0.9, 0.999), and weight decay was set to 5e-2. The training process lasted for 80,000 iterations, with linear learning rate for the first 1,500 iterations, and then the polynomial learning rate adjustment strategy was used, as shown in Table 2. Finally, if the average Dice coefficient of the model in the validation set did not increase after 10 iterations, the training was stopped and the model weight with the highest average Dice coefficient on the validation set was saved.

4   Results and Discussion

4.1   Quantitative Results on Validation Set

The metrics of the proposed model on the validation set are shown in Table 3.

4.2   Qualitative Results on Validation Set

Good Segmentation Cases. Figure 3 shows some examples of the proposed baseline model with good segmentation results on the validation set.

Failure Case Analysis. The difficulties encountered in the segmentation of the proposed baseline model mainly stem from the segmentation of the tooth details, especially in the marginal regions of the teeth, which is framed with red

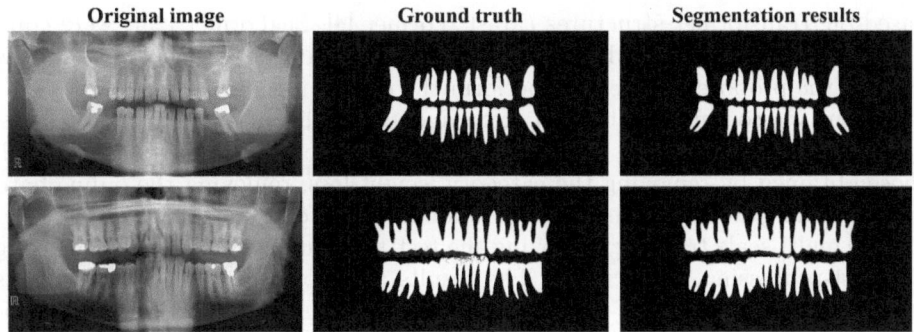

Fig. 3. Good segmentation results on the validation set. The model produces the segmentation mask for teeth instances.

circles and rectangles in Fig 4. This shows that although the proposed model is close to the doctor's annotation in terms of the overall segmentation effect of most images, the segmentation of the detail parts of some images is still not precise enough, which may affect the application of the model in the clinic. In the future, we will consider adopting a more advanced model for fine segmentation or applying post-processing techniques such as CRF [13] to refine the segmentation results.

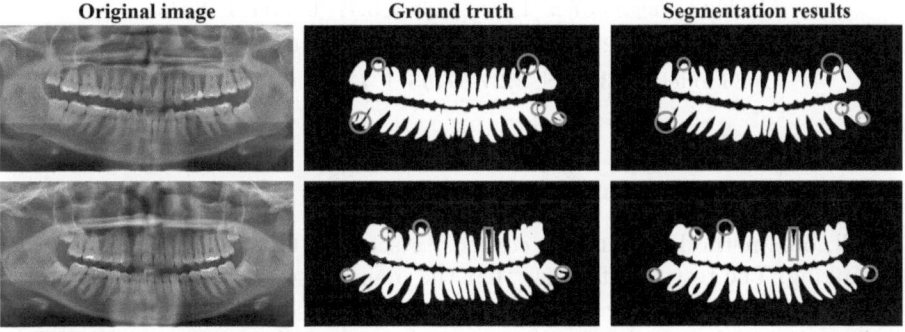

Fig. 4. Failure segmentation results on the validation set. Inaccuracies in the segmentation results are marked with red circles and rectangles. (Color figure online)

4.3 Results on Final Testing Set

We performed inference and ablation experiments on a final test set containing 1000 unlabeled panoramic dental radiographs to validate the effectiveness of the proposed model architecture and methodology. We compared the proposed baseline model with classical semantic segmentation models (DeepLabv3+ [3], PointRend [10]), classical medical image segmentation models (U-Net [18]), and up to the end of the competition with the latest semantic segmentation models based on Transformer structures (Mask2Former [4], SegFormer [23]) were comprehensively compared and the results are shown in Table 4. The results show that all the proposed models outperform the other model architectures.

Then, we conducted ablation experiments on the proposed key methods, specifically, the test results obtained using all the methods were compared with those obtained by removing the category weight loss, removing the online hard sample mining method, removing the random mosaic data augmentation, removing the multi-scale training, removing the test-time augmentation, and removing the post-processing, respectively. The results are shown in Table 5. The results show that removing any of the methods degrades the model results, which indicates the effectiveness of our proposed method. In addition, removing multi-scale training has the greatest impact on the model results, which indicates that multi-scale training provides the greatest model performance enhancement.

Table 4. Comparison of segmentation results of different key methods. The best results are shown in bold.

Method	Final Testing Set		
	Dice(%)	IoU(%)	HD(mm)
DeepLabv3+	92.51 ± 2.86	86.19 ± 4.67	0.0254 ± 0.0196
PointRend	92.91 ± 3.99	86.96 ± 5.37	0.0252 ± 0.0348
U-Net	90.68 ± 5.55	83.29 ± 6.93	0.0532 ± 0.0801
Mask2Former	93.07 ± 4.04	87.23 ± 5.47	0.0311 ± 0.0435
SegFormer	92.51 ± 3.94	86.25 ± 5.25	0.0308 ± 0.0438
Our Model	**93.22 ± 3.27**	**87.65 ± 4.98**	**0.0251 ± 0.0199**

4.4   Discussion, Limitation and Future Work

Overall, our method obtained a composite score of 0.9607 and ranked fifth in the ranking. The test results show that the main reason for the excellent performance of our model is the combination of UperNet and ConvNeXt-XL, which benefits from the powerful feature extraction capability of ConvNeXt-XL and the multi-task segmentation capability of UperNet, and ultimately outperforms other model combinations. In addition, the multi-scale training strategy, mosaic data augmentation, test-time augmentation, and the proposed post-processing strategy all improve the robustness of the model to varying degrees and provide ideas for subsequent research.

Despite the excellent performance of our model, there are still some limitations. First, although we tried some semi-supervised segmentation strategies [26], the final score is still not as good as the fully supervised method, and how to effectively utilize unlabeled data to further improve the segmentation effect of the model is the focus of our future research. Second, although the proposed test time enhancement as well as post-processing strategies improved the final score

Table 5. Comparison of segmentation results of different baseline models. The best results are shown in bold.

Method	Final Testing Set		
	Dice(%)	IoU(%)	HD(mm)
Results (without category weight loss)	93.08 ± 5.07	87.33 ± 6.25	0.0249 ± 0.0455
Results (without online hard sample mining)	93.01 ± 5.07	87.21 ± 6.25	0.0248 ± 0.0454
Results (without random mosaic)	93.10 ± 5.09	87.38 ± 6.28	0.0252 ± 0.0454
Results (without multi-scale training)	92.41 ± 6.19	86.35 ± 8.27	0.0256 ± 0.0460
Results (without test-time augmentation)	93.01 ± 3.55	87.11 ± 5.13	0.0253 ± 0.0240
Results (without post-processing)	92.80 ± 3.51	87.20 ± 4.82	0.0255 ± 0.0299
Results (all)	**93.41 ± 5.07**	**87.93 ± 6.28**	**0.0244 ± 0.0255**

of the model, the inference time of the model also increased by about 10 times. This may increase the difficulty of clinical application of the method. Therefore, in future work, we will explore how to reduce the model inference time without significant loss of inference accuracy in order to generalize the method to clinical applications.

5   Conclusion

In this study, we propose a semantic segmentation framework based on CNNs aimed at segmenting teeth in 2D panoramic radiograph. In order to improve the model performance, we propose a novel data augmentation strategy based on the combination of Mosaic and multi-scale image scaling and a post-processing strategy based on the model prediction probability map to improve the accuracy of the model prediction. The results of ablation experiments show that all the training strategies and post-processing strategies enhance the model prediction results. We believe that our method can reduce the workload of dentists, improve the accuracy of diagnostic results, and facilitate the development of computer-aided dental panoramic radiograph analysis in the future.

Acknowledgements. The authors of this paper declare that the segmentation method they implemented for participation in the STS 2023 challenge has not used any pre-trained models nor additional datasets other than those provided by the organizers. The proposed solution is fully automatic without any manual intervention. We thank all the data owners for making the X-ray images and CT scans publicly available and Alibaba Cloud for hosting the challenge platform.

References

1. Ambikathanaya, U.K., Swamy, K.R., Gujjari, A.K., Tejaswi, S., Shetty, S., Ravi, M.B.: Effect of acrylic removable partial denture in caries prevalence among diabetic and non-diabetic patients. J. Pharm. Bioallied Sci. **14**(Suppl 1) (2022). https://journals.lww.com/jpbs/fulltext/2022/14001/effect_ of_acrylic_removable_partial_denture_in.209.aspx

2. Ballikaya, E., Koc, N., Avcu, N., Cehreli, Z.C.: The quality of root canal treatment and periapical status of permanent teeth in Turkish children and teens: a retrospective CBCT study. Oral Radiol. **38**(3), 405–415 (2022)
3. Chen, L.C., Zhu, Y., Papandreou, G., Schroff, F., Adam, H.: Encoder-decoder with atrous separable convolution for semantic image segmentation. In: Ferrari, V., Hebert, M., Sminchisescu, C., Weiss, Y. (eds.) Computer Vision - ECCV 2018, pp. 833–851. Springer International Publishing, Cham (2018)
4. Cheng, B., Misra, I., Schwing, A.G., Kirillov, A., Girdhar, R.: Masked-attention mask transformer for universal image segmentation. In: 2022 IEEE/CVF Conference on Computer Vision and Pattern Recognition (CVPR), pp. 1280–1289 (2022). https://doi.org/10.1109/CVPR52688.2022.00135
5. Di Stefano, M., Polizzi, A., Santonocito, S., Romano, A., Lombardi, T., Isola, G.: Impact of oral microbiome in periodontal health and periodontitis: a critical review on prevention and treatment. Int. J. Mol. Sci. **23**(9) (2022)
6. Estes Bright, L.M., Garren, M.R.S., Ashcraft, M., Kumar, A., Husain, H., Brisbois, E.J., Handa, H.: Dual action nitric oxide and fluoride ion-releasing hydrogels for combating dental caries. ACS Appl. Mater. Interfaces **14**(19), 21916–21930 (2022). https://doi.org/10.1021/acsami.2c02301
7. Goh, V., Hassan, F.W., Baharin, B., Rosli, T.I.: Impact of psychological states on periodontitis severity and oral health-related quality of life. J. Oral Sci. **64**(1), 1–5 (2022)
8. Hajek, A., König, H.H.: Oral health-related quality of life, probable depression and probable anxiety: evidence from a representative survey in Germany. BMC Oral Health **22**(1), 9 (2022)
9. He, K., Gkioxari, G., Dollár, P., Girshick, R.: Mask r-CNN. In: 2017 IEEE International Conference on Computer Vision (ICCV), pp. 2980–2988 (2017). https://doi.org/10.1109/ICCV.2017.322
10. Kirillov, A., Wu, Y., He, K., Girshick, R.: Pointrend: image segmentation as rendering. In: 2020 IEEE/CVF Conference on Computer Vision and Pattern Recognition (CVPR), pp. 9796–9805 (2020). https://doi.org/10.1109/CVPR42600.2020.00982
11. Koch, T.L., Perslev, M., Igel, C., Brandt, S.S.: Accurate segmentation of dental panoramic radiographs with u-nets. In: 2019 IEEE 16th International Symposium on Biomedical Imaging (ISBI 2019), pp. 15–19 (2019). https://doi.org/10.1109/ISBI.2019.8759563
12. Krois, J., et al.: Generalizability of deep learning models for dental image analysis. Sci. Rep. **11**(1), 6102 (2021)
13. Lafferty, J.D., McCallum, A., Pereira, F.C.N.: Conditional random fields: probabilistic models for segmenting and labeling sequence data. In: Proceedings of the Eighteenth International Conference on Machine Learning, pp. 282–289. ICML '01, Morgan Kaufmann Publishers Inc., San Francisco, CA, USA (2001)
14. Li, C., et al.: Dcsegnet: deep learning framework based on divide-and-conquer method for liver segmentation. IEEE Access **8**, 146838–146846 (2020). https://doi.org/10.1109/ACCESS.2020.3012990
15. Lin, T.Y., Dollár, P., Girshick, R., He, K., Hariharan, B., Belongie, S.: Feature pyramid networks for object detection. In: 2017 IEEE Conference on Computer Vision and Pattern Recognition (CVPR), pp. 936–944 (2017). https://doi.org/10.1109/CVPR.2017.106
16. Liu, Z., Mao, H., Wu, C.Y., Feichtenhofer, C., Darrell, T., Xie, S.: A convnet for the 2020s. In: 2022 IEEE/CVF Conference on Computer Vision and Pattern Recognition (CVPR), pp. 11966–11976 (2022). https://doi.org/10.1109/CVPR52688.2022.01167

17. Pedregosa, F., et al.: Scikit-learn: machine learning in Python. J. Mach. Learn. Res. **12**, 2825–2830 (2011)
18. Ronneberger, O., Fischer, P., Brox, T.: U-net: convolutional networks for biomedical image segmentation. In: Navab, N., Hornegger, J., Wells, W.M., Frangi, A.F. (eds.) Medical Image Computing and Computer-Assisted Intervention - MICCAI 2015, pp. 234–241. Springer International Publishing, Cham (2015)
19. Shelhamer, E., Long, J., Darrell, T.: Fully convolutional networks for semantic segmentation. IEEE Trans. Pattern Anal. Mach. Intell. **39**(4), 640–651 (2017). https://doi.org/10.1109/TPAMI.2016.2572683
20. Silva, G., Oliveira, L., Pithon, M.: Automatic segmenting teeth in x-ray images: Trends, a novel data set, benchmarking and future perspectives. Expert Syst. Appl. **107**, 15–31 (2018)
21. Wirtz, A., Mirashi, S.G., Wesarg, S.: Automatic teeth segmentation in panoramic x-ray images using a coupled shape model in combination with a neural network. In: Frangi, A.F., Schnabel, J.A., Davatzikos, C., Alberola-López, C., Fichtinger, G. (eds.) Medical Image Computing and Computer Assisted Intervention - MICCAI 2018, pp. 712–719. Springer International Publishing, Cham (2018)
22. Xiao, T., Liu, Y., Zhou, B., Jiang, Y., Sun, J.: Unified perceptual parsing for scene understanding. In: Ferrari, V., Hebert, M., Sminchisescu, C., Weiss, Y. (eds.) Computer Vision - ECCV 2018, pp. 432–448. Springer International Publishing, Cham (2018)
23. Xie, E., Wang, W., Yu, Z., Anandkumar, A., Alvarez, J.M., Luo, P.: SegFormer: simple and efficient design for semantic segmentation with transformers. In: Advances in Neural Information Processing Systems (NeurIPS) (2021)
24. Xu, X., et al.: Attention mask R-CNN with edge refinement algorithm for identifying circulating genetically abnormal cells. Cytometry A **103**(3), 227–239 (2023)
25. Xu, X., et al.: A lightweight and robust framework for circulating genetically abnormal cells (CACS) identification using 4-color fluorescence in situ hybridization (fish) image and deep refined learning. J. Digit. Imaging **36**(4), 1687–1700 (2023)
26. Yang, L., Qi, L., Feng, L., Zhang, W., Shi, Y.: Revisiting weak-to-strong consistency in semi-supervised semantic segmentation. In: Proceedings of the IEEE/CVF Conference on Computer Vision and Pattern Recognition (CVPR), pp. 7236–7246 (2023)
27. Zhang, P., et al.: Dual-sensitive antibacterial peptide nanoparticles prevent dental caries. Theranostics **12**(10), 4818–4833 (2022)
28. Zhang, Y., et al.: Children's dental panoramic radiographs dataset for caries segmentation and dental disease detection. Sci. Data **10**(1), 380 (2023)

TB-FPN: Enhancing Tooth Segmentation with Cascade Boundary-Aware FPN

Xinxu Cai[ID], Yisong Zhang[ID], Zeyuan Guan[ID], Qi Sun[ID],
and Zhenshen Qu[✉][ID]

Harbin Institute of Technology, Harbin, CN, China
{23s004026,23s004040,23s004079,23s121074}@stu.hit.edu.cn, ocicq@126.com

Abstract. The semi-supervised deep learning algorithm for effective tooth segmentation greatly simplifies the consultation process for dentists, reduces the occurrence of misclassification and missed diagnoses, and improves the efficiency of medical work. To achieve this, we propose a Tooth Boundary-aware Feature Pyramid Network (TB-FPN), a semi-supervised deep learning method applied to tooth image segmentation. This method aims to significantly improve the segmentation capability of tooth structures by integrating boundary information, effectively addressing the challenges in tooth segmentation tasks. We utilized this method on the validation set of the dental panoramic radiographs dataset using NVIDIA 3060 for tooth segmentation. The average Dice score is 91.75%, the average IoU score is 97.70%, and the average Hausdorff distance (HD) error is 0.0250. The code is available at https://github.com/Dew026/TB-FPN.git.

Keywords: Segmentation · TB-FPN · Dental panoramic radiographs

1 Introduction

Dental diseases not only lead to serious oral problems but may also have adverse effects on other organs, thereby impacting overall health [7]. In current medical practice, the treatment of dental diseases still relies mainly on the dentist's on-site judgment, combined with panoramic X-rays and consultation diagnosis, to formulate corresponding treatment plans. However, as clinical practice deepens, many patients exhibit multiple dental diseases, which pose significant challenges for comprehensive analysis of etiology and precise planning of treatment strategies for dentists. Therefore, an effective deep learning algorithm for tooth segmentation would greatly simplify the diagnostic process for dentists, reduce the occurrence of misclassification and missed diagnoses, and thus improve the efficiency of medical work.

Currently, most advanced segmentation models typically employ deep and wide network structures, and their strong generalization capability often relies on large-scale and high-quality pixel-level annotated data [11]. However, manual pixel-level annotation of medical images is a time-consuming process, which hinders the practical application of deep segmentation models in clinical and healthcare settings. Therefore, it is crucial to build a powerful and robust segmentation model that can learn from limited annotated data and existing unlabeled data for the successful application of deep learning models in clinical use and healthcare.

The most common methods for semi-supervised medical image segmentation include utilizing general strategies such as image augmentation to expand the training data. For example, Panfilov et al. [10] employed Mixup image augmentation during training and tested its effectiveness in knee joint MRI segmentation, resulting in improved model robustness. Chaitanya et al. [3] proposed learning-based generative networks that synthesize new samples by simultaneously learning and applying realistic spatial deformation fields and additive intensity transformation fields from labeled and unlabeled data. Additionally, some researchers have addressed semi-supervised segmentation problems by incorporating prior domain knowledge into the segmentation model as strong regularization terms [14]. Dong et al. [5] introduced a deep graph network that includes a lightweight registration network and a multi-level information consistency constraint. For semi-supervised 3D segmentation of renal arteries, He et al. [8] proposed using multi-scale semantic features extracted from unlabeled data using autoencoders to assist the segmentation network. Furthermore, transfer learning is also a commonly used general strategy, but its reliability depends on the similarity of external large benchmark datasets. When transferring from natural image benchmark datasets to medical datasets, the advantages of transfer learning are not always significant due to relatively low data similarity [12].

In addition to the aforementioned methods, there are also numerous approaches that make full use of unlabeled data, such as self-training [1], adversarial learning [6], self-supervised learning [4], and consistency regularization [2]. Self-training directly increases labeled data by pseudo-labeling unlabeled data. Self-supervised learning follows a "pre-training, fine-tuning" process but performs model pre-training in an unsupervised or self-supervised manner on the current unlabeled data. On the other hand, consistency regularization introduces unsupervised losses on unlabeled data, which are learned together with supervised losses on labeled data.

In our current research, we selected a dental panoramic radiographs dataset derived from the STS 2023 challenge. Considering the limitations of tooth segmentation tasks, especially in dealing with fine-grained segmentation of tooth boundaries, we propose an innovative solution called the Cascade FPN based on tooth boundary information(TB-FPN). This network architecture aims to significantly improve the segmentation capability of tooth structures by integrating boundary information, effectively addressing the challenges in tooth segmentation tasks.

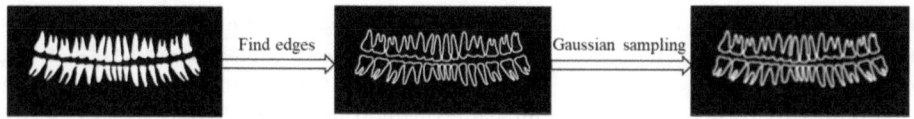

Fig. 1. The process of generating boundary information heatmaps for teeth.

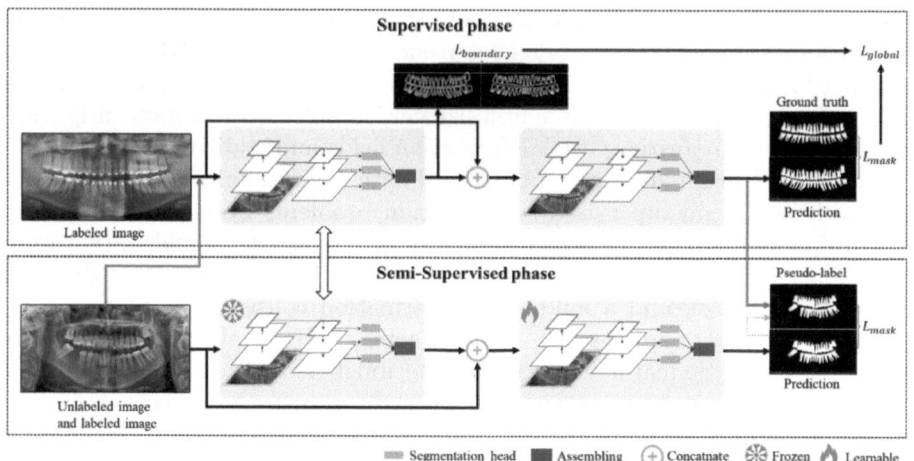

Fig. 2. The network structure of proposed TB-FPN. In the fully supervised phase, TB-FPN predicts the boundary information and segmentation mask of annotated tooth images, and predict pseudo labels for unlabeled images, which are then input into the semi-supervised part. In the semi-supervised phase, we predict the segmentation mask for unlabeled tooth images and iteratively update the pseudo labels.

2 Method

2.1 Pre-processing

Considering that all the tooth panoramic X-ray images in the dataset are three-channel images with a size of 320×640, we directly use the original images. Taking into account the variations in data distribution during the training process, the adaptability of the model to images of different scales and brightness, we choose image normalization techniques. It is worth noting that in this study, we fully consider the importance of tooth boundary information in tooth segmentation tasks. To achieve this, we extract masks from the original tooth images and obtained boundary information from them. Then, we generate a heatmap of tooth boundaries through Gaussian smoothing, as shown in Fig. 1.

2.2 Proposed Method

As shown in Fig. 2, our model consists of two main parts: the fully supervised part and the semi-supervised part, both of which are composed of stacked

Feature Pyramid Networks (FPN). The advantage of using FPN [9] is its ability to effectively capture information at different scales, which is crucial for the segmentation of both overall and detailed tooth structures. Additionally, considering the importance of tooth boundary prediction, we introduce the prediction of tooth boundaries as auxiliary information in the network to achieve more accurate tooth segmentation.

To achieve better results on the dental panoramic radiographs dataset in the fully supervised scenario, we train the model using labeled data. In this process, we generate tooth image segmentation boundaries after the first stacked FPN and input them together with the original images into the second FPN to generate the final tooth segmentation masks.

In the context of semi-supervised learning and the utilization of unlabeled data, we first predict the unlabeled data in the fully supervised part to obtain pseudo-labels, which are then used as input for training in the semi-supervised part. The first FPN in the semi-supervised part shares and freezes all the weights from the fully supervised part to ensure effective extraction of tooth boundary information, while the second FPN still outputs tooth segmentation masks. We iterate this process by continuously predicting unlabeled data and updating pseudo-labels.

Finally, during the testing phase, we input the test data into both the fully supervised part and the semi-supervised part. By weighting the two obtained tooth segmentation masks, we obtain the final test output.

In the fully supervised part, we use Dice loss and MSE loss to calculate the segmentation result loss and the predicted boundary loss respectively, which is calculated by:

$$L_{mask} = L_{Dice} \tag{1}$$

$$L_{boundary} = L_{MSE} \tag{2}$$

$$L_{global} = L_{mask} + L_{boundary} \tag{3}$$

where L_{Dice} and L_{MSE} represent Dice loss and MSE loss respectively. L_{mask} and $L_{boundary}$ represent the segmentation result loss and the predicted boundary loss respectively. L_{global} represents the total loss.

In the semi-supervised part, we only use Dice loss to calculate the segmentation result loss in Equation (1).

2.3   Post-processing

When using our network to obtain the final results, there may be small connected regions that are not the desired predicted results and need to be removed. As mentioned earlier, in our approach, the weighted combination of the output masks from the fully supervised part and the semi-supervised part can help address this issue to some extent.

3 Experiments

3.1 Dataset

For this study, we use the dataset from the STS-2023 Challenge. The competition includes a dental panoramic radiographs dataset [15], as shown in Fig. 3. The images in this dataset are of medical nature and are commonly used to assist doctors in diagnosis and treatment. The dataset consists of three-channel tooth X-ray panoramic images with dimensions of 320×640.

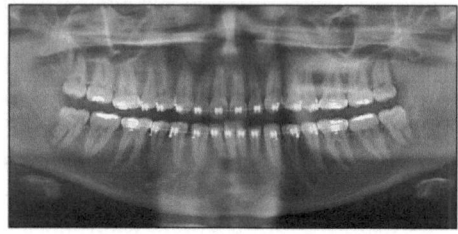
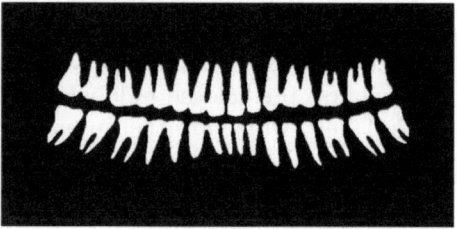

Dental panoramic radiograph   Ground truth

Fig. 3. Dental panoramic radiographs dataset. The white areas in the labeled images are teeth.

The dataset includes a training set and a test set. The training set contains 900 labeled tooth images and 2100 unlabeled tooth images. The test set contains 1000 unlabeled tooth images. To account for practical testing during the training process, we further divided the provided training set into a validation set. Our internal validation set consists of 200 labeled tooth images. Consequently, our training set consists of 700 labeled tooth images and 2100 unlabeled tooth images.

3.2 Evaluation Metrics

In this study, we use Dice coefficient, IoU (Intersection over Union), and 2D Hausdorff distance as evaluation metrics.

The Dice coefficient is the most commonly used metric in medical image competitions. It is a measure of set similarity and is typically used to calculate the similarity between two samples, which is calculated by:

$$Dice = \frac{2 \times |A \cap B|}{|A| + |B|} \tag{4}$$

where A and B represent the two masks respectively.

The IoU is define as the ratio between area of intersection and area of union, which is calculated by:

$$IoU = \frac{(A \cap B)}{(A \cup B)} \tag{5}$$

where A and B represent the two masks respectively.

Table 1. Development environments and requirements.

System	Windows 11
CPU	Intel(R) Core(TM) i9-12900H CPU 2.5GHz
RAM	16GB
GPU (number and type)	One NVIDIA 3060 8G
CUDA version	11.8
Programming language	Python 3.7.4
Deep learning framework	torch 1.13.1, torchvision 0.14.1

Table 2. Training protocols for the supervised phase.

Network initialization	
Batch size	16
Patch size	$3 \times 320 \times 640$
Total epochs	100
Optimizer	SGD
Initial learning rate (lr)	0.0001
Lr decay schedule	halved by 40 epochs
Training time	1.5 h
Loss function	Dice Loss, MSE Loss
Number of model parameters	46.31M
Number of flops	690.10G

Hausdorff distance is a measure that describes the similarity between two sets of points. It is a defined form of distance between two point sets, which is calculated by:

$$H(d) = min(|x_1 - x_2| + |y_1 - y_2|) \tag{6}$$

where (x_1, y_1) represents the pixel coordinates of a point on one image and (x_2, y_2) represents the pixel coordinates of a point on another image.

3.3 Implementation Details

The development environment and requirements are listed in Table 1. The operating system running on the system is Windows 11. The CPU used is 12th Gen Intel(R) Core(TM) i9-12900H with a clock speed of 2.50 GHz. The system has a total of 16GB of RAM. It is equipped with an NVIDIA 3060 8G GPU. The system has CUDA version 11.8 installed. The programming language used for development is Python 3.7.4. The deep learning frameworks used include torch 1.13.1 and torchvision 0.14.1.

Table 3. Training protocols for the semi-supervised phase.

Network initialization	
Batch size	8
Patch size	3×320×640
Total epochs	100
Optimizer	SGD
Initial learning rate (lr)	0.0001
Lr decay schedule	halved by 40 epochs
Training time	4.5 h
Number of model parameters	41.22M
Number of flops	345.05G

The strategies for fully supervised training are shown in Table 2. We used annotated data exclusively in this part. The strategies for semi-supervised training are shown in Table 3. In this part, we utilized both annotated and unlabeled data with their pseudo-labels. Considering the importance of local information for tooth boundary contour extraction and the displacement caused by the dataset acquisition, we applied a series of data augmentation operations such as image scaling, shifting, and mirroring to all training images. Our TB-FPN utilizes FPN as the baseline, which inherently possesses multi-scale detection capability. Therefore, we did not perform image block processing and used single images as input. Finally, we selected the model with the highest evaluation metrics on the validation set as our optimal model.

4   Results and Discussion

4.1   Quantitative Results on Validation Set

As shown in Table 4, we present the evaluation metrics calculated from internal validation and online validation. Our model performs well on the validation set, with a Dice score of 94.42%, an IoU score of 97.35%, and a Hausdorff distance of 0.0199. These metrics demonstrate superior performance compared to the classical segmentation algorithm U-Net [13] and the baseline model FPN that we used.

To assess the impact of unlabeled data on the model's results, we conduct ablation experiments, as shown in Table 5. Through training on unlabeled data, we attain impressive results, with a Dice score of 94.42%, an IoU score of 97.35%, and a Hausdorff distance of 0.0199. In contrast, without using unlabeled data for training, the corresponding metrics are a Dice score of 94.25%, an IoU score of 97.25%, and a Hausdorff distance of 0.0204. Although training with unlabeled data only results in a slight performance improvement, this result is still noteworthy.

Table 4. Total quantitative evaluation results.

Method	Internal Validation			Online Validation		
	Dice(%)	IoU(%)	HD(mm)	Dice(%)	IoU(%)	HD (mm)
U-Net	94.20 ± 0.10	97.24 ± 0.03	0.0225	91.36	97.55	0.0740
FPN	93.83 ± 0.08	97.08 ± 0.02	0.0218	91.23	97.49	0.0864
TB-FPN	**94.42** ± 0.10	**97.35** ± 0.03	**0.0199**	**91.75**	**97.70**	**0.0250**

Table 5. Results on ablation studies of unlabeled image.

Method	Internal Validation			Online Validation		
	Dice(%)	IoU(%)	HD(mm)	Dice(%)	IoU(%)	HD(mm)
TB-FPN(Supervise)	94.25 ± 0.10	97.25 ± 0.03	0.0204	91.31	97.46	0.0348
TB-FPN(Semi-supervise)	**94.42** ± 0.10	**97.35** ± 0.03	**0.0199**	**91.75**	**97.70**	**0.0250**

Table 6. Results on ablation studies of boundary information.

Method	Internal Validation			Online Validation		
	Dice(%)	IoU(%)	HD(mm)	Dice(%)	IoU(%)	HD(mm)
TB-FPN(no Bdy)	93.83 ± 0.08	97.08 ± 0.02	0.0218	91.23	97.49	0.0864
TB-FPN(Bdy)	**94.25** ± 0.10	**97.25** ± 0.03	**0.0204**	**91.31**	**97.46**	**0.0348**

Furthermore, we conduct another set of ablation experiments to assess the impact of incorporating boundary information on model performance, as detailed in Table 6. When training with boundary information, we observe a Dice score of 94.25%, an IoU score of 97.25%, and a Hausdorff distance of 0.0204. In comparison, without incorporating boundary information during training, the corresponding metrics are a Dice score of 93.83%, an IoU score of 97.08%, and a Hausdorff distance of 0.0218. This indicates that the inclusion of boundary information significantly influenced the training results of the model.

It is worth mentioning that our results are also validated on the online validation set, further confirming the excellent performance of our model.

4.2   Qualitative Results on Validation Set

We present the test results on the validation set in Fig. 4. In the case 0119 and the case 0306 shown in the figure, it can be observed that both the U-Net and FPN methods fail to accurately segment the boundaries of some teeth, especially when dealing with the segmentation of tooth roots. In contrast, the TB-FPN method successfully achieves accurate segmentation of the boundaries of tooth roots.

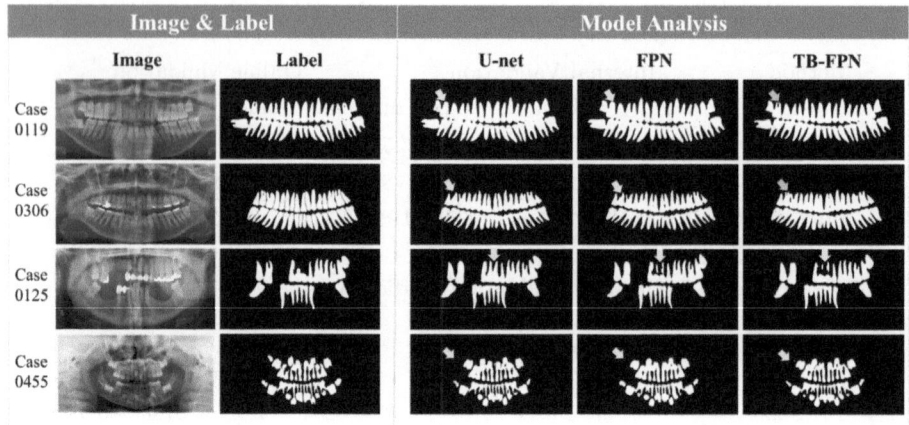

Fig. 4. Qualitative results on validation set. Inaccuracies in the segmentation results are marked with yellow and green arrows.

In the cases 0125 and the case 0455 in Fig. 4, none of the three methods are able to accurately segment the teeth. This can be attributed to the relatively small size of the wisdom teeth and the presence of large areas of tooth defects, which result in confusion and difficulties for all methods in handling these situations.

4.3   Results on Final Testing Set

Our research achieve a total score of 95.26% on the final online leaderboard. The Dice score is 91.75%, the IoU score is 97.70%, and the Hausdorff distance of is 0.0250.

4.4   Limitation and Future Work

In the current study, we only utilize two cascaded FPN for feature extraction and segmentation task learning. However, this setup may not fully exploit their potential in feature extraction and task learning, and we fail to effectively integrate the features extracted by these two networks.

In future research, to further improve the accuracy of the model, we can introduce more multi-scale feature extraction and fusion methods through in-depth experimentation. Additionally, it is worth considering the use of more advanced semi-supervised training models specifically designed for medical image segmentation tasks. Such adjustments are expected to enhance the model's representation capability and generalization performance on complex medical images, thereby driving progress in related fields.

5   Conclusion

In the current study, we employ the TB-FPN for tooth segmentation tasks, specifically applied to the dental panoramic radiographs dataset . Our algorithm performs remarkably well on the final test set, achieving a total score of 95.26% on the final online leaderboard. Through thorough comparisons with algorithms such as U-Net and FPN, we observe that our algorithm demonstrated superior performance in terms of segmentation effectiveness.

Upon closer examination, we discover that our algorithm can accurately capture boundary regions in tooth segmentation tasks, particularly in accurately segmenting tooth roots, surpassing the accuracy of other comparative algorithms. Additionally, the TB-FPN enables segmentation with a finer granularity, allowing for more precise tooth segmentation. This is an aspect that other comparative algorithms fail to achieve.

Acknowledgements. The authors of this paper declare that the segmentation method they implemented for participation in the STS 2023 challenge has not used any pre-trained models nor additional datasets other than those provided by the organizers. The proposed solution is fully automatic without any manual intervention. We thank all the data owners for making the X-ray images and CT scans publicly available and Alibaba Cloud for hosting the challenge platform.

References

1. Bai, W., et al.: Semi-supervised learning for network-based cardiac MR image segmentation. In: Medical Image Computing and Computer-Assisted Intervention-MICCAI 2017: 20th International Conference, Quebec City, QC, Canada, September 11-13, 2017, Proceedings, Part II 20, pp. 253–260. Springer (2017)
2. Bortsova, G., Dubost, F., Hogeweg, L., Katramados, I., De Bruijne, M.: Semi-supervised medical image segmentation via learning consistency under transformations. In: Medical Image Computing and Computer Assisted Intervention–MICCAI 2019: 22nd International Conference, Shenzhen, China, October 13–17, 2019, Proceedings, Part VI 22, pp. 810–818. Springer (2019)
3. Chaitanya, K., Karani, N., Baumgartner, C.F., Becker, A., Donati, O., Konukoglu, E.: Semi-supervised and task-driven data augmentation. In: Information Processing in Medical Imaging: 26th International Conference, IPMI 2019, Hong Kong, China, June 2–7, 2019, Proceedings 26, pp. 29–41. Springer (2019)
4. Doersch, C., Gupta, A., Efros, A.A.: Unsupervised visual representation learning by context prediction. In: Proceedings of the IEEE international conference on computer vision, pp. 1422–1430 (2015)
5. Dong, S.: Deep atlas network for efficient 3D left ventricle segmentation on echocardiography. Med. Image Anal. **61**, 101638 (2020)
6. Goodfellow, I., et al.: Generative adversarial nets. Adv. Neural Inf. Proce. Syst. **27** (2014)
7. Hao, Y., et al.: Eiseg: An efficient interactive segmentation annotation tool based on paddlepaddle. arXiv preprint arXiv:2210.08788 (2022)

8. He, Y., et al.: Dpa-densebiasnet: semi-supervised 3D fine renal artery segmentation with dense biased network and deep priori anatomy. In: Medical Image Computing and Computer Assisted Intervention–MICCAI 2019: 22nd International Conference, Shenzhen, China, October 13–17, 2019, Proceedings, Part VI 22, pp. 139–147. Springer (2019)

9. Lin, T.Y., Dollár, P., Girshick, R., He, K., Hariharan, B., Belongie, S.: Feature pyramid networks for object detection. In: Proceedings of the IEEE Conference on Computer Vision and Pattern Recognition, pp. 2117–2125 (2017)

10. Panfilov, E., Tiulpin, A., Klein, S., Nieminen, M.T., Saarakkala, S.: Improving robustness of deep learning based knee MRI segmentation: Mixup and adversarial domain adaptation. In: Proceedings of the IEEE/CVF International Conference on Computer Vision Workshops (2019)

11. Peng, J., Wang, Y.: Medical image segmentation with limited supervision: a review of deep network models. IEEE Access **9**, 36827–36851 (2021)

12. Raghu, M., Zhang, C., Kleinberg, J., Bengio, S.: Transfusion: Understanding transfer learning for medical imaging. Adv. Neural Inf. Proce. Syst. **32** (2019)

13. Ronneberger, O., Fischer, P., Brox, T.: U-net: convolutional networks for biomedical image segmentation. In: Medical Image Computing and Computer-Assisted Intervention–MICCAI 2015: 18th International Conference, Munich, Germany, October 5-9, 2015, Proceedings, Part III 18, pp. 234–241. Springer (2015)

14. Wang, S., et al.: Lt-net: label transfer by learning reversible voxel-wise correspondence for one-shot medical image segmentation. In: Proceedings of the IEEE/CVF Conference on Computer Vision and Pattern Recognition, pp. 9162–9171 (2020)

15. Zhang, Y., et al.: Children's dental panoramic radiographs dataset for caries segmentation and dental disease detection. Sci. Data **10**(1), 380 (2023)

Perform Special Post-processing After Tooth Segmentation

Bing Wang⬛, Chi Zhang⬛, and Weili Shi^(✉)⬛

School of Computer Science and Technology, Changchun University of Science and
Technology, Changchun, Jilin, China
shiweili@cust.edu.cn

Abstract. In the ever-evolving realm of dental imaging, the significance
of 2D dental panoramic images has undergone a notable surge, particularly in the realms of dental diagnosis and surgical planning. The
meticulous segmentation of these images stands out as a pivotal task,
endowing healthcare professionals with indispensable anatomical insights
and paving the way for the progression of computer-aided diagnosis.
Through a meticulously refined segmentation process, practitioners are
empowered to attain heightened precision in diagnosing dental lesions,
thereby fostering the evolution of more efficacious treatment plans. In
our research endeavors, we chose to leverage the nnU-Net as our baseline network. The post-processing stage within our methodology assumed
a role of paramount importance, integrating connected domain analysis. This strategic approach proved instrumental in honing the predicted
images, aligning them more closely with established medical prior knowledge, and ensuring a heightened level of consistency in the segmentation
outcomes. As a tangible testament to the efficacy of our approach, the
preliminary-round score ultimately is 0.9475. This numerical validation
underscores the success of our methodology in enhancing the precision of
dental image segmentation, thereby laying the groundwork for advancements in computer-aided diagnosis within the realm of dental care.

Keywords: tooth segmentation · prior knowledge · nnU-Net

1 Introduction

In recent years, with the continuous progress of technology and the rapid development of society, two-dimensional panoramic X-ray technology has been widely
applied, and the dental field has therefore received more attention and development [15]. The development of the dental industry is being driven by various
factors such as economic development and aging population trends, making it
increasingly important and urgent. In the field of dentistry, the accuracy of
dental imaging is crucial for diagnosis and treatment planning, and one of the
key tasks is tooth segmentation [3]. However, traditional manual segmentation
methods have some problems. This method requires a lot of time and high-level

professional knowledge, making it difficult to meet clinical needs in practical applications. Therefore, optimizing automatic segmentation methods has become an urgent task. With the continuous development of artificial intelligence and machine learning technologies, these technologies have been widely applied in the field of image processing and provide new solutions for tooth segmentation. In the field of dentistry, obtaining dental images is the foundation of diagnosis and treatment. By automatically segmenting tooth images, the shape, size, position, and other information of teeth can be quickly and accurately extracted, providing doctors with more accurate and reliable diagnostic basis and treatment plans [2]. At the same time, automatic segmentation methods can also reduce subjective errors and improper operations that may occur in manual segmentation, improving the quality and efficiency of diagnosis and treatment. Therefore, optimizing automatic segmentation methods for dental images is of great significance for improving the level of dental diagnosis and treatment [7].

After training the medical image segmentation model, post-processing has significant effects in guiding the model, helping to optimize its capture of task related features, thereby improving the robustness and accuracy of the model [6,10]. By introducing prior knowledge of post-processing, the segmentation model can be closer to human thinking logic, cleverly integrated into the construction process of the segmentation model, and effectively improve the diagnostic performance of the model. Currently, a lot of research has emerged in the field, focusing on post-processing based medical image segmentation methods and successfully applying them to the medical field [8,12]. These methods play an important role in enhancing model reasoning ability and optimizing output results, providing more reliable and effective solutions for medical image analysis.

Many tooth segmentation networks exist, but these networks often contain complex attention mechanisms [4] and uncertain parameters, making the reproduction process quite difficult. Therefore, the focus of our research is not on innovations in the network structure, but rather on optimising the post-processing part of the process. By focusing on the use of post-processing algorithms, we hope to provide more reliable solutions for research and practice in the field of tooth segmentation. Research in this direction is expected to improve the accuracy and stability of segmentation results, while simplifying the implementation of the model, bringing significant progress to the clinical and application fields.

To focus more on the post-processing part, we've chosen a robust baseline network called nnU-Net [5]. This network is equipped with powerful processing capabilities, including advanced pre-processing techniques, data fingerprinting mechanisms, and an adaptive network structure. By leveraging the strengths of the nnU-Net, we can focus on others beyond the intricacies of the network architecture.

The principal contributions of our study can be outlined as follows:

– We added special post-processing operations after training the network.
– We added a five-fold cross validation during the training process.

2   Method

2.1   Data Preprocessing

During the training process, our network employs a diverse set of data augmentation techniques to enhance its robustness and generalisation capabilities [14]. These techniques include random rotations, scaling, addition of Gaussian noise, Gaussian blur, random adjustments to brightness and contrast, simulation of low resolution through average pooling downsampling, gamma correction with randomly selected gamma values, and random mirroring in both horizontal and vertical directions. This combination of data augmentation strategies, implemented within the nnU-Net framework, serves as a fundamental and versatile approach to effectively augment the training dataset, ultimately improving the model's ability to generalize across various scenarios. For non-CT images, a crucial preprocessing step involves independent z-score normalisation for each individual image. This entails calculating the mean and standard deviation specific to each image. The grayscale values of the image are then adjusted by subtracting the mean and dividing by the standard deviation. This tailored approach effectively mitigates intensity distribution variations across different images. By applying this normalisation method, the disparities in intensity distribution are mitigated for each image, resulting in a more consistent and comparable representation of grayscale values. This becomes particularly significant in the context of non-CT images, as it ensures that each image undergoes a normalisation process customized to its unique intensity characteristics.

2.2   Architecture

In our study, we chose nnU-Net as the baseline network and conducted experiments with the following training framework as shown Fig. 1. In traditional approaches, researchers often face great challenges in adapting network structures and parameters to different datasets, requiring a large number of experiments, which makes it exceptionally difficult to reproduce experimental results. Previous research has mainly focused on developing new network structures, often by empirically fine-tuning them for specific training data, but this approach suffers from insufficient generalisation ability and easy overfitting. In contrast, our study introduces an innovative approach that incorporates a rational post-processing design. Before network training begins, we thoroughly analyse the data and perform post-processing based on any available prior knowledge. This approach significantly reduces the risk of over-tuning the network structure and parameters, resulting in models that are more consistent with dental segmentation. Our research looks at optimising the entire training process, focusing not only on the choice of network structure but also considering post-processing as a key step. Through this integrated approach, we achieve more effective control over the model, improving its generalisation and avoiding the problem of overfitting. This leads to more reliable and robust results for our research.

nnU-Net [5] represents an innovative framework designed for the automatic configuration and training of segmentation pipelines based on the U-Net architecture. Employing a meticulous analysis of the target dataset, nnU-Net seamlessly adapts crucial parameters such as patch size, batch size, preprocessing techniques, and network topology. Despite these dynamic adjustments, the fundamental network structure adheres to the proven encoder-decoder paradigm, featuring essential skip connection interlinking these two components. This approach ensures a robust and tailored segmentation solution, optimizing performance through intelligent parameter tuning based on dataset characteristics. We did not use unlabelled data during the training process.

We used five-fold cross-validation during training. Five-fold cross-validation is an effective method of validating training data, with the benefit of being able to more fully assess the performance of the model and improve the reliability of the results. This cross-validation method helps to reduce the randomness error caused by different data divisions, making the model evaluation more robust. At the same time, five-fold cross-validation also makes better use of limited data because each sample has a chance to be a validation set.

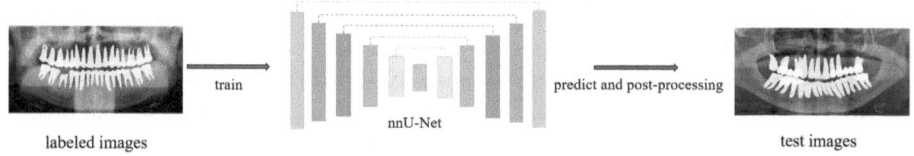

labeled images   nnU-Net   test images

Fig. 1. The overall framework of our proposed method, which is based on nnU-Net segmentation model.

2.3   Loss Function

Our approach involves integrating both the Dice Similarity Coefficient (DSC) loss and the cross-entropy loss into our training scheme [9]. The composite loss function is very effective in dealing with complex and diverse medical image segmentation tasks. By synergistically exploiting the strengths of DSC and cross-entropy, we enhance the robustness of our model, recognising the unique challenges posed by medical image data. This dual-loss strategy contributes to a more comprehensive and adaptive training process, fostering improved performance and accuracy in tooth segmentation scenarios.

$$L = L_{DSC} + L_{CE} \tag{1}$$

2.4   Post-processing

The implementation of Test Time Augmentation (TTA) [13] is straightforward yet highly effective. During the testing phase, a set of augmented samples is generated by applying suitable transformations to the original test dataset. These transformations can encompass various forms of geometric transformations, such as scaling, rotation, or affine transformations. Additionally, domain-specific transformations may also be employed to account for domain shifts or distribution mismatches. The generated augmented samples are then fed into the model, and predictions are obtained for each sample. By amalgamating these predictions, a consensus prediction is derived that is less susceptible to outliers or idiosyncrasies present in any individual prediction. This consensus prediction represents a more robust and reliable estimate of the true target value. The utilisation of TTA as a post-processing technique offers several advantages. Firstly, it provides an additional layer of robustness to the model, compensating for potential inaccuracies that may arise from variations in input data or distribution shifts. Secondly, TTA's ability to enhance generalisation performance makes it an invaluable tool for deploying models in uncontrolled environments where data may be scarce or unreliable. Finally, TTA's simplicity and ease of implementation render it a versatile and practical approach for enhancing model performance in a wide range of applications.

We have designed a special post-processing for this dataset, using depth analysis of the prediction results and morphological connected-domain analysis, which removes some isolated points and better matches the prediction results with the medical a prior knowledge of the dental images. In a binary image, spatially contiguous pixels that share the same value form a 'contiguous region'. The process begins with binarisation, which converts the image to a binary format with only two pixel values, typically 0 and 1. Each pixel is then examined in turn to determine whether it belongs to a connected region. This assessment uses an 8-connectivity approach, where pixels within the same region are given identical labels to indicate their connectivity. This processing method not only improves the accuracy of the prediction results, but also better preserves the detail information of the dental images, making the processed images more compatible with the needs of medical diagnosis.

3   Experiments

3.1   Dataset and Evaluation Measures

The dataset for dental panoramic radiographs, as referenced in [16], utilized in this competition was collaboratively contributed by Hangzhou Dental Group, Hangzhou Qiantang Dental Hospital, University of Electronic Science and Technology, and Queen Mary University of London. In the Preliminary Round, the training set comprises 2000 labelled panoramic radiograph images, with an additional 500 designated for testing.

The assessment criteria consist of three accuracy metrics: Dice coefficient (Dice), Intersection over Union (IoU), and Three-dimensional Hausdorff distance (H(d)). These metrics jointly contribute to the calculation of rankings. The weights assigned to each metric are defined by the following formula.

$$Score = 0.4 * Dice + 0.3 * IOU + 0.3 * (1 - H(d)) \qquad (2)$$

3.2   Implementation Details

Environment Settings. The development environments and requirements are presented in Table 1. The system is running CentOS Linux release 7.9.2009 as the operating system. The CPU in use is an Intel(R) Xeon(R) Gold 6338 CPU with a clock speed of 2.00 GHz. The system has a total of 16GB RAM, divided into 16 modules of 4 GB each, operating at a speed of 3200 MT/s. The system is equipped with one NVIDIA A100-PCIE-40 GB GPU. The CUDA version installed on the system is 11.7. The programming language used for development is Python 3.8.13. The deep learning framework employed includes torch 1.12.1, torchvision 0.13.1 [11]. These specifications provide insight into the hardware and software setup used for the development of a specific project or application.

Table 1. Development environments and requirements.

System	CentOS Linux release 7.9.2009
CPU	Intel(R) Xeon(R) Gold 6338 CPU @ 2.00 GHz
RAM	16 GB; 3200 MT/s
GPU	A100-PCIE-40 GB
CUDA version	11.7
Programming language	Python 3.8.13
Deep learning framework	Pytorch (torch1.12.1, torchvision0.13.1)
Specific dependencies	nnU-Net

Training Protocols. All training data are subjected to appropriate preprocessing based on their respective data sets, and the methods used for preprocessing are the standard processing methods of nnU-Net. Our training strategy combines the dice loss and cross-entropy loss functions, with the initial learning rate set to 0.01 and the number of training rounds set to 1000 for all experiments. The detailed settings are shown in Table 2.

4   Results and Discussion

The Dice coefficient(Dice), intersection over union (IoU), and Hausdorff distance(HD) scores for all experiments were acquired from the online validation leaderboard during Semi-supervised Tooth Segmentation on Panoramic X-ray Image.

Table 2. Training protocols.

Network initialisation	"HE" normal initialisation
Batch size	16
Patch size	320×640
Optimizer	SGD [1] with nesterov momentum ($\mu = 0.99$)
Total epochs	1000
Initial learning rate	0.01
Lr decay schedule	Poly learning rate policy:$(1 - epoch/1000)^{0.9}$
Training time	24 h
Loss function	Dice loss and Cross Entropy loss
Number of model parameters	29.3M

4.1 Preliminary-Round

The overall quantitative results in the preliminary-round are shown in Table 3. Meanwhile, ablation experiments were performed to verify the effect of the five-fold cross-validation method and post-processing. Table 4 shows the results with or without the use of post-processing and five-fold cross-validation. The results clearly demonstrate the effectiveness of this post-processing and five-fold cross validation. Example of segmentation of ablation experiments are given in Fig. 2. In Fig. 2, it is evident that implementing post-processing techniques significantly reduces the occurrence of false positive predictions.

Good and Failure Segmentation Cases. Figure 3 presents four representative segmentation results obtained from our final submission in the preliminary-round. The top two rows show case 140 and case 148, our network successfully achieved high-accuracy segment. However, in the bottom two rows, specifically case 4 and case 128, if other elements appear around the teeth, it can lead to misjudgment.

Table 3. Quantitative evaluation results in the preliminary-round.

Method	Internal Validation			Online Validation		
	Dice (%)	IoU (%)	HD (mm)	Dice (%)	IoU (%)	HD (mm)
Our	94.28 ± 5.1	89.54 ± 7.6	0.023 ± 0.019	91.89	96.38	0.0307

original image

nnU-Net

nnU-Net+five-fold

nnU-Net+five-fold+post-processing

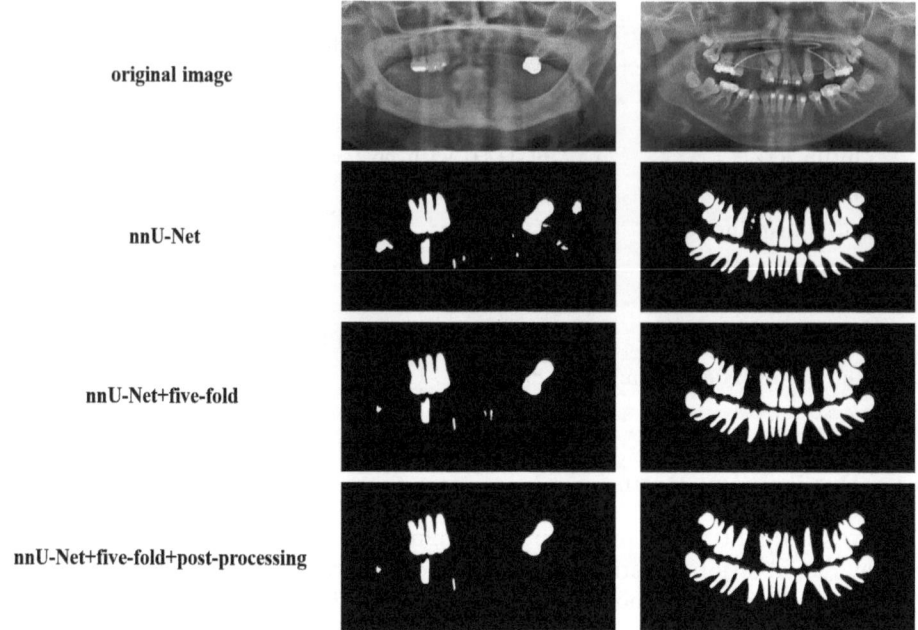

Fig. 2. Image segmentation example of ablation experiments in the preliminary-round.

Table 4. Ablation experiments in the preliminary-round.

Method	Dice(%)	IoU(%)	HD(mm)	score
nnU-Net	91.78	96.34	0.0310	0.9468
nnU-Net+five-fold	91.89	96.38	0.0310	0.9474
nnU-Net+five-fold+post-processing	91.89	96.38	0.0307	0.9475

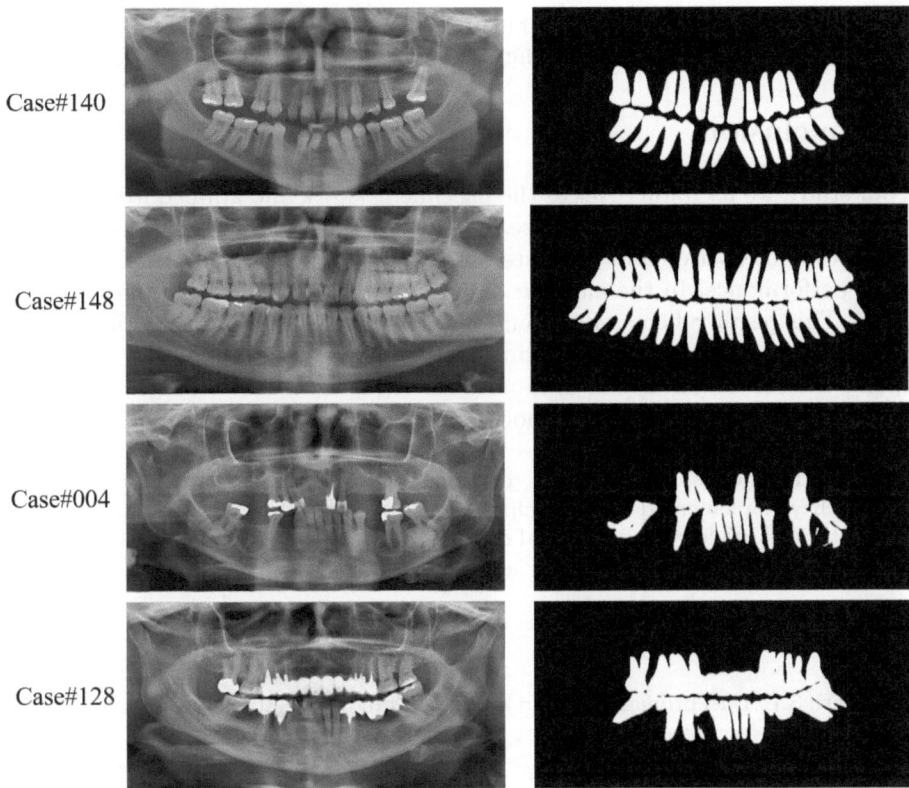

Fig. 3. Good and failure tooth segmentation cases. They highlight the differences in accuracy and areas where the segmentation process did not perform well.

Table 5. Quantitative evaluation of inference efficiency parameters

Image Size	Max GPU (MB)
(320, 640)	2189

4.2 Segmentation Efficiency Results on Validation Set

We ran our model on a docker with NVIDIA A100-PCIE-40 GB for inference on 500 validation cases in the preliminary-round In the preliminary-round, the average maximum GPU memory used for inference is 2189 MB. Table 5 shows the inference efficiency parameters of our model on some examples.

4.3 Limitation and Future Work

It is important to acknowledge that our method has certain limitations. As we only participated in the preliminary round, unlabelled data from the final round were not used. The model is prone to false positives in the presence of interference from other elements. Future work plans to use unlabelled data and filter out interfering elements in the data pre-processing.

5   Conclusion

In our study, we used nnU-Net as the baseline network and applied fivefold cross-validation during the training phase. In the post-processing stage, we introduced test time augmentation and connected component analysis to further improve the model performance. In the end, we achieved a satisfactory preliminary result of 0.9475. This result reflects our extensive optimisation work in network selection, training process and post-processing steps. In the future, we plan to further explore the use of unlabelled data and other improvement strategies to further improve the performance of the model.

Acknowledgements. The authors of this paper declare that the segmentation method they implemented for participation in the STS 2023 challenge has not used any pre-trained models nor additional datasets other than those provided by the organizers. The proposed solution is fully automatic.

References

1. Amari, S.I.: Backpropagation and stochastic gradient descent method. Neurocomputing **5**(4–5), 185–196 (1993)
2. Ballikaya, E., Koc, N., Avcu, N., Cehreli, Z.C.: The quality of root canal treatment and periapical status of permanent teeth in Turkish children and teens: a retrospective cbct study. Oral Radiol. **38**(3), 405–415 (2022)
3. Di Stefano, M., Polizzi, A., Santonocito, S., Romano, A., Lombardi, T., Isola, G.: Impact of oral microbiome in periodontal health and periodontitis: a critical review on prevention and treatment. Int. J. Mol. Sci. **23**(9), 5142 (2022)
4. Hou, S., Zhou, T., Liu, Y., Dang, P., Lu, H., Shi, H.: Teeth U-Net: a segmentation model of dental panoramic x-ray images for context semantics and contrast enhancement. Comput. Biol. Med. **152**, 106296 (2023)
5. Isensee, F., Jaeger, P.F., Kohl, S.A., Petersen, J., Maier-Hein, K.H.: NNU-Net: a self-configuring method for deep learning-based biomedical image segmentation. Nat. Methods **18**(2), 203–211 (2021)
6. Isensee, F., Ulrich, C., Wald, T., Maier-Hein, K.H.: Extending NNU-Net is all you need. In: Deserno, T.M., Handels, H., Maier, A., Maier-Hein, K., Palm, C., Tolxdorff, T. (eds.) BVM 2023, pp. 12–17. Springer, Wiesbaden (2023). https://doi.org/10.1007/978-3-658-41657-7_7
7. Kheraif, A.A.A., Wahba, A.A., Fouad, H.: Detection of dental diseases from radiographic 2D dental image using hybrid graph-cut technique and convolutional neural network. Measurement **146**, 333–342 (2019)
8. Larrazabal, A.J., Martinez, C., Ferrante, E.: Anatomical priors for image segmentation via post-processing with denoising autoencoders. In: Shen, D., et al. (eds.) MICCAI 2019. LNCS, vol. 11769, pp. 585–593. Springer, Cham (2019). https://doi.org/10.1007/978-3-030-32226-7_65
9. Ma, J., et al.: Loss odyssey in medical image segmentation. Med. Image Anal. **71**, 102035 (2021)

10. Mortazi, A., Bagci, U.: Automatically designing CNN architectures for medical image segmentation. In: Shi, Y., Suk, H.-I., Liu, M. (eds.) MLMI 2018. LNCS, vol. 11046, pp. 98–106. Springer, Cham (2018). https://doi.org/10.1007/978-3-030-00919-9_12

11. Paszke, A., et al.: Pytorch: an imperative style, high-performance deep learning library. In: Advances in Neural Information Processing Systems, vol. 32 (2019)

12. Ross-Howe, S., Tizhoosh, H.R.: The effects of image pre-and post-processing, wavelet decomposition, and local binary patterns on U-Nets for skin lesion segmentation. In: 2018 International Joint Conference on Neural Networks (IJCNN), pp. 1–8. IEEE (2018)

13. Shanmugam, D., Blalock, D., Balakrishnan, G., Guttag, J.: Better aggregation in test-time augmentation. In: Proceedings of the IEEE/CVF International Conference on Computer Vision, pp. 1214–1223 (2021)

14. Shorten, C., Khoshgoftaar, T.M.: A survey on image data augmentation for deep learning. J. Big Data 6(1), 1–48 (2019)

15. Silva, G., Oliveira, L., Pithon, M.: Automatic segmenting teeth in x-ray images: trends, a novel data set, benchmarking and future perspectives. Expert Systems with Applications p. S0957417418302252 (2018)

16. Zhang, Y., et al.: Children's dental panoramic radiographs dataset for caries segmentation and dental disease detection. Sci. Data 10(1), 380 (2023)

A Multi-stage Framework for 3D Individual Tooth Segmentation in Dental CBCT

Chunshi Wang[1], Bin Zhao[1,2](✉), and Shuxue Ding[1,2]

[1] School of Artificial Intelligence, Guilin University of Electronic Technology, Guilin, Guangxi 541004, China
zhaobinnku@mail.nankai.edu.cn
[2] Guangxi Colleges and Universities Key Laboratory of AI Algorithm Engineering, Guilin, Guangxi 541004, China

Abstract. Cone beam computed tomography (CBCT) is a common way of diagnosing dental related diseases. Accurate segmentation of 3D tooth is of importance for the treatment. Although deep learning based methods have achieved convincing results in medical image processing, they need a large of annotated data for network training, making it very time-consuming in data collection and annotation. Besides, domain shift widely existing in the distribution of data acquired by different devices impacts severely the model generalization. To resolve the problem, we propose a multi-stage framework for 3D tooth segmentation in dental CBCT, which achieves the third place in the "Semi-supervised Teeth Segmentation" 3D (STS-3D) challenge. The experiments on validation set compared with other semi-supervised segmentation methods further indicate the validity of our approach.

Keywords: Cone beam computed tomography · tooth segmentation · semi-supervised learning

1 Introduction

Advances in modern digital dentistry rely heavily on the acquisition and segmentation of three-dimensional (3D) imaging. In particular, cone beam computed tomography (CBCT) plays a crucial role in obtaining accurate 3D digital models of the jaws and teeth while keeping costs and radiation doses relatively low.

The acquisition and segmentation of 3D digital images has a variety of applications in the field of oral and maxillofacial disciplines, with the most prominent applications being orthodontic diagnosis and treatment planning. Specifically, these techniques are commonly used in 3D-guided implant surgery, guided endodontic and apical surgery, CBCT-based planning and fabrication of donor tooth replicas, etc. 3D tooth segmentation is an important part of the aforementioned treatment processes and can be used in orthodontics to develop treatment

---

Chunshi Wang and Bin Zhao contribute equally to this paper.

Y. Wang et al. (Eds.): STS 2023, LNCS 14623, pp. 36–45, 2025.
https://doi.org/10.1007/978-3-031-72396-4_4

plans and to follow the evolution of root resorption after treatment. However, precise tooth segmentation is challenging. The presence of a large number of teeth on each arch in the mouth complicates the segmentation process. Teeth in the emergence stage have some specialized structures that make them difficult to distinguish. Metal fillings and dental restorations can cause artifacts in CBCT, which can lead to aberrations in the segmentation results. In addition, the composition of the tooth itself is more complex, with elements consisting of cementum, dentin, pulp and enamel in close contact with other anatomical structures in the mouth, making it difficult to determine tooth edges. There is also a similar density between the alveolar bone and the tooth structure, which leads to separate the upper and lower teeth from each other difficultly [12].

Over the past decade, many attempts have been made to develop 3D tooth segmentation methods, most of which have been level-set based methods [8,13]. Unfortunately, these methods do not achieve fully automatic segmentation for the reason that they need to manually intervene in the initialization of the level-set and the complex image structure between adjacent teeth and bones further prevents automatic initialization. Besides, level-set based methods require a lot of mathematical operations and perform poorly for metal artifacts and upper-lower tooth separation. There are also some graph cut based methods for tooth segmentation [7,9], but they need priors to guide the segmentation process and lack robustness.

Recently, convolutional neural networks (CNNs) have been applied to 3D tooth segmentation aiming to overcome the limitations of traditional segmentation methods. The focus of researchers has shifted to the development of an algorithm for fully automated tooth segmentation without human intervention, striving for accuracy and speed [17]. For instance, Chen et al. propose a 3D full convolutional neural network (FCN) combined with the watershed transform for tooth segmentation [2]. Hsuet al. propose a 3.5D U-Net model to improve the performance of tooth segmentation [10]. Cui et al. propose Toothnet, a network that utilizes edge maps, similarity matrix and spatial relationships between teeth [6]. Cui et al. further develop an AI system for fully automated segmentation of teeth and alveolar bone using the 2-Stage scheme, which is validated on a large number of CBCT scans, demonstrating to some extent the effectiveness of AI technology in enhancing clinical workflow [5].

The above-mentioned methods are performed in fully supervised scenarios, where the data need to be labeled in detail by experts. However, the labeling process for 3D medical data is both complex and expensive. In addition, there are limited datasets available for 3D tooth segmentation studies [4], which severely limits its wide application in the field of tooth segmentation. To address this problem, semi-supervised learning (SSL) methods for medical image segmentation have emerged [23,24]. These methods require less expert annotation for model training, thus reducing the time and effort required for data annotation. But Since domain offsets exist widely in medical data, semi-supervised learning cannot directly obtain better segmentation results. Therefore, in this paper, we propose a multi-stage framework based on SSL and domain adaptation to segment tooth from CBCT, which achieves the third place in the "Semi-supervised

Teeth Segmentation" 3D (STS-3D) challenge. The extensive experiments compared with other semi-supervised segmentation methods further indicate the validity of our approach.

2   Materials and Method

2.1   Research Subjects

The experimental data used in this paper is provided by the STS-3D challenge where training set includes 12 CT scans with annotations and 300 CT scans without annotations [3,4]. There are 50 CT scans for test and they do not provided the annotations for participants.

2.2   Multi-stage Framework

Our proposed multi-stage framework is illustrated in the Fig. 1. As shown in the Fig. 1, in stage 1, we utilize supervised learning based on the 2D nnU-Net [11] model to generate pixel-level pseudo-annotations for a small number of randomly sampled unlabeled samples from the training set, and then combine these pseudo-annotated samples with the labeled samples in the training set to form new labeled samples. In stage 2, these new labeled samples are fed into the Improved-UniMatch model for parameter learning after domain adaptation together with the unlabeled samples in the training set.

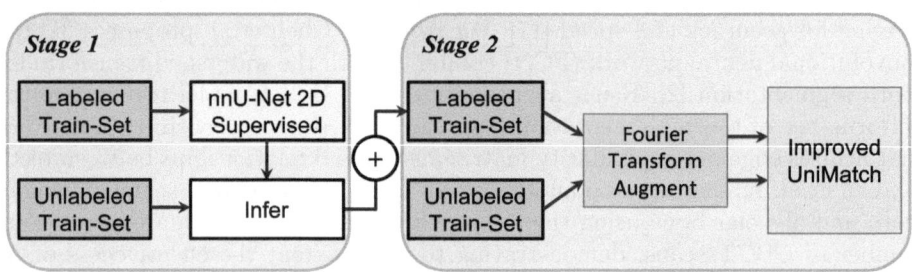

Fig. 1. The architecture of our proposed multi-stage framework. Best viewed in color.

In particular, in stage 1, the labeled samples is first used to train the 2D nnU-Net 20 epochs, and then the trained 2D nnU-Net is used to generate low-quality pixel-level pseudo-annotations for the 10 randomly selected unlabeled samples in the unlabeled set. These 10 pseudo-annotated samples are then merged with the labeled samples to form new labeled samples to train the stage 2. In stage 2, the new labeled samples and the remaining unlabeled samples are fed into Fourier Transform Augment (FTA) module to make the model learn the difference between two domains. The FTA module is presented in Fig. 2. During the training process, a labeled image x^w and a unlabeled image x^u are randomly

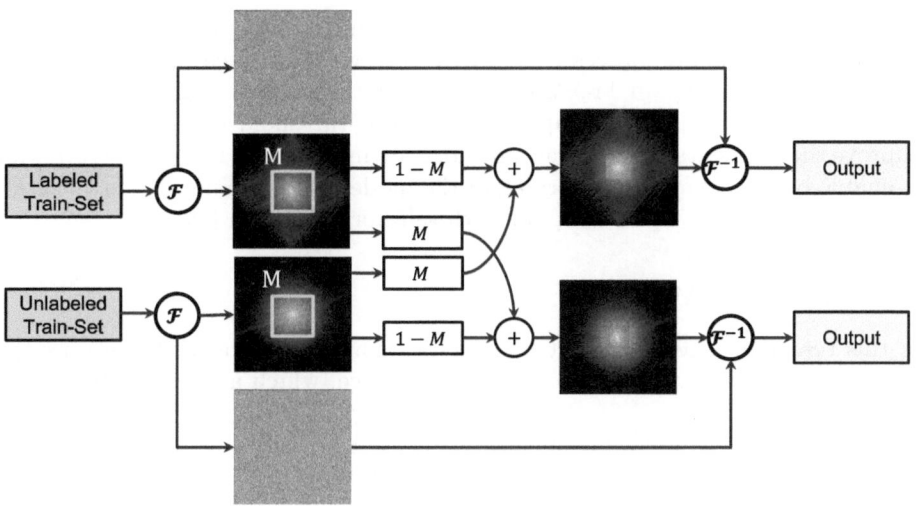

Fig. 2. The flowchart of FTA module. This module makes the model learn the difference between two domains

selected, and then a Fourier transform $\mathcal{F}$ is performed to transfer the images to the frequency domain and obtain the magnitude spectrum $\{A^w,\ A^u\}$ and the phase image $\{P^w,\ P^u\}$, where the magnitude spectrum contains the low-level statistics and the phase image includes the high-level semantics of the original signal [22]. The image x^w is then enhanced by merging the magnitude information of the image x^u,

$$A_{new}^w = (1 - \lambda)A^w * (1 - M) + \lambda A^u * M, \qquad (1)$$

where A_{new}^w is the newly generated phase map. λ is a parameter to adjust the ratio between the phase information of x^w and x^u . M is used to control the spatial extent of the magnitude spectrum to be exchanged, and here M is set to the center region of the magnitude spectrum containing low frequency information. After that, the merged samples are transformed from the frequency domain to the image domain by $\mathcal{F}^{-1}$ to obtain the image sample Z^w enhanced by Fourier transform and fused with the low-level information of the other sample,

$$Z^w = \mathcal{F}^{-1}(A_{new}^w, P^w). \qquad (2)$$

Similarly exchanging x^w and x^u gives Z^u:

$$Z^u = \mathcal{F}^{-1}(A_{new}^u, P^u). \qquad (3)$$

It is worth mentioning that Z^w and Z^u can be merged together for computation, which will greatly reduce the computational cost. That is, it is necessary to augment both x^u and x^w at the same time, and send the result of mutual augmentation into the subsequent training process.

The data performed through FTA are fed into the Improved-Unimatch for segmentation training process. In particular, we introduce the idea of self-adaptive thresholding in FreeMatch [20] into the current segmentation task, allowing UniMatch [21] to adaptive adjust the threshold during training and improve the segmentation accuracy. Besides, we improve the feature perturbation to enable better consistency learning of the model by replacing the perturbation of Dropout with an Alpha Dropout with self-normalization [14].

2.3   Evaluation Metrics

In this research, dice coefficient and intersection over union (IoU) are used to evaluate the pixel-level segmentation performance, which are formulated as

$$Dice = \frac{2 * |A \cap B|}{|A| + |B|},$$ (4)

and

$$IoU = \frac{A \cap B}{A \cup B},$$ (5)

respectively, where A and B indicate the predicted segmentation and the ground truth, respectively. In addition, the 3D Hausdorff distance is used to evaluate the voxel-level segmentation performance and is formulated as

$$H(d) = min(|x1 - x2| + |y1 - y2| + |z1 - z2|),$$ (6)

where $(x1, y1, z1)$ and $(x2, y2, z2)$ denote the coordinates of the two voxels. $|x1 - x2|$, $|y1 - y2|$ and $|z1 - z2|$ denote the distances on the corresponding axes.

For scoring purposes, the challenge uniformly normalizes the hausdorff distance to the range of [0, 1]. The final weighted average of the three metrics is taken and the specific scoring formula is

$$score = 0.4 * Dice + 0.3 * IoU + 0.3 * (1 - H(d)).$$ (7)

3   Experiment

3.1   Data Preprocessing

To take advantage of the pixel-level pseudo-annotations generated from unlabeled data and obtain rich tooth morphology, the training data are sliced in 3-axis. That is, the 3D tooth data are sliced in axial, coronal, and sagittal planes, e.g., a $640 \times 640 \times 400$ CT image would result in $640 + 640 + 400 = 1680$ slices. Using file suffixes as the division of slice axes, for simplicity, $\_x, \_y$ and $\_z$ are directly used as the suffixes of slice files [15]. In addition, the slices are normalized to a range of [0,1] and 10% of slices are used as the validation set.

In order to explore the effect of different thresholds of the input image on the performance of the proposed method, we conduct thresholding experiments to select the best threshold for training. In particular, to save time, we randomly

Table 1. Quantitative results of input images with different thresholds on the validation set

Bottom	Top	val1	val2	val3
0	1500	0.774	0.818	0.862
500	1500	0.817	0.826	0.876
500	1800	0.839	0.804	0.885
550	1950	0.725	0.850	0.873
500	2000	**0.816**	**0.848**	**0.884**
300	2000	0.813	0.854	0.879
450	2050	0.829	0.820	0.867
400	2100	0.747	0.813	0.845
0	2500	0.825	0.830	0.860

Table 2. The top five submission results of the STS-3D challenge. Our result has been highlighted in **bold**. The arrows indicate which direction is better.

Participant	Score (↑)	Dice (↑)	IoU (↑)	H(d) (↓)
RoboSurge	0.8497	0.8442	0.8661	0.1595
Yxx	0.8427	0.8343	0.8583	0.1615
GUET-IICI	**0.8256**	**0.8058**	**0.8376**	**0.1599**
IGIP-CBCT	0.8237	0.8070	0.8386	0.1689
sdkxd	0.8147	0.7932	0.8290	0.1708

select 25% of slices from the training slices to train our model. We train 3 epochs and the quantitative results on validation set of each epoch are shown in Table 1. From Table 1, it can be seen that when the combination of 500 and 2000 is chosen for the threshold value, the proposed method has the best segmentation results on the validation set, so this combination is chosen as the threshold value in the experiment.

3.2 Implementation Details

The optimizer is the AdamW method [16] with $weight_{decay} = 0.0001$. The initial learning rate is 10^{-4}. During training, the learning rate is updated using the following formula,

$$lr = lr_b \times (1 - \frac{i}{N})^{0.9} \tag{8}$$

where lr_b indicates the initial learning rate. i and N indicate the current number and the total number of iterations, respectively.

The experiments are performed on a computer with an Intel Core i7-6800K CPU, 64 GB RAM and NVIDIA Tesla V100 GPU with 32 GB memory. All networks are implemented in PyTorch.

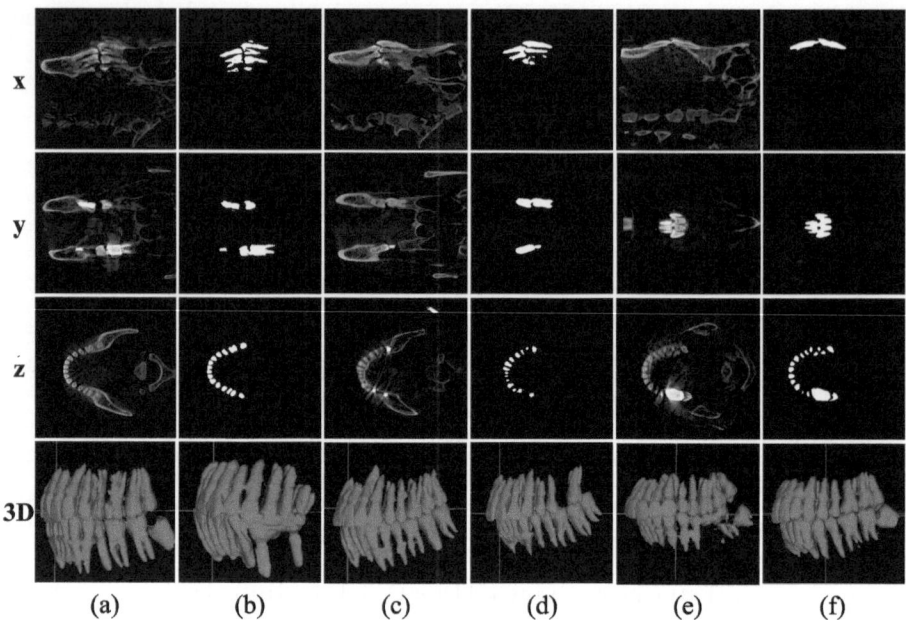

(a)   (b)   (c)   (d)   (e)   (f)

Fig. 3. Six examples showing segmentation results obtained from our method. The four rows from top to bottom denotes axial, coronal, sagittal and 3D views. Best viewed in color.

Table 3. The quantitative evaluation results of our method and the comparison methods on the validation set. Our result has been highlighted in **bold**. The arrows indicate which direction is better.

Method	Score (↑)	Dice (↑)	IoU (↑)	H(d) (↓)
CPS [1]	0.8582	0.8501	0.8078	0.0808
FixMatch [18]	0.8796	0.8713	0.8266	0.0563
MeanTeacher [19]	0.8737	0.8645	0.8210	0.0613
Ours	**0.8859**	**0.8801**	**0.8425**	**0.0632**

3.3   Results

We train our model only 3 epochs for limited time and submit the results to the challenge. Table 2 summaries the top five submission results of the STS-3D challenge and our result has been highlighted in bold. As shown in the Table 2, our proposed method achieves the third place in the challenge. In addition, we visualize some segmentation results in the Fig. 3. No matter from the axial, coronal and sagittal, our proposed method obtains the better segmentation results.

We further compared with other state-of-the-art (SOTA) semi-supervised segmentation methods using the challenge data. Specifically, we train and evaluate CPS [1], FixMatch [18] and MeanTeacher [19] using the same settings on the

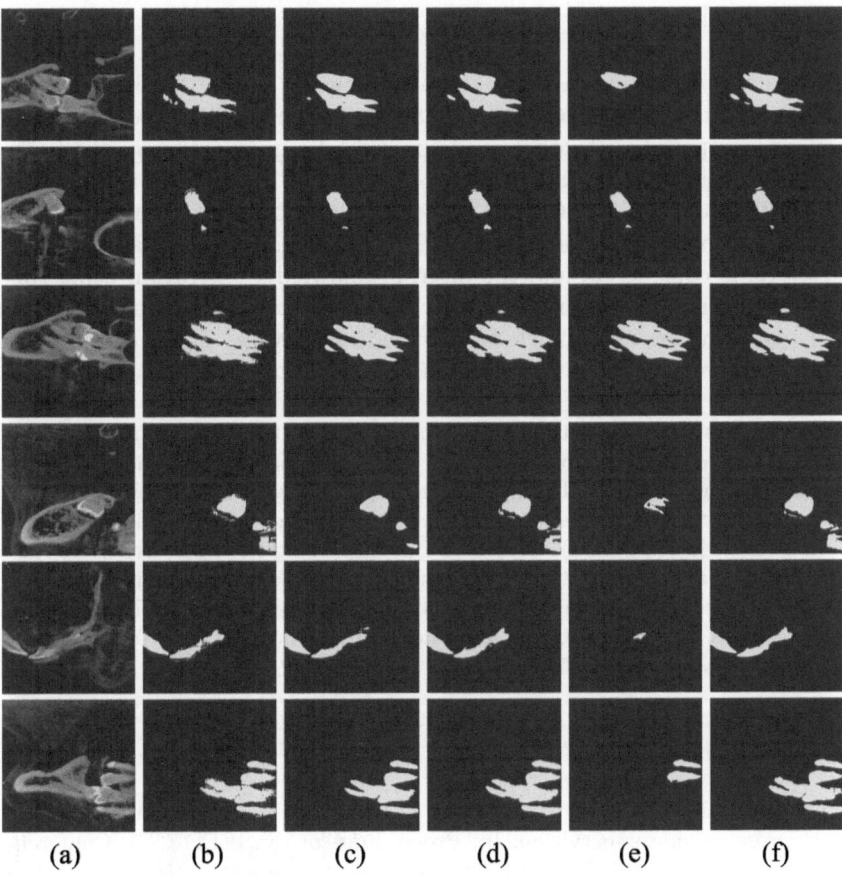

Fig. 4. Comparison of segmentation performance. (a-b) CBCT slices and their corresponding ground truth. (c-f) are the segmentation results of CPS [1], FixMatch [18], MeanTeacher [19] and our proposed method, respectively.

challenge data. In particular, we use the validation set as the test set to validate the proposed method and the comparison methods.

Figure 4 visualizes some slices of segmentation results and the ground truth. As the Fig. 4 shows, CPS [1] and MeanTeacher [19] ignore some tooth morphology and did not obtain complete segmentation results. FixMatch [18] is not accurate enough to segment the edges of the teeth. Instead, regardless of tooth morphology or edge information, our method achieves segmentation that is superior to comparison methods.

The quantitative evaluation results are summarized in Table 3. As Table 3 shows, our proposed method taking advantage of its multi-stage training and domain adaptation mechanism achieves a mean Dice of 0.8801, a mean IoU of 0.8425 and a mean Score of 0.8859, which exceeds the comparison methods.

4   Conclusion

In this paper, we propose a multi-stage framework for 3D tooth segmentation, which achieves the third place in the STS-3D challenge. The experiments on validation set compared with other semi-supervised segmentation methods further indicate the validity of our approach.

In the future work, in order to better utilize the information of the labeled data, the appropriate introduction of perturbations at the image level or the feature level is considered, and the internal knowledge migration using the predictive consistency of the model under different strengths of perturbations is carried out by using the knowledge distillation method, so as to optimize the learning effectiveness and generalization ability of the model on unlabeled data.

Acknowledgments. The authors of this paper declare that the segmentation method they implemented for participation in the STS 2023 challenge has not used any pre-trained models nor additional datasets other than those provided by the organizers. Besides, this work is supported in part by the National Natural Science Foundation of China (Grant No.62076077), the Project of Improving the Basic Scientific Research Ability of Young and Middle-Aged Teachers in Universities of Guangxi Province (Grant No.2023KY0223), Youth Science Foundation of Guangxi Natural Science Foundation (Grant No.2023GXNSFBA026018) and the Guangxi Science and Technology Major Project (Grant No.AA22068057).

References

1. Chen, X., Yuan, Y., Zeng, G., Wang, J.: Semi-supervised semantic segmentation with cross pseudo supervision. In: Proceedings of the IEEE/CVF Conference on Computer Vision and Pattern Recognition, pp. 2613–2622 (2021)
2. Chen, Y.: Automatic segmentation of individual tooth in dental CBCT images from tooth surface map by a multi-task FCN. IEEE Access **8**, 97296–97309 (2020)
3. Cui, W., et al.: Ctooth+: a large-scale dental cone beam computed tomography dataset and benchmark for tooth volume segmentation. In: MICCAI Workshop on Data Augmentation, Labelling, and Imperfections, pp. 64–73 (2022)
4. Cui, W., et al.: Ctooth: a fully annotated 3D dataset and benchmark for tooth volume segmentation on cone beam computed tomography images. In: International Conference on Intelligent Robotics and Applications, pp. 191–200 (2022)
5. Cui, Z., et al.: A fully automatic AI system for tooth and alveolar bone segmentation from cone-beam CT images. Nat. Commun. **13**(1), 2096 (2022)
6. Cui, Z., Li, C., Wang, W.: Toothnet: automatic tooth instance segmentation and identification from cone beam CT images. In: Proceedings of the IEEE/CVF Conference On Computer Vision And Pattern Recognition, pp. 6368–6377 (2019)
7. Evain, T., Ripoche, X., Atif, J., Bloch, I.: Semi-automatic teeth segmentation in cone-beam computed tomography by graph-cut with statistical shape priors. In: 2017 IEEE 14th International Symposium on Biomedical Imaging (ISBI 2017), pp. 1197–1200 (2017)
8. Gao, H., Chae, O.: Individual tooth segmentation from CT images using level set method with shape and intensity prior. Pattern Recogn. **43**(7), 2406–2417 (2010)

9. Hiew, L., Ong, S., Foong, K.W., Weng, C.: Tooth segmentation from cone-beam CT using graph cut. In: Proceedings of the Second APSIPA Annual Summit and Conference, pp. 272–275 (2010)

10. Hsu, K., et al.: Improving performance of deep learning models using 3.5 D u-net via majority voting for tooth segmentation on cone beam computed tomography. Sci. Reports **12**(1), 19809 (2022)

11. Isensee, F., Jaeger, P.F., Kohl, S.A., Petersen, J., Maier-Hein, K.H.: NNU-net: a self-configuring method for deep learning-based biomedical image segmentation. Nat. Methods **18**(2), 203–211 (2021)

12. Jang, T.J., Kim, K.C., Cho, H.C., Seo, J.K.: A fully automated method for 3D individual tooth identification and segmentation in dental CBCT. IEEE Trans. Pattern Anal. Mach. Intell. **44**(10), 6562–6568 (2021)

13. Ji, D.X., Ong, S.H., Foong, K.W.C.: A level-set based approach for anterior teeth segmentation in cone beam computed tomography images. Comput. Biol. Med. **50**, 116–128 (2014)

14. Klambauer, G., Unterthiner, T., Mayr, A., Hochreiter, S.: Self-normalizing neural networks. Adv. Neural Inf. Proce. Syst. **30** (2017)

15. Liu, Z., Cao, C., Ding, S., Liu, Z., Han, T., Liu, S.: Towards clinical diagnosis: automated stroke lesion segmentation on multi-spectral MR image using convolutional neural network. IEEE Access **6**, 57006–57016 (2018)

16. Loshchilov, I., Hutter, F.: Decoupled weight decay regularization. arXiv preprint arXiv:1711.05101 (2017)

17. Polizzi, A., et al.: Tooth automatic segmentation from CBCT images: a systematic review. Clin. Oral Inv. 1–16 (2023)

18. Sohn, K.: Fixmatch: simplifying semi-supervised learning with consistency and confidence. Adv. Neural. Inf. Process. Syst. **33**, 596–608 (2020)

19. Tarvainen, A., Valpola, H.: Mean teachers are better role models: weight-averaged consistency targets improve semi-supervised deep learning results. Adv. Neural Inf. Proce. Syst. **30** (2017)

20. Wang, Y., et al.: Freematch: self-adaptive thresholding for semi-supervised learning. In: The Eleventh International Conference on Learning Representations (2022)

21. Yang, L., Qi, L., Feng, L., Zhang, W., Shi, Y.: Revisiting weak-to-strong consistency in semi-supervised semantic segmentation. In: Proceedings of the IEEE/CVF Conference on Computer Vision and Pattern Recognition, pp. 7236–7246 (2023)

22. Yao, H., Hu, X., Li, X.: Enhancing pseudo label quality for semi-supervised domain-generalized medical image segmentation. In: Proceedings of the AAAI Conference on Artificial Intelligence. vol. 36, pp. 3099–3107 (2022)

23. Zhao, B., et al.: Automatic acute ischemic stroke lesion segmentation using semi-supervised learning. Int. J. Comput. Intell. Syst. **14**(1), 723–733 (2021)

24. Zhao, B., et al.: Combine unlabeled with labeled MR images to measure acute ischemic stroke lesion by stepwise learning. IET Image Proc. **16**(14), 3965–3976 (2022)

Preprocessing of Prior Knowledge Before Semi-supervised Tooth Segmentation

Bing Wang⬤, Chi Zhang⬤, and Weili Shi[(✉)]⬤

School of Computer Science and Technology, Changchun University of Science and Technology, Changchun, Jilin, China
shiweili@cust.edu.cn

Abstract. In the realm of dental imaging, the utilisation of 3D dental cone-beam computed tomography (CBCT) scans has gained significant prominence, particularly in the fields of orthodontics and endodontics. These scans, characterized by their lower radiation exposure, have proven instrumental in clinical diagnosis. A crucial aspect of their application involves the precise segmentation of teeth, as it provides vital anatomical information for medical practitioners and serves as a cornerstone in computer-aided diagnosis. While the nnU-Net architecture has gained popularity for medical image segmentation, the practical integration of unlabelled medical image data remains a significant challenge. In response to this, our paper introduces a semi-supervised approach rooted in the foundational nnU-Net structure. This method incorporates the preprocessing of data with prior knowledge and iterative optimisation of pseudo-labels to enhance the accuracy of tooth segmentation.A key insight from our research is the pivotal role played by morphological opening and closing operations as preprocessing steps, capitalizing on the wealth of a prior information available. This strategic approach culminated in remarkable results, with a preliminary-round score of 0.9381 and a final-round score of 0.8427, demonstrating the effectiveness of our proposed technique.

Keywords: tooth segmentation · prior knowledge · pseudo-label · semi-supervision

1 Introduction

In recent years, with the continuous advancement of 3D dental cone beam computed tomography technology, as well as the combined effects of multiple factors such as economic upgrading and the trend of aging population, the development of the dental field is increasingly emphasizing its importance and urgency. In dental imaging, tooth segmentation is a crucial task for diagnosis and treatment planning. However, traditional manual segmentation methods consume a lot of time and require a high level of expertise, so the optimisation of automatic segmentation methods is imminent [6].

© The Author(s), under exclusive license to Springer Nature Switzerland AG 2025
Y. Wang et al. (Eds.): STS 2023, LNCS 14623, pp. 46–57, 2025.
https://doi.org/10.1007/978-3-031-72396-4_5

Medical image segmentation methods based on prior knowledge medical knowledge can effectively guide the model and help it to better capture task-relevant features, thus improving the robustness and accuracy of the model. By introducing prior knowledge, the segmentation model can be made more compatible with the logic of human thinking and integrated into the construction process of the segmentation model in an appropriate way, thus improving the diagnostic performance of the model. Currently, there have been many research works exploring medical image segmentation methods based on prior knowledge and applying them successfully in the medical field. These ways [7,14] of introducing prior knowledge can be classified as constraints based on the optimisation problem, model architecture design, or a combination of these two ways.

Fully supervised deep learning methods have demonstrated remarkable success in computer vision, particularly in the realm of computer-aided diagnosis [3], including the differentiation between benign and malignant tumors and the segmentation of various organs. However, fully supervised segmentation requires expensive and time-consuming manual annotation and requires medical expertise and clinical skills of the annotator, which creates difficulties and challenges in the field of fully supervised segmentation. Given the challenges outlined above, the use of semi-supervised methods for medical image segmentation, which capitalise on a wealth of unlabelled data and only a limited number of labelled examples, holds great promise. This approach has attracted considerable interest in the academic community. To illustrate, numerous researchers have introduced techniques for augmenting unlabelled data by incorporating predicted pseudo-labels [1,12]. For the problem of lack of quality labelled data, selecting high-confidence segmentation results as pseudo-labels to supervise the prediction of unlabelled data is also a common approach in medical image processing. Wu et al. [15]proposed a network with one encoder and two decoders of different structures to generate trustworthy predictions. These factors combine to make supervised learning methods more difficult to apply in practical scenarios. Therefore, it is essential to employ semi-supervised learning methods for unlabelled medical image data to enhance model performance. Unlike fully supervised methods, semi-supervised learning focuses on efficiently utilising both labelled and unlabelled data [2,13]. Furthermore, hybrid semi-supervised learning [8,10] has gained significant attention and application, where diverse methods are integrated to optimize the model and enhance segmentation performance. These methods fully utilise the vast amount of unlabelled data, thereby enhancing the generalisation performance and robustness of the model. The use of semi-supervised learning methods shows significant promise in the area of dental image segmentation, aiding in tackling obstacles posed by data labelling and expediting advancements in disease diagnosis and treatment planning.

In both fully supervised and semi-supervised learning, the focus is on the training process, often without adapting to the specific characteristics of the data. However, detailed analysis and tailored pre-processing of the data prior to training can significantly influence the results. This approach is particularly useful for unlabelled data in semi-supervised settings, where such preprocessing can greatly improve learning efficiency. In this paper, we present a novel approach that combines nnU-Net [9] with medical prior knowledge, allowing the use of unlabelled data to improve model performance in tooth segmentation.

The principal contributions of our study can be outlined as follows:

- We employ medical prior knowledge, and pre-process the label data to effectively minimize erroneous segmentation area.
- We apply pseudo-labelling based semi-supervised learning to tooth segmentation, effectively exploiting unlabelled data.

2 Method

2.1 Data Preprocessing

There are many excellent preprocessing methods integrated in nnU-Net, which are simple and effective, can automatically adapt to different data, and are an important support for the generalisation capability of nnU-Net. For CBCT images, z-score normalisation is performed independently for each image. z-Score normalisation is a commonly used data normalisation method, which aims to model data with different distributions onto a uniform scale, which is beneficial for model training. Meanwhile, during the training process, nnU-Net employs a variety of data enhancement techniques: e.g., rotating, scaling, adding Gaussian noise, and etc. Therefore we borrowed these excellent preprocessing techniques to preprocess the data.

In our research, we found that achieving regional smoothness in dental image segmentation is crucial. To achieve this, we integrated this prior knowledge into our approach by incorporating morphological opening and closing operations alongside the nnU-Net network architecture. Morphological open and close operations are two basic morphological operations in digital image processing that use structural elements to process the image. These operations are very useful in image denoising, segmentation and feature extraction. Morphological opening is used to remove small objects or details, such as noise dots, from an image while preserving its overall structure. This process involves an initial erosion operation followed by an expansion operation. The erosion removes pixels from the edges of the image, and the expansion restores the main image structure without the small objects that were eroded. Consequently, this technique effectively removes small or thin objects while preserving larger ones. Morphological closure is used to seal small holes and fractures in an image while preserving the larger structure. This procedure starts with an expansion operation followed by an erosion operation. The expansion operation effectively closes small gaps and fractures, while the subsequent erosion operation aims to restore the original size of the object. As a result, this technique fills small holes and gaps in the image while maintaining the overall structural integrity. This valuable knowledge is particularly useful for medical image segmentation, and enhances algorithm accuracy. Since medical images frequently feature complicated anatomical structures and tissues, prior knowledge may help algorithms to capture target structures with greater precision, substantially reducing the likelihood of segmentation errors. Meanwhile, another role is to decrease dependency on extensive labelled data. Within the medical domain, obtaining high-quality labelled data often involves a significant expense and consumes time. This improves the performance and robustness of the model while also reducing costs. Furthermore, it aligns with the data-driven principle of deep learning, making the model more feasible for practical applications.

2.2   Architecture

For our study, we selected nnU-Net as the baseline network, and Fig. 1 presents the complete training framework. To suit different datasets, researchers have typically had to modify network structures and parameters. This undertaking necessitates substantial experimentation and is reliant on the researcher's professional expertise. Moreover, results can be challenging to reproduce successfully. Previous research has typically concentrated on developing novel network structures, yet these models are frequently empirically calibrated using specific training data, lack generalisation and tend to result in overfitting. However, our study's primary innovation is our rational design process. We first analyse the data and pre-process any prior knowledge before starting network training. This approach significantly reduces the over-tuning of the network structure and parameters, thus resulting in a more generalised model. A training framework designed and the effective use of unlabelled data sensibly will enable the realisation of nnU-Net's full potential, leading to a more robust and dependable solution for medical image segmentation tasks.

nnU-Net adopts a symmetric encoder-decoder architecture based on skip connections. In addition, nnU-Net determines the input patch size and input spacing according to dataset properties. Then, the dataset-sensitive patch size and spacing are used to set the hyper-parameters related to network architecture, like the number of resolution stages, convolution kernels and down-sample/up-sample ratios. As a result, these architecture-related hyperparameters can vary across tasks, resulting in distinct network architectures for each specific task. This adaptive structure enables the quick creation of a fundamental model, serving as a strong starting point for subsequent optimisation steps.

2.3   Loss Function

We combine the Dice Similariy Coefficient(DSC) loss and crossentropy loss because compound loss functions have been proven to be robust in various medical image segmentation tasks. [11]

$$L = L_{DSC} + L_{CE} \qquad (1)$$

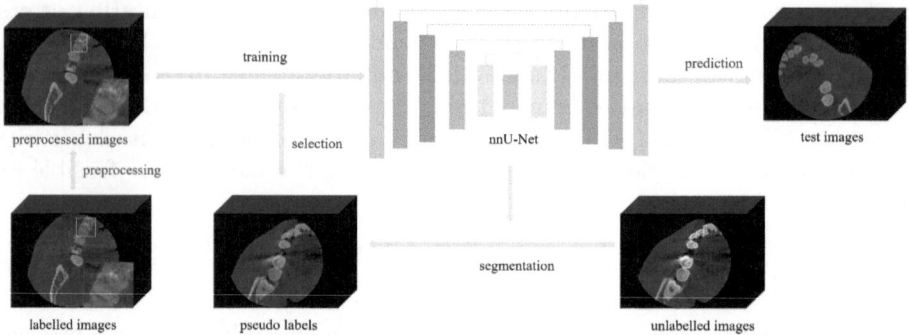

Fig. 1. The architecture of our training framework, which is based on nnU-Net.

2.4   Post-processing

Test Time Augmentation (TTA) was selected as an excellent post-processing. It generates more diverse samples during testing, and the aggregation of multiple predictions corrects some of the incorrect predictions, ultimately achieving the goal of improving the generalisation performance of the model on the test set.

2.5   Training Strategy Innovation

We adopt a simple and effective method for generating pseudo-labels, which facilitates the use of unlabelled data to train our model. The specific method for generating pseudo-labels is as follows:

1. Train a five-fold cross-validation model based on the pre-processed labelled data.
2. Use the network model trained in the first step to make predictions on unlabelled data.
3. Combine the labelled data with the unlabelled data to retrain a network model.

For five-fold cross-validation, the first two folds of 3 data are used as the validation set, and the last three folds of 2 data are used as the validation set. We use a composite loss function of dice loss and cross entropy loss in the training process.

2.6   Related Configurations

In order to improve the segmentation accuracy of the network, we have developed a new set of configurations based on the default 3d-fullres configuration of nn-UNet. These new configurations implement larger input slice sizes and a higher batch size. Given that the competition has two phases, namely the preliminary-round and the final-round, with datasets that significantly differ between them,

Table 1. Input data specific settings.

Configuration	Preliminary-round		Final-round	
	Default	Our	Default	Our
Input Patch Size	(112, 160, 128)	(112, 160, 160)	(160, 96, 160)	(160, 96, 160)
Input Batch Size	2	4	2	4
Input Spacing	(0.3, 0.3, 0.3)	(0.3, 0.3, 0.3)	(0.3, 0.3, 0.3)	(0.3, 0.3, 0.3)

separate configurations were executed for the preliminaries and the rematches. These configurations, as demonstrated in Table 1, were performed in the respective datasets.

3   Experiments

3.1   Dataset and Evaluation Measures

The CTooth+ [4,5] dataset used in this competition was jointly provided by Hangzhou Dental Group, Hangzhou Qiantang Dental Hospital, University of Electronic Science and Technology, and Queen Mary University of London. In the Preliminary Round, the training set comprises data from 12 labelled 3D CBCT scans, 200 unlabelled 3D CBCT dental scans, and 10 CBCT scans for testing. For the Final Round, an additional 100 unlabelled 3D CBCT dental scans and 50 CBCT scans for testing were included.

The evaluation metrics encompass three accuracy Dice coefficient(Dice), Intersection over Union(IoU) and Three-dimensional Hausdorff distance(H(d)). These metrics collectively contribute to the ranking computation.The following formula describes their respective weights.

$$Score = 0.4 * Dice + 0.3 * IOU + 0.3(1 - H(d)) \qquad (2)$$

3.2   Implementation Details

Environment Settings. The development environments and requirements are presented in Table 2.

Training Protocols. All training data are subjected to appropriate preprocessing based on their respective data sets, and the methods used for preprocessing are the standard processing methods of nnU-Net. Our training strategy combines the dice loss and cross-entropy loss functions, with the initial learning rate set to 0.01 and the number of training rounds set to 1000 for all experiments. The detailed settings are shown in Table 3.

Table 2. Development environments and requirements.

System	CentOS Linux release 7.9.2009
CPU	Intel(R) Xeon(R) Gold 6338 CPU @ 2.00 GHz
RAM	16GB;3200MT/s
GPU	A100-PCIE-40 GB
CUDA version	11.7
Programming language	Python 3.9.16
Deep learning framework	Pytorch (torch2.0.1,torchvision0.15.2)
Specific dependencies	nnU-Net

Table 3. Training protocols.

Network initialisation	"HE" normal initialisation
Optimizer	SGD with nesterov momentum ($\mu = 0.99$)
Total epochs	1000
Initial learning rate	0.01
Lr decay schedule	Poly learning rate policy:$(1 - epoch/1000)^{0.9}$
Training time	24/48 h
Loss function	Dice loss and cross entropy loss
Number of model parameters	30.5M

Table 4. Quantitative evaluation results in the preliminary-round.

Method	Internal Validation			OnlineValidation		
	Dice(%)	IoU(%)	HD(mm)	Dice(%)	IoU(%)	HD(mm)
Our	98.79±2.8	97.74±4.9	0.0158±0.014	93.00	93.30	0.0462

Table 5. Ablation experiments in the preliminary-round.

Method	Dice (%)	IoU (%)	HD (mm)	Score
nnU-Net	90.81	91.36	0.0479	0.9229
nnU-Net+pre-process	91.91	92.35	0.0488	0.9300
nnU-Net+pre-process+unlabel	93.00	93.30	0.0462	0.9381

4   Results and Discussion

The Dice coefficient(Dice), intersection over union (IoU), and Hausdorff distance(HD) scores for all experiments were acquired from the online validation leaderboard during the MICCAI 2023 Semi-supervised Teeth Segmentation Challenge.

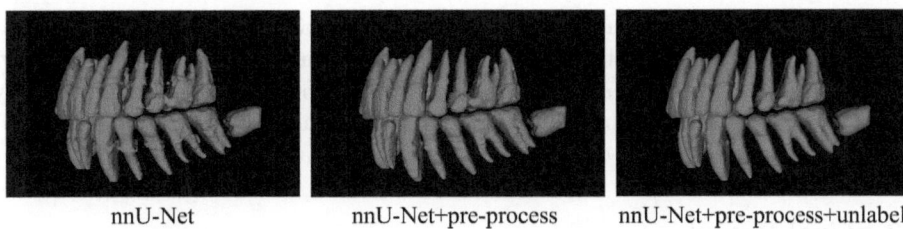

| nnU-Net | nnU-Net+pre-process | nnU-Net+pre-process+unlabel |

Fig. 2. Segmentation examples of ablation experiments in the preliminary-round.

Table 6. Quantitative evaluation results in the final-round.

Method	Internal Validation			OnlineValidation		
	Dice (%)	IoU (%)	HD (mm)	Dice (%)	IoU (%)	HD (mm)
Our	99.42±0.3	98.84±0.5	0.0125±0.009	83.43	85.83	0.1615

Table 7. Ablation experiments in the final-round.

Method	Dice (%)	IoU (%)	HD (mm)	Score
preliminary-round	76.59	81.15	0.2679	0.7694
preliminary-round+post-process	81.62	84.55	0.1806	0.8259
preliminary-round+post-process+unlabel	83.43	85.83	0.1615	0.8427

4.1 Preliminary-Round

The overall quantitative results in the preliminary-round are shown in Table 4. Meanwhile, ablation experiments were performed to verify the effect of the pre-process method and the use of unlabel data. Table 5 shows the results with or without the use of pre-process and unlabelled data. In our first experiment, the network was trained using a conventional supervised approach, resulting in a performance score of 0.9229. To improve this, we introduced a semi-supervised learning strategy. This involved iteratively feeding the network's predictions on unlabelled data back into the training set. As the network continued to learn from this ever-expanding pool of unlabelled data, we observed a significant improvement in its performance, with the score rising to 0.9381. Furthermore, Fig. 2.provides a visual representation of this process. It clearly shows that as the network was exposed to more data through these iterative cycles, there was a clear trend towards producing smoother and more refined images. This trend is indicative of the network's increasing ability to generalise from the data, a key benefit of incorporating semi-supervised learning into the training regime. The evolution of image smoothness over iterations, as shown in Fig. 2, visually represents the advanced learning and adaptation capabilities of the network through this semi-supervised approach.

Good and Failure Segmentation Cases. Figure 3 presents four representative segmentation results obtained from our final submission in the preliminary-round. The top two rows show case 13 and case 16, our network successfully achieved high-accuracy segmentation. However, in the bottom two rows, specifically case 15 and case 19, over-segmentation errors are apparent.

4.2   Final-Round

In the final-round, the model with the highest score in the preliminary-round are used to directly predict the test data of the final-round. Through analysis, we found that the data of the preliminary-round and the final-round are quite different, we therefore post-processed the results above and use unlabel data. This post-processing operation focuses on applying ROI restrictions. The overall quantitative results in the final-round are shown in Table 6. Meanwhile, ablation experiments were performed to verify the effect of the post-process method and the use of unlabel data. Table 7 shows the results with or without the use of pre-process and unlabelled data. The results clearly show that this semi-supervised learning approach leads to improved performance compared to models trained only on labelled data. Examples of segmentation of ablation experiments are given in Fig. 4.

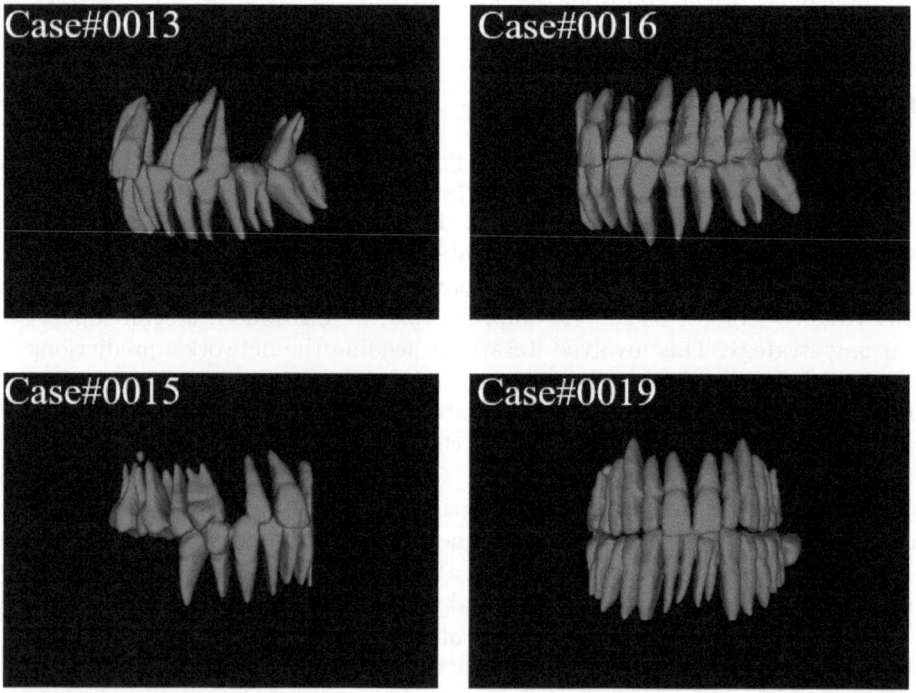

Fig. 3. Segmentation examples of good and poor cases in the preliminary-round.

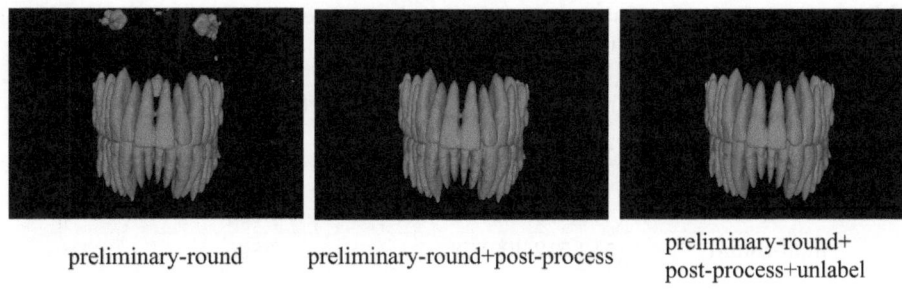

preliminary-round   preliminary-round+post-process   preliminary-round+
post-process+unlabel

Fig. 4. Segmentation examples of ablation experiments in the final-round.

Good and Failure Segmentation Cases. Figure 5 presents four representative segmentation results obtained from our final submission in the final-round. For the final-round test data, our model encountered difficulties in segmenting teeth with implants and peripheral parts of teeth.

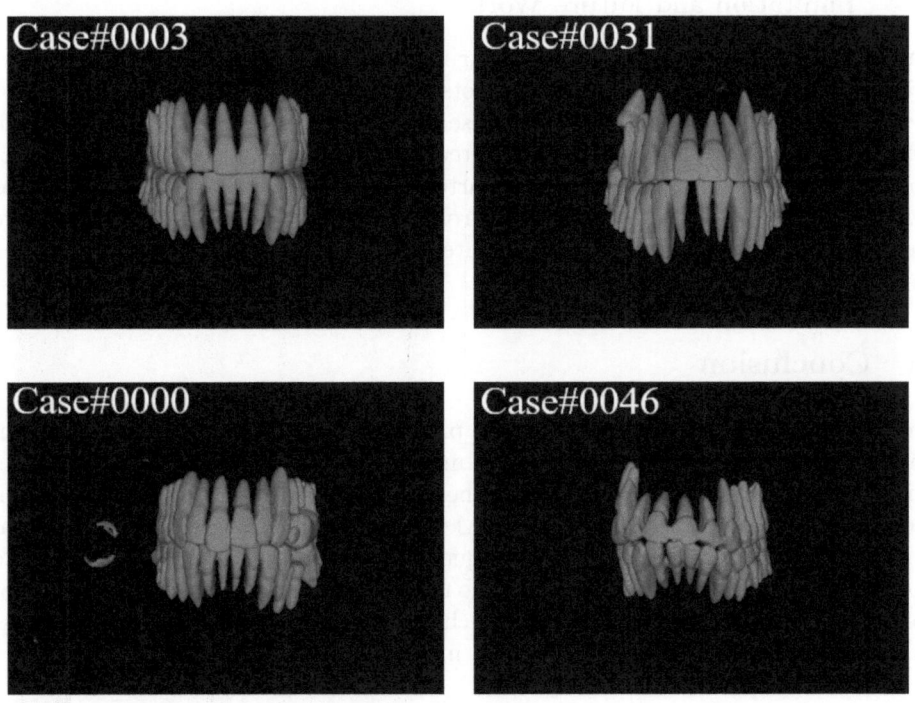

Fig. 5. Segmentation examples of good and poor cases in the final-round.

Table 8. Quantitative evaluation of segmentation efficiency in terms of the running time and GPU memory consumption. Evaluation GPU platform: A100-PCIE-40GB

	Image Size	Running Time (s)	Max GPU (MB)
preliminary-round	(200,200,300)	11	3249
	(266,266,200)	29	3349
	(400,400,300)	29	3353
final-round	(512,512,400)	78	3895

4.3   Segmentation Efficiency Results on Validation Set

We ran our model on a docker with NVIDIA A100-PCIE-40GB for inference on 10 validation cases in the preliminary-round and 50 validation cases in the final-round. Table 8 shows the inference efficiency parameters of our model on some examples.

4.4   Limitation and Future Work

It is important to acknowledge that our method has certain limitations. In particular, when dealing with new datasets of varying resolutions, we may need to retrain the model to adapt to these changes. Future work should include exploring advanced data augmentation techniques, employing sophisticated postprocessing methods and Designing smarter semi-supervised strategies to further enhance the model's performance and robustness. Additionally, we plan to give more attention to understanding the interplay between preprocessing strategies and architectural decisions.

5   Conclusion

In this study, we cleverly incorporate prior knowledge in the medical domain based on nnU-Net and effectively use unlabelled data to participate in model training, thus significantly improving the model's performance in the 3D CBCT teeth segmentation task of the MICCAI 2023 Challenge. By leveraging medical expertise and image processing techniques, our approach not only improves the accuracy of tooth segmentation, but also reduces the reliance on large amounts of labelled data. Ultimately, our method achieved an average score of 0.8427 across all the online test data, placing second in the final-round.

Acknowledgements. The authors of this paper declare that the segmentation method they implemented for participation in the STS 2023 challenge has not used any pre-trained models nor additional datasets other than those provided by the organizers. The proposed solution is fully automatic without any manual intervention. We thank all the data owners for making the X-ray images and CT scans publicly available and Alibaba Cloud for hosting the challenge platform.

References

1. Bai, W., et al.: Semi-supervised learning for network-based cardiac MR image segmentation. In: Descoteaux, M., Maier-Hein, L., Franz, A., Jannin, P., Collins, D.L., Duchesne, S. (eds.) MICCAI 2017. LNCS, vol. 10434, pp. 253–260. Springer, Cham (2017). https://doi.org/10.1007/978-3-319-66185-8_29

2. Chen, X., Yuan, Y., Zeng, G., Wang, J.: Semi-supervised semantic segmentation with cross pseudo supervision. In: Proceedings of the IEEE/CVF Conference on Computer Vision and Pattern Recognition, pp. 2613–2622 (2021)

3. Clark, K., et al.: The cancer imaging archive (tcia): maintaining and operating a public information repository. J. Digit. Imaging **26**, 1045–1057 (2013)

4. Cui, W., et al.: Ctooth+: a large-scale dental cone beam computed tomography dataset and benchmark for tooth volume segmentation. In: MICCAI Workshop on Data Augmentation, Labelling, and Imperfections, pp. 64–73. Springer (2022). https://doi.org/10.1007/978-3-031-17027-0_7

5. Cui, W., et al.: Ctooth: a fully annotated 3d dataset and benchmark for tooth volume segmentation on cone beam computed tomography images. In: International Conference on Intelligent Robotics and Applications, pp. 191–200. Springer (2022). https://doi.org/10.1007/978-3-031-13841-6_18

6. Heimann, T., Meinzer, H.P.: Statistical shape models for 3d medical image segmentation: a review. Med. Image Anal. **13**(4), 543–563 (2009)

7. Huang, H., et al.: Medical image segmentation with deep atlas prior. IEEE Trans. Med. Imaging **40**(12), 3519–3530 (2021)

8. Huang, W., et al.: Semi-supervised neuron segmentation via reinforced consistency learning. IEEE Trans. Med. Imaging **41**(11), 3016–3028 (2022)

9. Isensee, F., Jaeger, P.F., Kohl, S.A., Petersen, J., Maier-Hein, K.H.: nnu-net: a self-configuring method for deep learning-based biomedical image segmentation. Nat. Methods **18**(2), 203–211 (2021)

10. Lai, X., et al.: Semi-supervised semantic segmentation with directional context-aware consistency. In: Proceedings of the IEEE/CVF Conference on Computer Vision and Pattern Recognition, pp. 1205–1214 (2021)

11. Ma, J., et al.: Loss odyssey in medical image segmentation. Med. Image Anal. **71**, 102035 (2021)

12. Wang, G., et al.: Semi-supervised segmentation of radiation-induced pulmonary fibrosis from lung ct scans with multi-scale guided dense attention. IEEE Trans. Med. Imaging **41**(3), 531–542 (2021)

13. Wu, Y., et al.: Mutual consistency learning for semi-supervised medical image segmentation. Med. Image Anal. **81**, 102530 (2022)

14. Zheng, H., et al.: Semi-supervised segmentation of liver using adversarial learning with deep atlas prior. In: Shen, D., et al. (eds.) MICCAI 2019. LNCS, vol. 11769, pp. 148–156. Springer, Cham (2019). https://doi.org/10.1007/978-3-030-32226-7_17

15. Zhu, S., Brazil, G., Liu, X.: The edge of depth: explicit constraints between segmentation and depth. In: Proceedings of the IEEE/CVF Conference on Computer Vision and Pattern Recognition, pp. 13116–13125 (2020)

A Semi-supervised Tooth Segmentation Method Based on Entropy-Guided Mean Teacher and Weakly Mutual Consistency Network

Mingqian Li[ID], Zhiqian Yan[ID], Qinghang Lu[ID], Qiongxiong Ma[(✉)][ID], Liang Guo[ID], and Qingmao Zhang[(✉)][ID]

Guangdong Provincial Key Laboratory of Nanophotonic Functional Materials and Devices, School of Optoelectronic Science and Engineering, South China Normal University, Guangzhou, China
maqx@m.scnu.edu.cn, zhangqm@scnu.edu.cn

Abstract. Accurate tooth CBCT segmentation is a crucial step in providing complete dental structure information for computer-aided diagnosis. Despite the emergence of many fully supervised deep learning tooth segmentation methods in recent years, annotating all teeth is a time-consuming and laborious task due to the large number of teeth and the similarity of tooth roots to surrounding bone density. Therefore, the application of semi-supervised learning in tooth segmentation has received increasing attention from researchers. In this study, we propose a semi-supervised tooth segmentation method combining the entropy-guided mean-teacher (EG-MT) and the weakly mutual consistency network (WMC-Net). Diverging from MC-Net+, we replace the last up-sampling layer with two up-sampling layers using different up-sampling methods on the basis of V-Net to provide consistency information and enhance local information attention through the CBAM module. The EG-MT strategy is designed to effectively guide the network in learning pixels that are difficult to recognize, such as boundaries. In addition, we perform post-processing operations such as erosion and dilation on the segmentation results to improve accuracy. On the validation set, we achieved an average DSC of 88.39%, an average IoU of 89.32%, and an average HD95 distance of 0.0934. On the test set of the MICCAI STS 2023 Challenge, we achieved an average DSC of 77.49%, an average IoU of 81.61%, and an average HD95 distance of 0.1580. Our code is available at https://github.com/59-lmq/STS2023-WMCNet.

Keywords: Semi-supervised learning · Tooth segmentation · STS2023

1 Introduction

Computer-Aided Design (CAD) tools are becoming increasingly popular in modern dental practice, especially for treatment planning and comprehensive prognostic assessment. Three-dimensional dental Cone Beam Computed Tomography

© The Author(s), under exclusive license to Springer Nature Switzerland AG 2025
Y. Wang et al. (Eds.): STS 2023, LNCS 14623, pp. 58–71, 2025.
https://doi.org/10.1007/978-3-031-72396-4_6

(CBCT) scans are widely used in dentistry and endodontics due to their low radiation dose. Tooth segmentation is an important task in the field of medical image analysis, providing essential dental structural information to doctors, and is a crucial step in enhancing clinical diagnosis and surgical planning. In recent years, there has been progress in deep learning for CBCT tooth segmentation. Some methods [6] have applied Mask R-CNN [8] for tooth segmentation. Others [5] utilize a multi-stage V-Net [11] segmentation network to locate the tooth's Region of Interest (ROI) before proceeding to instance segmentation of the tooth. However, these methods are conducted under fully supervised learning and evaluated on private dental datasets, making it difficult to guarantee the reproducibility of their model's accuracy. Currently, automatic tooth segmentation remains a formidable challenge for several reasons [2]: (1) The volume and annotations of open-source datasets are insufficient to support the training of a robust model; (2) The density of the tooth root is similar to that of the surrounding bone tissue; (3) There are continuous boundaries at the crowns of adjacent teeth.

In the task of tooth image segmentation, fully annotating a large number of teeth requires the domain knowledge of dental experts and is time-consuming and labor-intensive. Semi-supervised learning leverages the existing labeled samples to pseudo-label the remaining unlabeled data, thus extracting useful information from unlabeled samples [1,7], making it more practical against the current backdrop of data annotation difficulties. As a result, an increasing number of researchers are focusing on the application of semi-supervised learning in the field of tooth segmentation.

In this paper, we propose a novel method using an Entropy-Guided Mean Teacher [12] (EG-MT) semi-supervised strategy to guide the Weakly Mutual Consistency Network (WMC-Net) for the complex task of semi-supervised tooth segmentation. Differing from the Mutual Consistency Network (MC-Net+ [14]), we introduce CBAM [13] modules in the top skip connections of V-Net [11], replacing the last up-sampling layer with two different types of up-sampling layers to provide consistency information. The CBAM [13] modules enable the model to understand tooth structure and filter out irrelevant data such as background noise, further focusing on the information relevant to the segmentation task. Additionally, combining tooth structure information, we optimize the segmentation results with post-processing methods like erosion, dilation, and the maximum connected domain, and evaluate our proposed method on the MICCAI STS 2023 challenge dataset [4,4]. The experimental results prove the effectiveness of our method.

The contributions of this paper can be summarized as follows:

- We adopt an Entropy-Guided Mean Teacher [12] (EG-MT) semi-supervised learning strategy. This strategy guides the network in learning difficult pixels through entropy, effectively utilizing unlabeled data.
- We propose WMC-Net, a weakly mutual consistency network combined with CBAM [13] modules. By incorporating CBAM [13] modules into the top skip connection, the network's ability to capture teeth on a large scale is enhanced.

We replace the last up-sampling layer with two different types of up-sampling layers to provide weakly consistency information.
- We combine tooth structure information for post-processing of segmentation results, effectively reducing erroneous segmentation areas.

2   Method

2.1   Proposed Method

Our approach includes two parts: a weakly mutual consistency network combining CBAM [13] and the entropy-guided MT [12] semi-supervised strategy, as shown in Fig. 1 and 2, respectively.

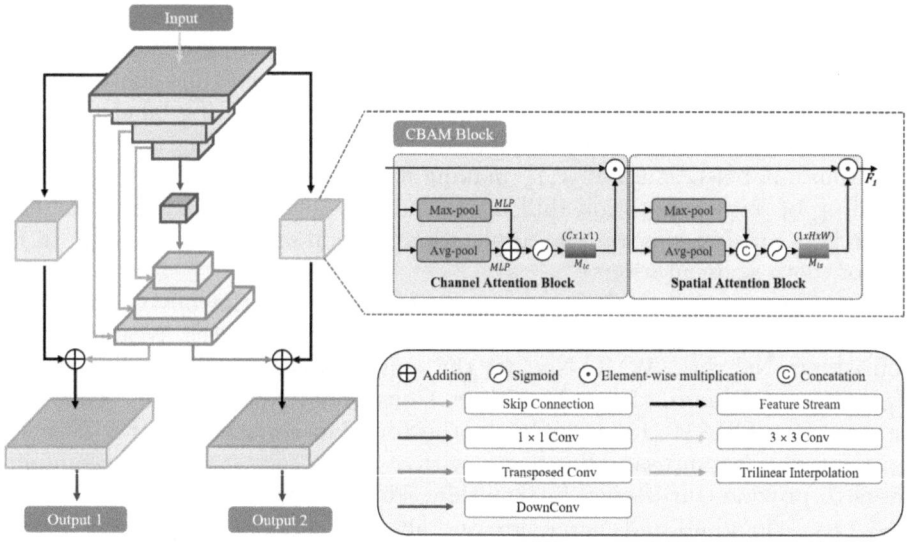

Fig. 1. Illustration of the weakly mutual consistency network(WMC-Net). Based on the original last layer of V-Net [11], we add the up-sampling method of Trilinear Interpolation to provide weakly mutual consistency, and add CBAM [13] module to the top skip connection to enhance local attention.

Network Architecture. For tooth segmentation, the tooth shape is similar, but there is the problem of the root and the surrounding bone density, which is easy for the network to identify bone into teeth. To solve this problem, we improve on V-Net [11] to propose a weakly mutual consistency network combining CBAM [13] to improve the model's ability of the model to capture features at large scales, as shown in Fig. 1. MCNet+ [14] is a method that arranges mutuality into the same network in semi-supervised learning, but the multiple decoding branches of the method lead to an increase in the number of network model parameters. Unlike MC-Net+ [14], we add the CBAM [13] module in the top-level jump connection, and only divide the last layer up-sampling into two branches with different up-sampling methods, ConvTransposed and Trilinear Interpolation.

Different up-sampling methods enable the network to output similar results under the same input, and the results are complementary. Through these branches, we can increase the consistency loss during the training process, and restrain the model to further learn the tooth features, as shown in Fig. 2. The CBAM [13] module captures the local feature, which improves the segmentation ability of the tooth and the remaining bone boundaries well, while reducing the attention to noise or irrelevant information.

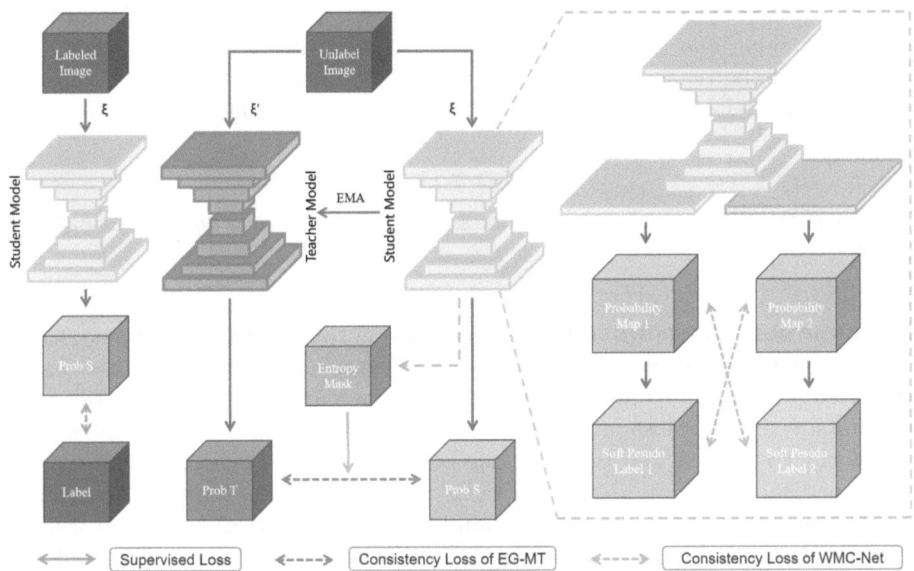

Fig. 2. Illustration of the semi-supervised learning strategy. For labeled data, the outputs of the student model computes the supervised learning loss with true labels. For unlabeled data, the consistency loss includes two parts: 1) the consistency loss between the student model's segmentation results; 2) the consistency loss between the averaged segmentation results of student model and teacher model, guided by entropy mask that calculated by the student model segmentation results.

Semi-supervised Learning Strategies. The semi-supervised learning strategy in this paper includes two parts: the entropy-guided mean-teacher(EG-MT) and consistency learning between the outputs of WMC-Net, as shown in Fig. 2. First, the output probabilities of WMC-Net satisfy the smoothness assumption, and the pseudo-labels can be generated to calculate the consistency loss. Second, EG-MT can make full use of the unlabeled data and use entropy mask to guide the consistency loss to notice the high entropy region during training [16].

Denoting p_s as the predicted probability of the student model at a voxel, we can measure the normalized entropy ne_v for the voxel as:

$$ne_v = -\sum_{c \in C} p_s^c log(p_s^c)/log(|C|) \in [0,1], \tag{1}$$

where $c \in C$ is the semantic class. A high entropy value means that the model is disordered at this voxel, implying that this voxel is likely difficult [16]. We select the voxels with $ne_v > H$ to obtain the entropy mask for calculation of consistency loss at the current training step, where H is an empirical ranging from 0.75 to 0.95 using a Gaussian ramp-up paradigm [16].

Briefly, during training, we use the labeled data and unlabeled data to train the student model, calculate the entropy of the student model output and the mutual consistency loss, and employ the entropy to guide the consistency loss between student and the teacher model. At the current training step t, the parameters of the teacher model's weights $\tilde{\theta}_t$ are updated using the exponential moving average(EMA) [12] of the student model's weights θ_t, which can be formulated as:

$$\tilde{\theta}_t = \alpha\tilde{\theta}_{t-1} + (1-\alpha)\theta_t, \tag{2}$$

where α is the EMA decay that controls the updating rate and empirically set to 0.99.

Loss Function. As shown in Fig. 2, our loss function includes two parts, supervised loss and consistency loss. For the supervised loss, the supervised loss is calculated as the predicted probability of the student model and the true label. We combine the Dice loss and the cross-entropy loss to calculate the supervised loss, as the composite loss function has been shown to remain robust in a variety of medical image segmentation tasks [10]. To the consistency loss, mainly divides into two parts. First, the probability map of the two outputs of the student model obtains the pseudo-labels, and the consistency loss is calculated with the segmentation probability of the pseudo-labels and another branch, denoted as L_{C1}. The second is the consistency loss between the average probability map output by the student model and that of the average probability map output by the teacher model, denoted as L_{C2}. The entropy is calculated from the averaged predicted probability map of student model by formula 1. We employed MSE Loss to calculate all consistency loss. The total Loss is a superposition of supervised and consistency loss:

$$L_{sup} = \gamma * L_{Dice} + (1-\gamma) * L_{CE} \tag{3}$$

$$L_{C1} = \sum_{i \in N}^{i} \sum_{j \in N}^{j} L_{MSE}(P_i^s, \tilde{Y}_j^s), i \neq j \tag{4}$$

$$L_{C2} = \frac{1}{N} \sum_{i \in N}^{i} L_{MSE}(P_i^t, P_i^s) \tag{5}$$

$$L_{C2} = (\sum \mathbb{I}(ne_v > H) * L_{C2}) / \sum \mathbb{I}(ne_v > H) \tag{6}$$

$$Loss = L_{sup} + \lambda(L_{C1} + L_{C2}) \tag{7}$$

$$\lambda(t) = 0.1 * e^{-5(1-\frac{t}{t_{max}})^2} \tag{8}$$

where γ is a balanced factor, set to 0.5; N is the number of model's output; P_i^s and P_i^t mean the i predicted probability of student and teacher model respectively; $\mathbb{I}(ne_v > H)$ is the entropy mask; $\mathbb{I}(\cdot)$ is the indicator function; $\tilde{Y}_j^s$ is the pseudo label generated by the j predicted probability of student model. Following [9,12], we use a time-dependent Gaussian warming up function(see Eq. 8) to control the balance between the supervised loss and consistency loss, where t denotes the current training step and t_{max} is the maximum training step.

2.2   Training Strategy

The following is the overall training strategy for our method:

- For the labeled data, the two predicted probabilities of student model are calculated supervised Loss with the true label.
- For unlabeled data, consistency loss L_{C2} is calculated as the averaged predicted probability of the student and teacher models. The entropy is calculated by equation. 1, guiding the consistency loss L_{C2}.
- For unlabeled data, computing the consistency loss L_{C1} between predicted probabilities of of student model.
- With the training iteration, the time-dependent Gaussian ramp-up function is used to gradually increase the threshold of entropy H and the coefficient λ of consistency loss, and the weights $\tilde{\theta}$ of the teacher network model is updated through the EMA algorithm [9,12].

2.3   Post-processing

To avoid the influence of noise, we use erosion operation to smooth the segmentation results, and the expanded the tooth with a larger Gaussian nucleus to merge the tooth into a connected region. Then we analyze the connectivity component, and select the maximum connected component except background as the final segmentation result.

3   Experiments

3.1   Dataset and Evaluation Measures

MICCAI STS 2023 Challenge aims to promote the development of semi-supervised dental segmentation methods and find robust methods to promote the development of computer-assisted diagnostic techniques in dentistry. All the 3D CBCT scans were acquired with a OP300, manufactured by Instrumentarium Orthopantomograph®. CBCT slices were acquired in the DICOM format

Table 1. Development environments and requirements.

System	Microsoft Windows 10 Professional
CPU	Intel(R) Xeon(R) W-2175 CPU @ 2.50 GHz
RAM	8×32GB
GPU (number and type)	2 * Nvidia GeForce RTX 3090Ti 24 GB
CUDA version	11.6
Programming language	Python 3.9.13
Deep learning framework	Pytorch (torch 1.12.1)
Specific dependencies	Nibabel, h5py

at the University of Electronic Science and Technology of China Hospital. All CBCT slices were scanned before dental operations, with a resolution of 266 × 266 pixels in the axial view. The in-plane resolution is about 0.25 × 0.25mm^2 and the slice thickness range from 0.25 mm to 0.3 mm. Data are acquired by orthodontists with more than five years of professional experience. Scans were annotated by fifteen dentists. Twelve junior dentists with at least two years of experience manually marked all teeth regions. The tooth labeling process used the ITK-SNAP [17] and Adobe Photoshop. The training set consisted of 312 CBCT scans, including 12 with labels and 300 data without labels, and the test set included 50 CBCT scans. In the experiment, we divided the 12 data with labels into training and validation sets by 8:2.

The evaluation metrics include three aspects, Dice similarity coefficient(Dice), IoU score and HD95 distance. The Dice similarity coefficient (Dice) and IoU score are used to evaluate the similarity of the two sets. HD95 distance measures the maximum deviation between the predicted boundary and the true boundary.

$$Dice = \frac{2 * |A \cap B|}{|A| + |B|} \tag{9}$$

$$IOU = \frac{|A \cap B|}{|A| + |B|} \tag{10}$$

$$HD95(d) = \frac{1}{\sqrt{a^2 + b^2 + c^2}} min(|x1 - x2| + |y1 - y2| + |z1 - z2|) \tag{11}$$

where A and B are the predicted label of model and the true label respectively; $(x1, y1, z1)$ and $(x2, y2, z2)$ present the coordinates of A and B; a, b, c are the height, weight, depth of label image respectively.

3.2   Implementation Details

Environment Settings. The development environments and requirements are presented in Table 1.

Table 2. Training protocols.

Network Initialization	"He" normal initialization
Batch size	4
Patch size	112×112×80
Total iterations	20000
Optimizer	SGD with nesterov momentum(μ= 0.9)
Initial learning rate (lr)	0.01
Lr decay schedule	Multiplied by 0.1 every 2500 iter
Training time	4.5 h
Loss function	cross-entropy Loss, Dice loss, MSE loss

Training Protocols. The training protocol of the proposed method is shown in Table 2.

Data Processing. We resample the images to the median spacing (spacing=0.3) of all data and then crop the non-zero regions of the image labels. Referring to the pre-processing method of [5], the images are processed with 2500 and 500 as pixel upper and lower bounds. We use the minimum-maximum normalization to normalize images:

$$x' = \frac{x - min}{max - min} \tag{12}$$

Data Augmentation. We use random cropping and random flipping as our data augmentation methods.

4   Results and Discussion

4.1   Quantitative Results on Validation Set

Table 3 shows the results of this work and the networks such as V-Net [11], MC-Net [15], MC-Net+ [14] on the validation set. We used V-Net [11] as baseline and compared it with the method of MC-Net [15], MC-Net+ [14]. Meanwhile, we also compared the results of MC-Net [15], MC-Net+ [14] trained on EG-MT strategy. From the results, our proposed method is better than MC-Net [15] and MC-Net+ [14] methods in the validation set, with Dice and IOU increasing by about 3%, respectively. The post-processing method is very effective in improving the segmentation results, with Dice and IOU generally increasing by about 10%. As shown in Fig. 3, our proposed method has higher accuracy and lower standard deviation compared to other methods.

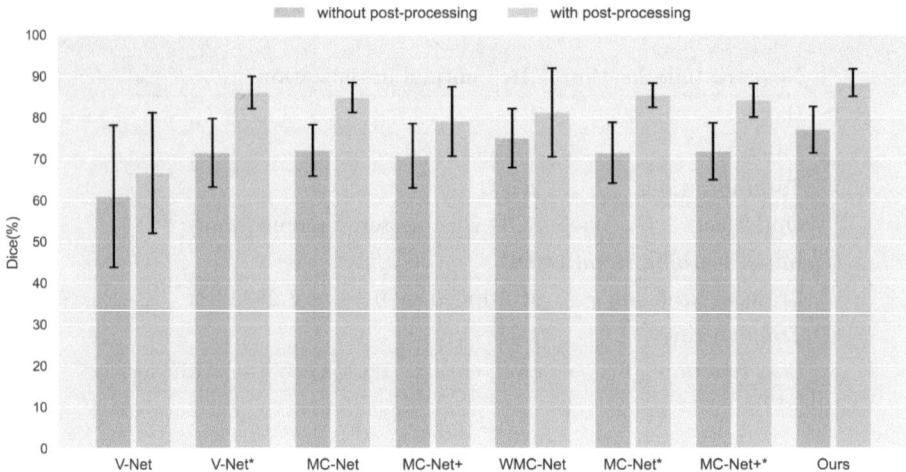

Fig. 3. With and without post-processing, Dice for different models on the validation set. Noted that * represents the network being trained on EG-MT strategy.

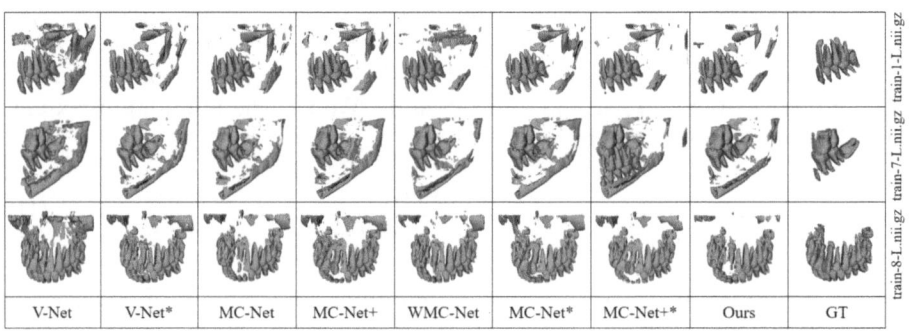

Fig. 4. Without post-processing, the segmentation results of different models on the validation set.

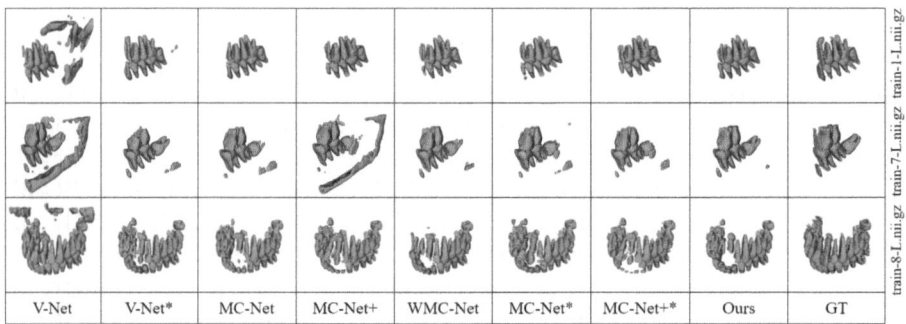

Fig. 5. With post-processing, the segmentation results of different models on the validation set.

Table 3. Results on the validation set with different networks . Noted that V-Net [11] means only trained on supervised leaning; * represents the network being trained on EG-MT strategy. All results are presented with the mean score and standard deviation of the metrics.

Method	Without post-processing			With post-processing		
	Dice (%)↑	IOU (%)↑	HD95(voxel)↓	Dice (%)↑	IOU(%)↑	HD95 (voxel)↓
V-Net [11]	60.87 ± 17.16	71.74 ± 10.24	0.3775 ± 0.1041	66.51 ± 14.55	74.94 ± 8.95	0.3281 ± 0.0696
V-Net [11]*	71.40 ± 8.26	77.31 ± 5.12	0.3616 ± 0.0961	86.00 ± 3.92	87.44 ± 3.30	0.1151 ± 0.0442
MC-Net [15]	71.97 ± 6.18	77.54 ± 3.78	0.3608 ± 0.0954	84.75 ± 3.66	86.43 ± 3.06	0.0901 ± 0.0557
MC-Net+ [14]	70.71 ± 7.78	76.84 ± 4.73	0.3601 ± 0.0955	79.02 ± 8.41	82.49 ± 5.80	0.1553 ± 0.1364
WMC-Net	74.94 ± 7.13	79.58 ± 4.70	0.3877 ± 0.1204	81.18 ± 10.71	84.24 ± 7.74	0.1663 ± 0.0884
MC-Net*	71.44 ± 7.35	77.27 ± 4.54	0.3639 ± 0.0967	85.34 ± 2.95	86.86 ± 2.53	0.0927 ± 0.0523
MC-Net+*	71.78 ± 6.85	77.44 ± 4.14	0.3843 ± 0.1114	84.10 ± 4.07	85.93 ± 3.34	0.0966 ± 0.0511
WMC-Net*(our)	**76.98 ± 5.59**	**80.86± 3.74**	**0.3596 ± 0.0947**	**88.39 ± 3.32**	**89.33 ± 2.90**	**0.0935 ± 0.0484**

Table 4. The ablation study of proposed method on the validation set. Noted thatt V-Net [11] means only trained on supervised leaning; WMC-Net/CBAM [13] represents WMC-Net withou CBAM [13] module; * represents the network being trained on EG-MT strategy.

Method	Design			Without post-processing			With post-processing		
	EG-MT	CBAM	Trilinear	Dice(%)↑	IOU(%)↑	HD95(voxel)↓	Dice(%)↑	IOU(%)↑	HD95(voxel)↓
V-Net [11]	-	-	-	60.87 ± 17.16	71.74 ± 10.24	0.3775 ± 0.1041	66.51 ± 14.55	74.94 ± 8.95	0.3281 ± 0.0696
V-Net [11]*	√	×	×	71.40 ± 8.26	77.31 ± 5.12	0.3616 ± 0.0961	86.00 ± 3.92	87.44 ± 3.30	0.1151 ± 0.0442
V-Net [11]+CBAM [13]*	√	√	×	71.70 ± 6.90	77.4 ± 4.23	0.3638 ± 0.0981	78.77 ± 12.49	82.7 ± 8.69	0.1587 ± 0.0998
WMC-Net/CBAM [13]*	√	×	√	74.91 ± 5.41	79.41 ± 3.45	0.3695 ± 0.0984	80.81 ± 12.96	84.25 ± 9.17	0.1429 ± 0.0932
WMC-Net/CBAM [13]	×	×	√	74.22 ± 6.16	79.01 ± 3.82	0.3747 ± 0.103	78.11 ± 13.06	82.31 ± 9.01	0.1801 ± 0.0916
WMC-Net	×	√	√	74.94 ± 7.13	79.58 ± 4.70	0.3877 ± 0.1204	81.18 ± 10.71	84.24 ± 7.74	0.1663 ± 0.0884
WMC-Net*(our)	√	√	√	**76.98 ± 5.59**	**80.86 ± 3.74**	**0.3596 ± 0.0947**	**88.39 ± 3.32**	**89.33 ± 2.90**	**0.0935 ± 0.0484**

Table 5. The ablation study of balanced factor γ between cross-entropy loss and Dice loss.

γ	Without post-processing			With post-processing		
	Dice(%)↑	IOU(%)↑	HD95(voxel)↓	Dice(%)↑	IOU(%)↑	HD95(voxel)↓
0.00	74.26 ± 0.79	79.21 ± 3.72	0.3660 ± 0.1009	85.65 ± 4.48	87.17 ± 3.69	0.1060 ± 0.0586
0.25	75.85 ± 3.72	79.78 ± 2.49	0.3632 ± 0.1014	80.86 ± 11.94	84.15 ± 8.51	0.1256 ± 0.1053
0.50	**76.98 ± 5.59**	**80.86 ± 3.74**	**0.3596 ± 0.0947**	**88.39 ± 3.32**	**89.93 ± 2.90**	**0.0953 ± 0.0484**
0.75	75.12 ± 5.92	80.17 ± 3.98	0.3674 ± 0.0978	88.19 ± 2.45	89.55 ± 3.21	0.0998 ± 0.0550
1.00	74.45 ± 7.64	78.59 ± 4.94	0.3736 ± 0.1077	87.47 ± 2.32	89.61 ± 3.10	0.1012 ± 0.0499

4.2   Qualitative Results on Validation Set

Figure 4 and Fig. 5 show the segmentation results of different models with or without post-processing on the validation set, respectively. As can be seen from Fig. 4, the segmentation results of our method contain the least noise and the tooth are more complete. As shown in Fig. 5, after post-processing, the segmentation results of our method can effectively remove the background such as the jaw bone when compared with the other methods.

Table 6. The segmentation results of proposed method on the test set (with post-processing).

Method	Dice(%)↑	IOU(%)↑	HD95(voxel)↓
WMC-Net*	77.49	81.61	0.1580

4.3   Ablation Study

Table 4 presents the results of the ablation study in this work on the validation set. We trained in the divided training set and validated our method in the validation set. We performed ablation experiments from four aspects, namely whether to use EG-MT, whether to use CBAM [13] module, whether to add Trilinear Interpolation up-sampling method and whether to use post-processing method. As shown in Table 4, the Dice of adding CBAM [13] module increased by 0.3%; training the WMC-Net with the EG-MT strategy is 2% higher than Dice with only trained WMC-Net; with training with the EG-MT strategy, the Dice of employing the Trilinear Interpolation up-sampling method is 3.5% higher than V-Net [11]; with post-processing method, all metrics have promoted obviously. Finally, our method achieves the largest boost, obtaining 88.39% averaged Dice, 89.32% averaged IoU, and 0.0934 averaged HD95 distance in the validation set.

Table 5 presents the impact on the validation set when there are different balanced factors among the loss functions in the supervised learning loss function. It can be observed that, in the supervised learning section, results obtained using only cross-entropy loss (γ=0.00) or only Dice Loss (γ=1.00) are inferior to those obtained using a combined loss function. However, when using a combined loss function, the optimal results are achieved when both are equally weighted in a one-to-one ratio (γ=0.50).

4.4   Results on Final Testing Set

The results of proposed method on the test set are shown in Table 6 and Fig. 6. We finally achieved an average DSC of 77.49%, an average IoU of 81.61%, and an average HD95 distance of 0.1580 on the test set of the MICCAI STS 2023 Challenge rematch.

4.5   Limitation and Future Work

From the above results, the proposed method can segment most of the teeth in CBCT images. However, as shown in Fig. 7, the segmentation effect is not satisfactory in CBCT with metal artifacts, and there is still a problem of poor segmentation of teeth and background. In the future, we may remove metal artifact noise by Generative Adversarial Networks [3], and combine it with semi-supervised methods, so that the network can catch the features of metal artifacts from a large number of unlabeled data.

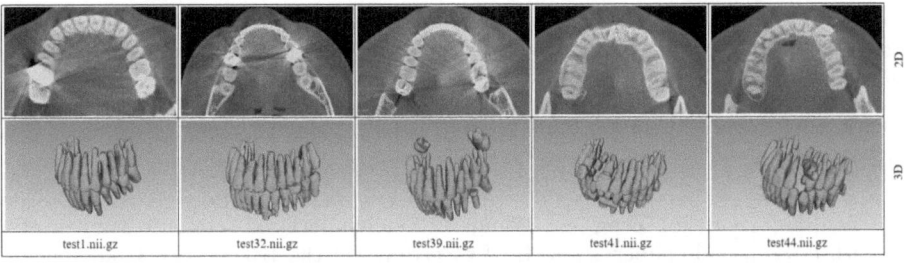

Fig. 6. The segmentation results of our method on the test set.

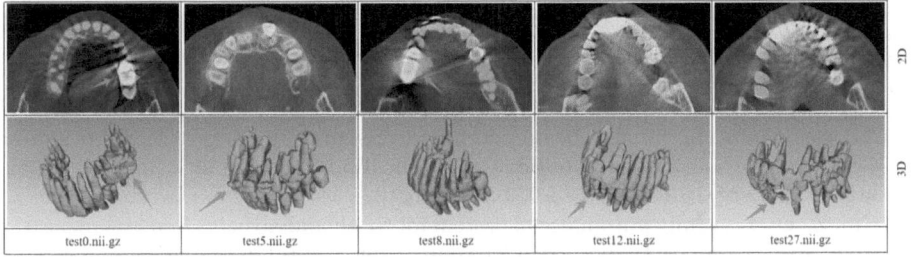

Fig. 7. Poor segmentation cases on the test set.

5   Conclusion

In this paper, we propose a weakly mutual consistency network (WMC-Net) and guide the network to learn difficult pixels through an entropy-guided MT semi-supervised strategy (EG-MT). WMC-Net replaces the last up-sampling layer with two different up-sampling methods to provide consistency information, and replaces the top skip connections with the local attention mechanism CBAM [13] module to focus more on the tooth information at large scales. EG-MT calculates the predicted probabilities of the student model to obtain a high entropy Mask, which guides the consistency loss between the student model and the teacher model. We developed and tested the entire framework on the MICCAI STS 2023 Challenge rematch dataset, achieving 77.49% average Dice, 81.61% mean IoU and 0.1580 average HD95 distance in the test set.

Acknowledgements. The authors of this paper declare that the segmentation method they implemented for participation in the MICCAI STS 2023 Challenge did not use any pre-trained model or anything other than the dataset provided by the organizer. The proposed solution is automated and required without any human intervention. We thank all data owners for making publicly available CT scans and the sponsor for curating and collecting the data. This work was supported by the Guangdong Basic and Applied Basic Research Foundation (2023A1515012966, 2023A1515011641, and 2021A1515011932), the Key-Area Research and Development Program of Guangdong

Province (2020B090922006), the Key field research projects in Foshan City(Grant No. 2120001009232), and the Young Talent Support Project of Guangzhou Association for Science and Technology (QT-2023-007).

References

1. Chen, X., Yuan, Y., Zeng, G., Wang, J.: Semi-supervised semantic segmentation with cross pseudo supervision. In: Proceedings of the IEEE/CVF Conference on Computer Vision and Pattern Recognition, pp. 2613–2622 (2021)
2. Chen, Y., et al.: Automatic segmentation of individual tooth in dental cbct images from tooth surface map by a multi-task fcn. IEEE Access **8**, 97296–97309 (2020)
3. Creswell, A., White, T., Dumoulin, V., Arulkumaran, K., Sengupta, B., Bharath, A.A.: Generative adversarial networks: an overview. IEEE Signal Process. Mag. **35**(1), 53–65 (2018)
4. Cui, W., et al.: Ctooth: a fully annotated 3d dataset and benchmark for tooth volume segmentation on cone beam computed tomography images. In: International Conference on Intelligent Robotics and Applications, pp. 191–200. Springer (2022). https://doi.org/10.1007/978-3-031-13841-6_18
5. Cui, Z., et al.: A fully automatic ai system for tooth and alveolar bone segmentation from cone-beam ct images. Nat. Commun. **13**(1), 2096 (2022)
6. Cui, Z., Li, C., Wang, W.: Toothnet: automatic tooth instance segmentation and identification from cone beam ct images. In: Proceedings of the IEEE/CVF Conference on Computer Vision and Pattern Recognition, pp. 6368–6377 (2019)
7. French, G., Laine, S., Aila, T., Mackiewicz, M., Finlayson, G.: Semi-supervised semantic segmentation needs strong, varied perturbations. arXiv preprint arXiv:1906.01916 (2019)
8. He, K., Gkioxari, G., Dollár, P., Girshick, R.: Mask r-cnn. In: Proceedings of the IEEE International Conference on Computer Vision, pp. 2961–2969 (2017)
9. Laine, S., Aila, T.: Temporal ensembling for semi-supervised learning. arXiv preprint arXiv:1610.02242 (2016)
10. Ma, J., et al.: Loss odyssey in medical image segmentation. Med. Image Anal. **71**, 102035 (2021)
11. Milletari, F., Navab, N., Ahmadi, S.A.: V-net: fully convolutional neural networks for volumetric medical image segmentation. In: 2016 Fourth International Conference on 3D Vision (3DV), pp. 565–571. IEEE (2016)
12. Tarvainen, A., Valpola, H.: Mean teachers are better role models: weight-averaged consistency targets improve semi-supervised deep learning results. Adv. Neural Inform. Process. Syst. **30** (2017)
13. Woo, S., Park, J., Lee, J.-Y., Kweon, I.S.: CBAM: convolutional block attention module. In: Ferrari, V., Hebert, M., Sminchisescu, C., Weiss, Y. (eds.) ECCV 2018. LNCS, vol. 11211, pp. 3–19. Springer, Cham (2018). https://doi.org/10.1007/978-3-030-01234-2_1
14. Wu, Y., et al.: Mutual consistency learning for semi-supervised medical image segmentation. Med. Image Anal. **81**, 102530 (2022)
15. Wu, Y., Xu, M., Ge, Z., Cai, J., Zhang, L.: Semi-supervised left atrium segmentation with mutual consistency training. In: de Bruijne, M., Cattin, P.C., Cotin, S., Padoy, N., Speidel, S., Zheng, Y., Essert, C. (eds.) MICCAI 2021. LNCS, vol. 12902, pp. 297–306. Springer, Cham (2021). https://doi.org/10.1007/978-3-030-87196-3_28

16. Xu, Z., et al.: Ambiguity-selective consistency regularization for mean-teacher semi-supervised medical image segmentation. Med. Image Anal. **88**, 102880 (2023)
17. Yushkevich, P.A., Gao, Y., Gerig, G.: Itk-snap: an interactive tool for semi-automatic segmentation of multi-modality biomedical images. In: 2016 38th Annual International Conference of the IEEE Engineering in Medicine and Biology Society (EMBC), pp. 3342–3345. IEEE (2016)

MsNet: Multi-stage Learning from Seldom Labeled Data for 3D Tooth Segmentation in Dental Cone Beam Computed Tomography

Xuewei Kang[1,4], Bingjiang Qiu[2,3,4], Lisha Yao[3,4,5], Zhihong Chen[4,6], Chu Han[3,4], and Zaiyi Liu[1,3,4,5(✉)]

[1] School of Computer Science and Information Security, Guilin University of Electronic Technology, Guilin 541004, China
[2] Guangdong Cardiovascular Institute, Guangdong Provincial People's Hospital, Guangdong Academy of Sciences, Guangzhou 510080, China
[3] Department of Radiology, Guangdong Provincial People's Hospital (Guangdong Academy of Medical Sciences), Southern Medical University, Guangzhou 510080, China
liuzaiyi@gdph.org.cn
[4] Guangdong Provincial Key Laboratory of Artificial Intelligence in Medical Image Analysis and Application, Guangzhou 510080, China
[5] The School of Medicine, South China University of Technology, Guangzhou, Guangdong 510006, China
[6] Institute of Computing Science and Technology, Guangzhou University, Guangzhou 510006, China

Abstract. Automatic and accurate 3D segmentation of teeth in dental cone beam computed tomography (CBCT) images is a prerequisite for computer-aided dental analysis. However, due to variations in dental anatomy, different imaging protocols, and limitations in accessing public datasets, developing an automated algorithm for dental analysis is challenging. This paper introduces a multi-stage learning-based method, named MsNet, utilizing a small amount of labeled data and a large amount of unlabeled data to achieve precise and effective 3D tooth segmentation in CBCT. In the initial stage, the nnU-Net model, incorporating both high and low-resolution modalities, undergoes training on the dataset of 12 labeled cases. Its subsequent application involves the generation of pseudo-labels for an expansive cohort of 200 unlabeled cases. By integrating the labeled and pseudo-labeled data, an optimal training dataset is constructed to train a full-resolution refined nnU-Net model for accurate and efficient 3D tooth segmentation. In two rounds of online validation, the results using MsNet are as follows: In the preliminary round, the Dice Similarity Coefficient (DSC), Intersection over Union (IoU) and Hausdorff Distance (HD) values for 3D tooth segmentation are 91.72%, 92.20% and 4.70 mm, respectively; During the final round, the values of DSC, IoU and HD are 75.08%, 80.11% and 25.55 mm, respectively.

Keywords: Tooth segmentation · Semi-supervised learning · Cone beam computed tomography · Deep learning

Y. Wang et al. (Eds.): STS 2023, LNCS 14623, pp. 72–82, 2025.
https://doi.org/10.1007/978-3-031-72396-4_7

1   Introduction

Dental cone beam computed tomography (CBCT) has emerged as an indispensable tool in modern dentistry due to its high-definition vision and low radiation dose [3]. Especially in the field of orthodontics, three-dimensional (3D) teeth segmentation from CBCT images has significantly enhanced the efficiency of dental professionals. Traditionally, 3D teeth segmentation was achieved through manual manning. However manual tooth annotation is labor-intensive and necessitates expert knowledge. In order to help improve the efficiency of manual annotation, robust and accurate automatic teeth segmentation algorithms are highly demanded for orthodontics.

Existing dental segmentation algorithms are generally classified into two primary categories: traditional algorithms and those based on deep learning. Traditional algorithms have been widely investigated for automatic tooth segmentation in CBCT. Akhoondali et al. [1] proposed a threshold-based segmentation algorithm that separates the teeth, alveolar bone, and periodontal tissues based on the grayscale difference between them in CBCT images, by selecting an appropriate threshold. Barandiaran et al. [2] determined multiple thresholds using the within-class variance minimization algorithm and between-class variance maximization algorithm and then segmented the dental images based on the selected thresholds. Nevertheless, weak and false boundaries of teeth in CBCT, often appear in the detected images, which frustrate the accurate segmentation of the teeth [4]. Consequently, the accuracy of traditional teeth segmentation models still remains challenging.

With the rapid development of deep learning, an increasing number of deep learning-related methods are developed for teeth segmentation [10]. Most of the above deep learning-based methods have been proven to be effective in tooth segmentation. Zan et al. [11] proposed the Mask-MCNet, which locates each tooth by predicting the 3D bounding box for each tooth and simultaneously segments each tooth instance. This model retains the original spatial resolution of the input 3D point cloud. Cui et al. [7] proposed a new automatic segmentation method for three-dimensional tooth models called TSegNet. This method first detects all the teeth based on the center of each tooth and then performs precise segmentation on the detected teeth. However, these methods require a large amount of labeled data for training. It is impractical to manually segment these teeth one by one in CBCT images for the training preparation.

In this study, to address the aforementioned challenges, we have made improvements to nnU-Net [8], proposing a multi-stage learning framework of MsNet from seldom labeled data for 3D tooth segmentation. The framework is composed of two principal components: the pseudo-label generation phase, which generates annotations absent in the actual labels, and the semi-supervised learning segmentation phase, which leverages the generated pseudo-labeled images to achieve more precise segmentation. Experiments show the effectiveness of the proposed MsNet for the seldom labeling problem.

2   Method

In this study, we design two phases to effectively address the segmentation problem of CBCT. Our framework mainly consists of two stages, as detailed in Fig. 1. In the first stage, the model is trained with limited annotated data to generate pseudo-labels for unannotated data. In the second stage, precise segmentation is achieved by combining pseudo-labeled images.

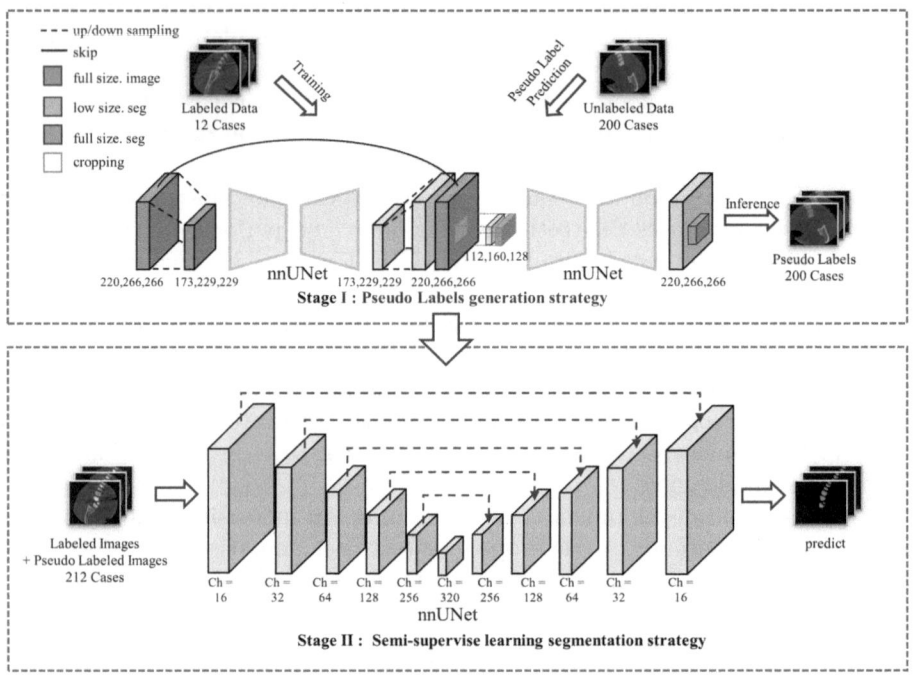

Fig. 1. Overall framework of the proposed method. (Stage I) Using 12 labeled data, the nnU-Net model with high and low-resolution fusion was trained to generate pseudo-labels for 200 unlabeled data. (Stage II) Using the final data set (12 precisely labeled cases + 200 pseudo-labeled data), a full-resolution fine nnU-Net model was trained, and efficient inference was performed.

2.1   Preprocessing

Data Preprocessing. To eliminate the invalid boundary regions of 3D CBCT scans and reduce the consumption of computer memory, all data is initially resampled to a voxel size of $0.3000 \times 0.3000 \times 0.3000 \, \text{mm}^3$ and subsequently cropped to a patch including $112 \times 168 \times 128$ voxels based on the central location of CBCT. Data normalization is then performed by clipping the intensity values of foreground voxels between 0.5% and 99.5%, aiming to enhance the robustness and convergence speed of the model. Additionally, various data augmentation techniques, including random rotation, random scaling, and random noise, are employed during the training process to expand the scale of the training data.

Data Augmentation. In order to prevent the model from over-fitting, data augmentation is used in this study. The augmentation approaches of nnU-Net methodology [8] have been utilized. In this methodology, no form of postprocessing is conducted. This approach remains consistent across all settings.

2.2 Proposed Method

Pseudo labele generation strategy At this stage, high-quality pseudo-labels are generated for unlabeled images, and we initially train using a small amount of labeled data. We first downsample the input images to a lower resolution and then train with a lower-resolution full-scale nnU-Net model. After obtaining a low-resolution segmentation map, we upsample it to the original resolution and use it as an additional input channel (one-hot encoded) for the second nnU-Net model, which trains on patches at full resolution. This results in our pre-teaching model. Following this, pseudo-label inference is conducted on 200 unlabeled images to produce pseudo-label images. Refer to Fig. 1 for stage 1. The hyperparameters of the nnU-Net were tuned to effectively segment teeth in CBCT scans. Table 1 displays the values utilized by nnU-Net, wherein "low" denotes low resolution and "full" indicates the original resolution.

Semi-supervised Learning Segmentation Strategy. Pseudo-labels contain valuable information about the location and boundary of target organs and tumors during training, which enhances the model's discriminative ability. By incorporating pseudo-labels, the pseudo-label generator augments the datasets and promotes the model to learn more boundary information from unlabeled organs in the actual labels. In this study, we design a semi-supervised learning segmentation strategy that improves the segmentation performance by integrating 12 labeled data and 200 pseudo-labeled data as the final training data and modifying the hyperparameters of the existing nnU-Net. The detailed values of the model are listed in Table 2.

Loss Function. We use the summation between Dice loss and cross-entropy (CE) loss because compound loss functions have been proven to be robust in various medical image segmentation tasks [9], which is defined as follows:

$$L_{total} = L_{Dice} + L_{CE} \tag{1}$$

3 Experiments

3.1 Dataset

In this study, We use the STS challenge 2023 dataset [5,6] provided consists of a total of 212 CBCT scans for training, encompassing approximately 42,400 slices.

Table 1. nnU-Net Hyperparameters.

	(low) nnU-Net
Base number of features	16
Ori size (D,W.H)	220,266,266
Patch size (D,W.H)	173,229,229
Target spacing (mm^3)	0.3778, 0.3778, 0.3778
Number of stages	6
Convolution kernel sizes	[[3,3,3], [3,3,3], [3,3,3], [3,3,3], [3,3,3], [3,3,3]]
Pooling operation kernel sizes	[[1,1,1], [2,2,2], [2,2,2], [2,2,2], [2,2,2], [1,2,2]]
(full) nnU-Net	
Base number of features	16
Ori size (D,W.H)	220,266,266
Patch size (D,W.H)	112,160,128
Target spacing (mm^3)	0.3000, 0.3000, 0.3000
Number of stages	6
Convolution kernel sizes	[[3,3,3], [3,3,3], [3,3,3], [3,3,3], [3,3,3], [3,3,3]]
Pooling operation kernel sizes	[[1,1,1], [2,2,2], [2,2,2], [2,2,2], [2,2,2], [1,2,2]]

Table 2. nnU-Net Hyperparameters

Base number of features	16
Ori size (D,W.H)	220,266,266
Patch size (D,W.H)	112,160,128
Target spacing (mm^3)	0.3000, 0.3000, 0.3000
Number of stages	6
Convolution kernel sizes	[[3,3,3], [3,3,3], [3,3,3], [3,3,3], [3,3,3], [3,3,3]]
Pooling operation kernel sizes	[[1,1,1], [2,2,2], [2,2,2], [2,2,2], [2,2,2], [1,2,2]]

Within the training set are 12 labeled CBCT with around 2,400 annotated slices and 200 unlabeled CBCT accounting for nearly 40,000 slices. Additionally, the online test set is composed of 10 CBCT scans, equivalent to about 2,000 slices. These scans are annotated, but the labels are withheld from the participants. This collection serves as an ideal resource for those delving into semi-supervised or unsupervised learning paradigms in medical imaging, reflecting real-world situations where acquiring annotations can be resource-intensive.

3.2 Evaluation Metrics

The evaluation metrics encompass three accuracy measures-Dice Similarity Coefficient(DSC) (Eq. 2), Intersection over union(IoU) (Eq. 3) and Hausdorff Distance

(HD) (Eq. 4). For scoring purposes (Eq. 5), the competition uniformly normalizes HD so that its value is between 0 and 1. The final weighted average of the three metrics is taken, and the specific scoring formula and metrics are as follows:

$$DSC = \frac{2 * |A \cap B|}{|A| + |B|} \tag{2}$$

$$IoU = \frac{A \cap B}{A \cup B} \tag{3}$$

$$HD(A, B) = \max \left\{ \sup_{a \in A} \inf_{b \in B} d(a, b), \sup_{b \in B} \inf_{a \in A} d(a, b) \right\} \tag{4}$$

$$Score = 0.4 * DSC + 0.3 * IoU + 0.3 * (1 - HD) \tag{5}$$

3.3   Implementation Details

Environment Settings. The development environments and requirements are presented in Table 3.

Table 3. Development environments and requirements.

System	Ubuntu 20.04 LTS
CPU	Intel(R) Core(TM) i9-10900X CPU@3.70 GHz
RAM	4×32 GB; 2933MT/s
GPU	NVIDIA GeForce RTX 3090 24G
CUDA version	11.4
Programming language	Python 3.9.16
Deep learning framework	torch 2.0, torchvision 0.2.2

Training Protocols. During the training stage, we set the batch size to 2 and randomly select all samples within each epoch. For each sample, we perform random patch cropping with patch sizes of (112, 160, 128). As for the optimizer, we utilize AdamW with a learning rate of 1e-3 and a weight decay of 1e-5. The learning rate updating follows the default mechanism of AdamW. Additional details are presented in Table 4.

(1) **Processing of the unlabeled images** We used 12 labeled data, and the pre-teacher nnU-Net model with high and low-resolution fusion is trained to generate pseudo-labels for 200 unlabeled data.

(2) **Data augmentation** We use augmentation approaches of the nnU-Net [8] methodology. These approaches include elastic deformation, rotation, scaling, brightness and contrast adjustment, and gamma transformation during the training process.

Table 4. Training protocols.

Network initialization	"He" normal initialization
Batch size	2
Patch size	112×160×128
Total epochs	1000
Optimizer	AdamW with weight decay($\mu = 1e - 5$)
Initial learning rate (lr)	1e-3
Lr decay schedule	halved by 200 epochs
Training time	25 h
Loss function	Adaptive Loss
Number of model parameters	27.7M[7]
Number of flops	556.78G[8]
CO_2eq	2.68 Kg[9]

https://github.com/sksq96/pytorch-summary.
https://github.com/facebookresearch/fvcore.
https://github.com/lfwa/carbontracker/.

4　Results and Discussion

The best fold is selected via the results in the internal validation, as shown in Table 5. The internal validation outcomes were obtained from 12 labeled datasets utilizing five-fold cross-validation, with each fold consisting of 9 cases for training and 3 for validation. We selected fold3, the best fold of Full_nnU-Net to infer unlabeled data and obtain pseudo-labeled data.

Table 5. Segmentation results of five-fold from Internal Validation.

Taget	Low_nnU-Net			Full_nnU-Net		
	Dice (%)	IoU (%)	HD (mm)	Dice (%)	IoU(%)	HD (mm)
fold0	92.02	85.26	10.04	92.52	86.08	2.56
fold1	**93.15**	**87.26**	**2.83**	93.49	87.86	6.83
fold2	92.17	85.52	3.77	92.19	85.57	8.36
fold3	92.58	86.20	2.81	**92.68**	**86.38**	**2.68**
fold4	92.21	85.63	4.29	92.09	85.41	4.29
Mean	92.42	85.97	4.74	92.59	86.26	4.94

4.1　Quantitative Results on Validation Set

As shown in Table 6, the quantitative experiments have been carried out for more comprehensive ablation studies on the MsNet and nnU-Net. For the tooth

Table 6. Results of quantitative experiments

Method	Internal Validation			Online Validation		
	Dice(%)	IoU (%)	HD (mm)	Dice (%)	IoU (%)	HD (mm)
nnU-Net	92.59	86.26	4.94	91.15	91.68	4.72
MsNet	98.03	96.16	5.01	91.72	92.2	4.70

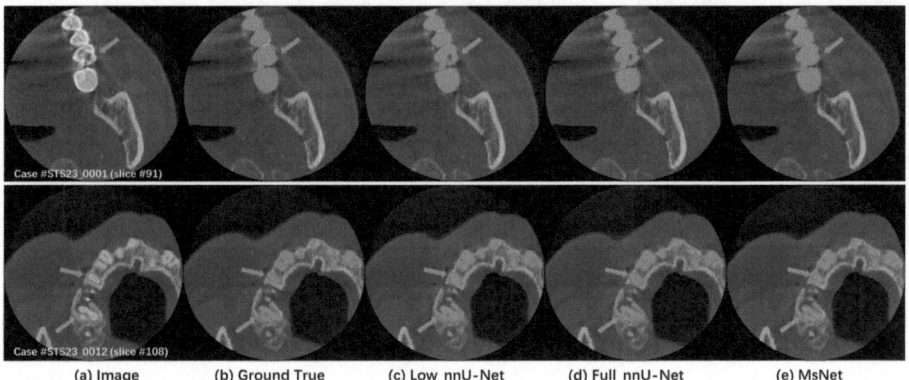

(a) Image   (b) Ground True   (c) Low_nnU-Net   (d) Full_nnU-Net   (e) MsNet

Fig. 2. Good segmentation cases from 12 validation sets.

segmentation, the MsNet model using a semi-supervised approach performs better than the full supervision nnU-Net model, with an improvement of at least 0.62% and 0.56% in DSC and IoU scores, respectively, and HD values decreasing from 4.72 mm to 4.70 mm.

4.2 Qualitative Results on Validation Set

In this section, we show the two good segmentation cases and two bad segmentation cases.

Failure Segmentation Cases Analysis. In case 0003 and 0006 in Fig. 3, Both the Low_nnU-Net and Full_nnU-Net methods encountered difficulties in splitting crowded (closely touching) teeth, and the improved MsNet method also failed to segment accurately. This can be explained by the fact that crowded teeth have confused all methods, preventing them from effectively recognizing edge information.

Good Segmentation Cases Analysis. As shown by the red arrow in Fig. 2, case 0001, both the Low_nnU-Net and Full_nnU-Net cannot segment individual teeth completely. Our method performs better in terms of the completeness of tooth segmentation. In case 00012, as indicated by the red arrow in Fig. 2,

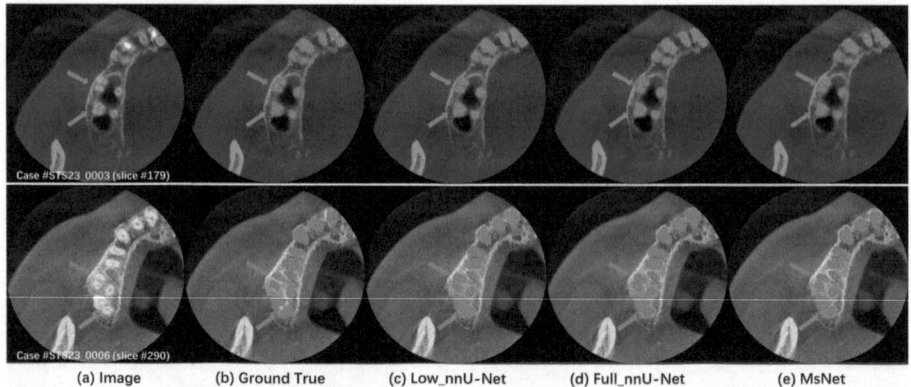

Fig. 3. Failure segmentation cases from 12 validation sets.

both the low nnU-Net and full nnU-Net cannot accurately identify the edges of the teeth, while our method demonstrates a better capability to highlight the segmentation of tooth edges. The results indicate that tooth segmentation has been improved.

4.3   Results on Final Test Set

We comprehensively demonstrated the final results of our method on the online leaderboard test set. Please refer to Table 7 for the format.

Table 7. In online validation, segmentation outcomes from 10 test sets were compared to those from 50 test sets in the final validation.

Method	Online Validation			Final Validation		
	Dice (%)	IoU (%)	HD (mm)	Dice (%)	IoU(%)	HD (mm)
MsNet	91.72	92.2	4.70	75.08	80.11	25.55

4.4   Limitation and Future Work

Upon reflecting on our study, it becomes evident that we encounter certain limitations in the following aspects.

Effect of different Preprocessing Strategies. Different preprocessing strategies were found to impact the contrast of the images. Future work may involve training on a fusion of images processed using various preprocessing methods.

Limitations of the Pseudo-marking Method. The aim of semi-supervised learning is to harness unlabeled data to enhance generalization performance. Not all pseudo-labels are valid. For instance, erroneous pseudo-labels can introduce excessive noise, leading to misguidance in model training. Overconfident pseudo-labels don't provide new insights, causing the model to continually learn pre-existing knowledge, which results in overfitting. Thus, the selection of pseudo-labels is an area for potential future refinement. We anticipate utilizing a pseudo-label selection approach based on uncertainty awareness to better pinpoint and sidestep pseudo-labels that may mislead the model. Furthermore, with the right pseudo-label selection strategy, we can bolster the model's generalization ability, mitigate overfitting risks, and ensure the model's stability and dependability in real-world applications.

5   Conclusion

For utilizing a small amount of labeled data and a large amount of unlabeled data in CBCT for 3D tooth segmentation, we have developed MsNet, a multi-stage semi-supervised learning framework. Quantitative and qualitative results show that MsNet can efficiently learn tooth information from unlabeled datasets. In the STS challenge 2023, we validated our approach on the online platform test sets and demonstrated that the proposed MsNet outperforms two nnU-Net segmentation methods in tooth segmentation tasks.

Acknowledgements. This study was supported by the National Key R&D Program of China [grant number 2021YFF1201003], Guangdong Provincial Key Laboratory of Artificial Intelligence in Medical Image Analysis and Application [grant number 2022B1212010011]. The authors of this paper declare that the segmentation method they implemented for participation in the STS 2023 challenge has not used any pre-trained models or additional datasets other than those provided by the organizers. The proposed solution is fully automatic without any manual intervention. We thank all the data owners for making the X-ray images and CT scans publicly available and Alibaba Cloud for hosting the challenge platform.

References

1. Akhoondali, H., Zoroofi, R., Shirani, G.: Rapid automatic segmentation and visualization of teeth in ct-scan data. J. Appl. Sci. **9**(11), 2031–2044 (2009)
2. Barandiaran, I., et al.: An automatic segmentation and reconstruction of mandibular structures from CT-Data. In: Corchado, E., Yin, H. (eds.) IDEAL 2009. LNCS, vol. 5788, pp. 649–655. Springer, Heidelberg (2009). https://doi.org/10.1007/978-3-642-04394-9_79
3. Caruso, P., Silvestri, E., Sconfienza, L.M.: Cone beam CT and 3D imaging: A practical guide. Springer (2013)
4. Chrcanovic, B.R., Nilsson, J., Thor, A.: Survival and complications of implants to support craniofacial prosthesis: a systematic review. J. Cranio-Maxillofacial Surgery **44**(10), 1536–1552 (2016)
5. Cui, W., et al.: Ctooth+: A large-scale dental cone beam computed tomography dataset and benchmark for tooth volume segmentation. In: MICCAI Workshop on Data Augmentation, Labelling, and Imperfections, pp. 64–73. Springer (2022). https://doi.org/10.1007/978-3-031-17027-0_7

6. Cui, W., et al.: Ctooth: a fully annotated 3d dataset and benchmark for tooth volume segmentation on cone beam computed tomography images. In: International Conference on Intelligent Robotics and Applications, pp. 191–200. Springer (2022). https://doi.org/10.1007/978-3-031-13841-6_18

7. Cui, Z., et al.: Tsegnet: an efficient and accurate tooth segmentation network on 3d dental model. Med. Image Anal. **69**, 101949 (2021)

8. Isensee, F., Jaeger, P.F., Kohl, S.A., Petersen, J., Maier-Hein, K.H.: nnu-net: a self-configuring method for deep learning-based biomedical image segmentation. Nat. Methods **18**(2), 203–211 (2021)

9. Ma, J., et al.: Loss odyssey in medical image segmentation. Med. Image Anal. **71**, 102035 (2021)

10. Reiß, S., Seibold, C., Freytag, A., Rodner, E., Stiefelhagen, R.: Every annotation counts: Multi-label deep supervision for medical image segmentation. In: Proceedings of the IEEE/CVF Conference on Computer Vision and Pattern Recognition, pp. 9532–9542 (2021)

11. Zanjani, F.G., et al.: Mask-mcnet: tooth instance segmentation in 3d point clouds of intra-oral scans. Neurocomputing **453**, 286–298 (2021)

Diffusion-Based Conv-Former Dual-Encode U-Net: DDPM for Level Set Evolution Mapping MICCAI STS 2023 Challenge

Junlin Li[1,2], Weixin Tian[1,2(✉)], Junliang Li[1,2], Yuan He[1,2], and Wanglin Ke[3]

[1] Hubei Key Laboratory of Intelligent Vision Based Monitoring for Hydroelectric Engineering, China Three Gorges University, Hubei, Yichang 443002, China
t_wxin@126.com
[2] College of Computer and Information Technology, China Three Gorges University, Hubei, Yichang 443002, China
[3] Advanced Research Department, FUSSEN Inc, Guangdong, Shenzhen 518000, China

Abstract. We propose the Diffusion-Based Conv-Former U-Net (DCFDU-Net) model for panoramic CT segmentation tasks. Our model primarily employs a dual-encode structure, comprising the CMT and PVT modules. To enhance boundary precision, we incorporated a novel boundary learning module inspired by DDPM and level set. This module constructs the level set function by initially predicting the boundary in a high-dimensional space projection. Then uses the DDPM model to evolve this projection, facilitating the accurate delineation of the zero level set. Finally, the boundaries and mask outcomes are refined through an efficient, cost-effective network architecture. Our method achieved an average DICE score of 91.81% and an average IOU score of 96.35%, with an average HD distance of 0.0332 for teeth segmentation on the validation set using an NVIDIA GeForce RTX 3090 GPU. The average running time was 0.91 s per image. The code is available at https://github.com/aoxipo/AITOOTH.

Keywords: Deep Learning · Tooth segmentation · Diffusion · Level Set

1 Introduction

Panoramic X-ray is often used for human dental examinations due to its cost-effectiveness, low radiation dose, and the ability to accurately segment teeth. The development of deep learning and advancements in computer computing power have made it possible to automatically segment teeth with high precision. The availability of various datasets has further improved the automatic segmentation capabilities in panoramic X-rays.

Y. Wang et al. (Eds.): STS 2023, LNCS 14623, pp. 83–95, 2025.
https://doi.org/10.1007/978-3-031-72396-4_8

Shen Dingang and his team introduced a multi-level, morphology-guided dental segmentation network enabling the precise extraction of tooth crown and root information for creating high-precision 3D dental models [1]. Tomáš Kunzo et al. presented a weakly supervised dental segmentation method which minimizes manual annotations and uses key point detection network outputs for segmentation refinement [2]. Li et al. proposed a CNN-Transformer hybrid architecture Group Transformer network (GT U-Net) for tooth root segmentation to effectively solve problems such as fuzzy boundary segmentation of tooth root [4].

The existing methods can not control the boundary fine and speculate the boundary effectively, so in order to better refine the boundary, we propose the Convolution Mix Transformer Module (CMT) module and a boundary learning module based on Denoising Diffusion Probabilistic Model(DDPM) [7]. The Convolution Mix Transformer Module effectively captures high-frequency features through convolution and low-frequency features through group Former, ultimately integrating these acquired features using SK model [3]. The distinguishing feature of the boundary learning model lies in its ability to acquire the optimal position for the zero level set within the predicted level set function through DDPM. Although the boundary learning module is based on diffusion, the boundary learning module is based on two parts:

1) Used model to predict the level set function to determine the boundary set.

2) Learned by the diffusion model to find suitable zero level set position.

It is noteworthy that in the second part, despite being based on the diffusion model, the model primarily focuses on predicting slice thresholds within a specific range of the level set function. The associated time overhead and computing power requirements are negligible. In summary, our main contributions are as follows:

1. We propose the CMT module, which can learn the potential features of different distributions and frequencies in the features, and extract and reconstruct them.

2. We propose a boundary learning model based on DDPM, where the level set is constructed by predicting the level set function of the projection in the high latitude space at the boundary. Subsequently, we employ the DDPM model to find the optimal zero level set, which enabling us to effectively learn all potential boundary features and select an appropriate partition boundary as our final outcome.

To visualise how our boundaries have evolved, see the https://github.com/aoxipo/AITOOTH.

2   Method

Our model primarily employs a dual encode structure consisting of the CMT and PVT [8] structures. it also follows the overall **U-Net** [6] structure. Where use the CMT module and PVT-v2-b2 as the dual encoders of the U-Net model, only the CMT module be used in the decoders. The boundary learning module

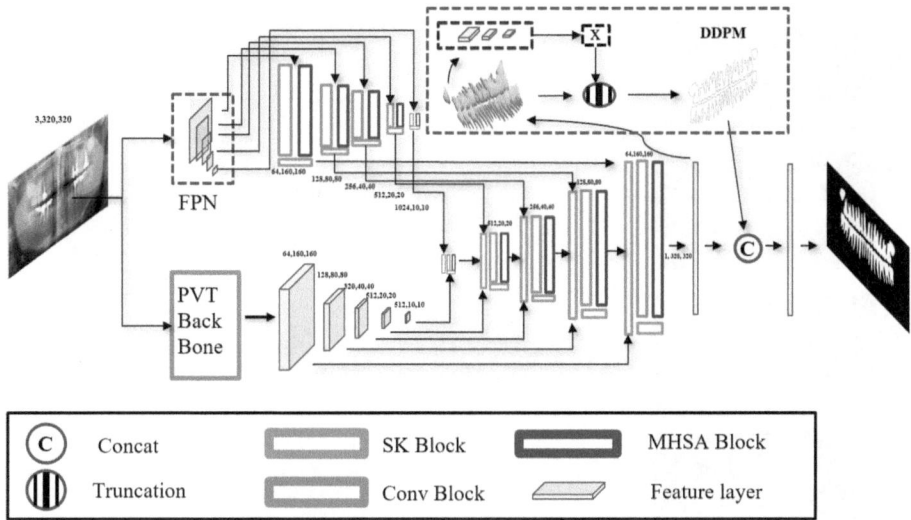

Fig. 1. Dual encode with CMT and PVT **U-Net** (The PVT structure is used to encode the image, and the CMT structure is used to encode the image pyramid. The results of both are decoded using the corresponding CMT structure. At the same time, the generated 3D evolution surface is used for DDPM prediction slice, and the results are spliced into the cross section of the evolution surface as the final output)

contains a simple generator and a learnable threshold for the DDPM. Our pipline is shown in Fig. 1, The proposed method is described in full detail below.

2.1 Preprocessing

Good data makes good performance. To take full advantage of all the detail in the data and construct a possible set of boundaries, we extract the boundaries of the label data through the corrosion operation, and use erode and dilate operation to build the level set function.

Data Preparation. We use histogram equalization, Mosaic enhancement to enhance the data, and randomly flip the data and rotate the angle, our execution sequence is as follows. All of the above operations have a probability of 0.5.

- histogram equalization
- normalization
- use mosaic to enhancement data or not
- Random horizontal flip
- Random vertical flip
- Random rotation

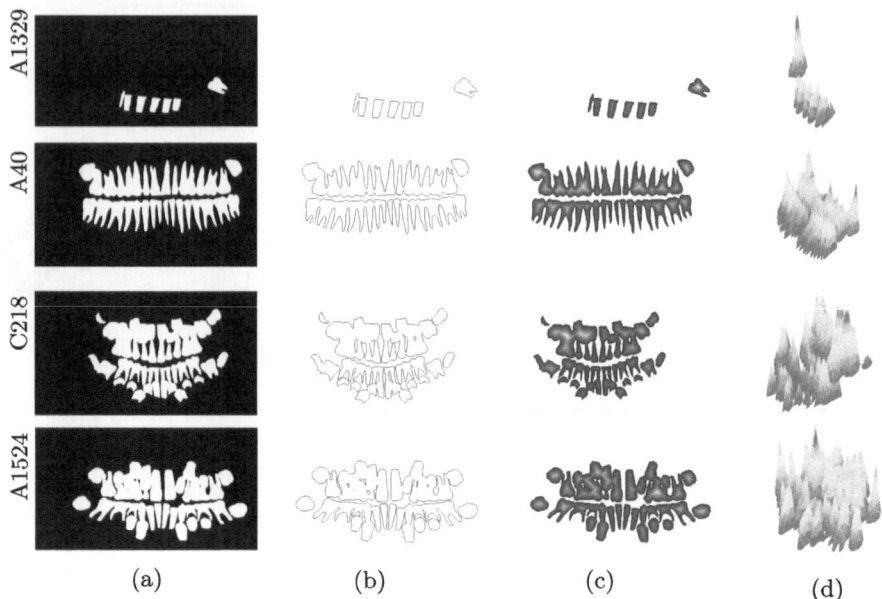

Fig. 2. The level set function generated by the corrosion operation. (a) is Ground True, (b) is a slice projection of (c), (c) is the level set function by erode operation, (d) is the 3D view of (c)

Level Set Generation. In this section, we use labels to generate possible boundary evolution surfaces by operate on the label through a corrosion expansion operation to generate our desired boundaries which can be formulated as follows:

$$g_{erode}(x)_{(i,j)} = Min(x)_{(i,j)} \tag{1}$$

$$f_{edge}(x) = x - g_{erode}(x) \tag{2}$$

where $Min(x)$ is minimum value in the window i, j is the filtering result of the whole window. in this paper, we set the windows size as three. x is the ground true for image.

We generate a boundary distance image by calculating the distance of each boundary pixel to the center point on the generated boundary, where each different distance denote a possible inner boundary case. An expansion operation of N times is performed on all the obtained boundaries, which is used to generate outer boundaries and inner boundaries is defined as:

$$g_{dilate}(x, N)_{(i,j)} = Max(x)_{(Ni,Nj)} \tag{3}$$

$$f_{outedge}(x_{edge}, x, N) = g_{dilate}(x, N) - x_{edge} \tag{4}$$

where N times the expansion filtering operation on x,x is same as the Eq. 2, x_{edge} denote the outermost boundary. The boundary set we generated by the above method is shown in the Fig. 2.

2.2 Proposed Method

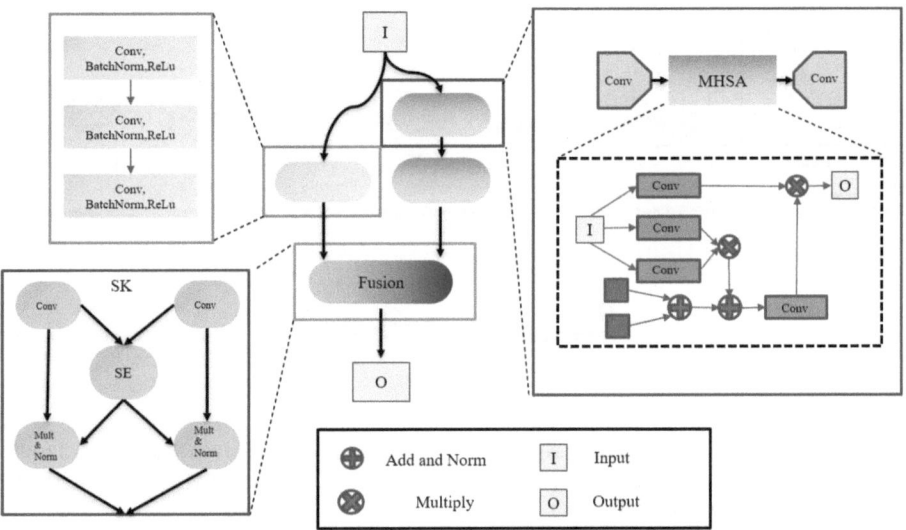

Fig. 3. CMT Module structure(Encoded by parallel three-layer convolution and two-layer group former structure, and then fed into SK layer for feature fusion)

CMT Module. Convolution Mix Transformer Module(CMT Module) is a structure used to extract the distribution of different features separately. This work proposes the features of the convolutional structure and transformer structure are used to independently learn the input features, and each module is responsible for learning the features of different data distributions. Finally, the feature pairs obtained by the fusion of SK module are used. Compared with using convolution or transformer structure alone, this parallel structure can help different modules to learn some data features that need deeper networks to learn when used alone. Detail structure as shown in the Fig. 3. Usually, channel splicing or addition methods are employed for fusing different feature layers, followed by the application of activation functions or Batch-Norm layer to smooth the fused data.We advocate the utilization of SK modules to adapt to diverse acceptance domains, rather than relying solely on the activation function or Channel addition which is equivalent to a simplistic linear layer with a weight of $1/2$ and a bias of 0. The primary objective is to compress and aggregate two or more feature layers in order to calculate respective weight coefficients for each input feature layer. This adaptive weight calculation approach for different feature layers ensures smoother fusion compared to simplistic superposition methods. Hence, we employ the SK module within the CMT module for diverse feature fusion purposes.

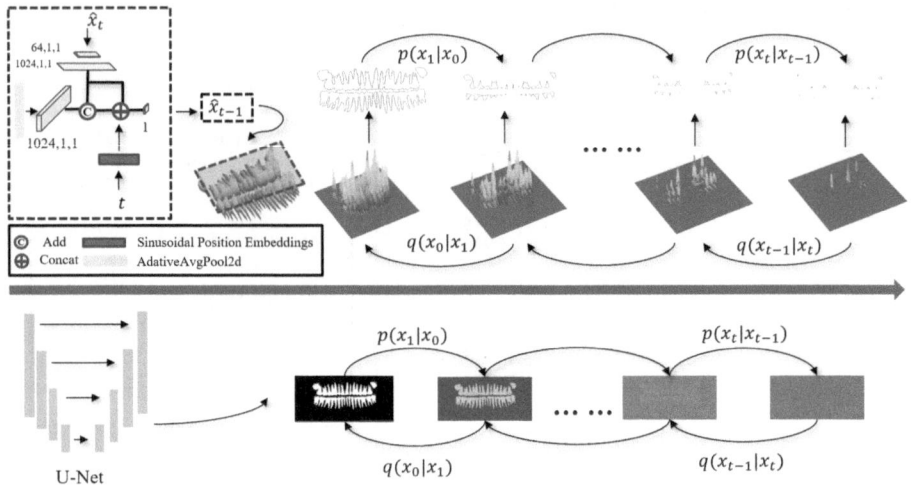

Fig. 4. The directed graphical about DDPM and level set evolution mapping (The top represents the mapping between the DDPM and the evolution of the level set, and at the bottom is the classic DDPM.)

Boundary Module. In the panoramic image, achieving convergence in the tooth root canal becomes challenging due to the presence of blurred boundaries, particularly when there are pathological gingiva inflammation, tooth decay, and other issues depicted. These factors contribute to an unclear boundary within the panoramic image. Our objective is to enhance the model's ability to predict boundary changes through low cost-effective learning. By deducing the changing trend of unclear boundaries from clear boundary segments, we propose a simple boundary module based on DDPM to help the model control fineness convergence on the boundary. In general, DDPM model needs to fit the process from real image to random noise image, and then reverse the process to generate new image. This process is affected by time step, which leads to a long time overhead, but its excellent complex dynamic modeling ability can make up for this shortcoming. Detail structure as shown in the Fig. 4.

We map the process of adding and reducing noise in DDPM to level set evolution of the boundary, the increase of the boundary corresponds to the noise reduction process of the diffusion model, and the reduction of the boundary corresponds to the noise addition process of the diffusion model. To reduce computational effort, we employ the model to directly predict all potential evolutions and subsequently utilize a simple parameter to discern which zero-level sets align more consistently with the actual evolution outcomes. Essentially, this process equ acquiring a specific slice within an appropriate levels set, given by formulated as follows:

$$\alpha_t = 1 - \beta_t, \beta_t \in t, t \in (0, T) \tag{5}$$

$$q(x_t|x_{t-1}) \sim N(x_t; \sqrt{\alpha_t}x_{t-1}, (1 - \alpha_t)) \tag{6}$$

where x_t represents the noise slice range with time t added, T represents the total evolution time, $q(x_t|x_{t-1})$ represents the conditional probability distribution of the current time step x_t given the previous time step x_{t-1}. β_t given the noise factor used at time step t. We reformulate the evolution of x from time t to time $t-1$ in 6 as :

$$f_{noise}(x, y, t) = g_{dec}(y + f_{embed}(x_t)) \tag{7}$$

$$x_{t-1} = x_t - f_{noise}(x_t, y, t) \tag{8}$$

where f_{noise} represents the noise formula of x at time step t, y represents the feature layer from CMT and PVT Block. g_{dec} represents the linear decode layer, f_{embed} represents the encode layer block of x.

Loss Function. We use the summation between Dice loss, cross-entropy loss and IOU loss because compound loss functions have been proven to be robust in various medical image segmentation tasks [5]. The loss function can be written by:

$$loss_{dice} = 1 - \frac{2|x \cap y|}{|x| + |y|} \tag{9}$$

$$loss_{cross} = -[y \log x + (1 - y) \log(1 - x)] \tag{10}$$

$$loss_{iou} = 1 - \frac{x \cap y}{x \cup y} \tag{11}$$

$$loss_{edge} = |x - y| \tag{12}$$

where x denote by predict result for given image, y denote by ground true. Our final loss consists of the above three elements:

$$loss = aloss_{iou} + bloss_{cross} + closs_{dice} + dloss_{edge} \tag{13}$$

where a parameters were set to 0.3, b set to 0.2, c set to 0.4, d set to 0.1.

Data Utilization Strategy. In the data set, we find that a small part of data has been post-processed. so, we carried out histogram equalization in the data preprocessing stage to avoid gray unbalance, but it is still impossible to avoid some samples with poor performance due to excessive post-processing. Unlabeled images were not used in our train stage. We generate a level set function for each sample using the label, which will be used in our boundary module. We compress the time steps required by the DDPM process to reduce the inference time.

2.3　Post-processing

During the training stage, we did not do overly complicated operations on the output results of the model, because we believe that an excellent model should output a perfect result instead of over-relying on the post-processing process. Therefore, we directly calculated the loss between the model results and true label during the training. In the test stage, only the output results were binary-coded with a threshold value of 0.5.

3　Experiments

3.1　Dataset

The dental data set we used came from children's dental panoramic radiographs dataset for caries segmentation and dental disease detection [9]. All of which are X-ray images of panoramic images of children's teeth. There are 7500 tooth images in this data set, among which 6000 are used for training. In the training data, there were only 4000 labeled tooth images, and the remaining 2000 were unlabeled tooth images. In the test set, there were a total of 1500 tooth images, among which 500 were labeled. All sample images are single-channel images with a bit depth of 24, and the corresponding label images are single-channel images with a bit depth of 8, and the size of all images is 640 pixel weight and 320 pixel height.

3.2　Evaluation Metrics

On 2D Datasets, We used Dice Similarity Coefficient(DICE), Intersection Over Union(IOU) and Hausdorff Distance(HD) respectively to evaluate the mask accuracy of prediction segmentation. The formula was shown in the following:

$$Score_{Dice} = \frac{2\,A \cap B|}{|A| + |B|} \tag{14}$$

$$Score_{Iou} = \frac{A \cap B}{A \cup B} \tag{15}$$

$$Score_{hd} = min(|x_A - x_B| + |y_A - y_B|) \tag{16}$$

Table 1. Development environments and requirements.

System	Ubuntu 20.04 LTS
CPU	Intel(R) Core(TM) i7-10700 CPU @ 2.90GHz
RAM	32GB;1.37MT/s
GPU (number and type)	NVIDIA 3090 (24G)
CUDA version	11.0
Programming language	Python 3.9
Deep learning framework	torch 1.4.0, torchvision 0.4.0

where, A denote the predicted mask, B denote the ground true, $Score_{hd}$ denote the maximum distance between the gt edge point and the most recently predicted mask edge point. x_A, y_A and x_B, y_B denote the horizontal and vertical coordinates of the point that is farthest from the phase in the image. Finally, our evaluation criteria are weighted by the above three indicators:

$$Score = \alpha Score_{Dice} + \beta Score_{Iou} + \Gamma Score_{hd} \tag{17}$$

where α, β, Γ were 0.4, 0.3, 0.3 in our experiment.

3.3 Implementation Details

Environment Settings. The development environments and requirements are presented in Table 1.

Training Protocols. We conduct data cleansing, discard samples that are only in gt or images, In order to better fit the model, we chose Adam optimizer, use learning rate as 0.001 and set betas as (0.5, 0.999), and set early-stop to avoid over-fitting. When training, to avoid the error boundary information provided when the model is not convergent, we only enable boundary losses when dice loss and mse loss are less than 0.1.

4 Results and Discussion

In this section, We divide the labelled data into a training set and a validation set in a 2.2:1, verify the effectiveness across different modules, and present the ablation results of our method and comparison with those of U-Net.

4.1 Quantitative Results on Validation Set

In order to better verify the precision of the boundary, we calculate Negtive Recall(NR) and Positive Recall as the convergence metrics of the boundary precision. To verify the validity of SK module in CMT module, We use channel splicing as an experimental comparison with SK module, The experimental results are shown in the table below:

Table 2. Training protocols.

Network initialization	"He" normal initialization
Batch size	4
Patch size	$1\times320\times640$
Total epochs	100
Optimizer	Adaptive Moment Estimation
Initial learning rate (lr)	0.001
early-stop	15
Training time	$26.9\,h(21.1 + 5.89)$
Loss function	$MSE, Dice, L1$
Number of model parameters	41.22M[1]
Number of flops	59.32G[2]
CO_2eq	1 Kg[3]

[1]https://github.com/sksq96/pytorch-summary
[2]https://github.com/facebookresearch/fvcore
[3]https://github.com/lfwa/carbontracker/

Table 3. Quantitative evaluation results

Method	Internal Validation			Online Validation			Time(s)
	Dice (%)	IoU(%)	HD (mm)	Dice(%)	IoU (%)	HD (mm)	
U-Net	89.03	95.35	0.0312	87.84	94.91	0.0340	0.13
DCFDU-Net	95.74	97.93	0.0196	91.81	96.35	0.0332	0.91

Table 4. Results on Our validation set.

Method	Score (%)	Dice (%)	IoU (%)	HD (mm)	NR (%)	PR (%)	Time(s)
U-Net	94.52	92.03	96.35	0.0401	97.72	94.42	0.14
U-Net++	96.65	93.02	98.12	0.0116	98.85	95.56	0.74
GT-U-Net	91.62	88.23	94.83	0.0706	98.81	83.56	0.58
Ours	97.23	95.97	98.08	0.0192	98.88	96.72	0.91

Table 5. SK module ablation experiment.

Method	Score (%)	Dice (%)	IoU (%)	HD (mm)	NR (%)	PR (%)
CMT Module with SK Module	96.15	94.14	97.18	0.0220	98.47	94.50
CMT Module without SK Module	93.35	90.88	94.10	0.0491	98.97	87.91

Table 6. Boundary module ablation experiment.

Method	Score (%)	Dice (%)	IoU (%)	HD (mm)	NR (%)	PR (%)
CMT Module + Boundary Module	97.09	95.74	97.93	0.0196	99.05	95.16
CMT Module	96.15	94.14	97.18	0.0220	98.47	94.50

In order to verify the validity of the boundary model, we compared the boundary module with the non-boundary module, and to evaluate the loss function, the result show in Table 6 and Table 7.

Good Segmentation Cases. In case 0073 and 0988 in Fig. 5, our results show that better segmentation results can be obtained under different gray scale distributions.

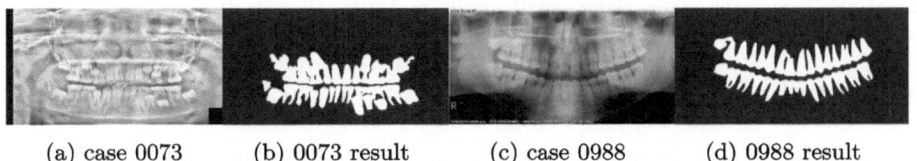

(a) case 0073   (b) 0073 result   (c) case 0988   (d) 0988 result

Fig. 5. Good case by our pipline

Table 7. Loss weight ratio ablation experiment.

Weight	IOU	DICE	HD	EDGE	**Score**(%)
Case 1	0.2	0.5	0.1	0.1	96.15
Case 2	0.5	0.3	0.1	0.1	94.07
Case 3 (Best)	0.3	0.4	0.2	0.1	**97.23**

Failure Case Analysis. In Fig. 6, for examples case 0288, such as when the model is difficult to converge due to inappropriate post-processing, and is affected by some over light areas, the model confuses it as a tooth. For example case 0993, the tooth root canal site close to the background is more difficult to converge, metal ear pendants were also used as positive samples.

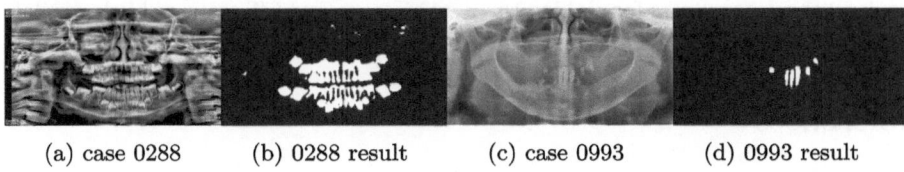

(a) case 0288   (b) 0288 result   (c) case 0993   (d) 0993 result

Fig. 6. Failure case by our pipline

4.2 Results on Final Testing Set

The results in Table 3 show that our model has a good performance on the comprehensive indicators, especially the HD distance and the IoU score.

4.3   Limitation and Future Work

In this task to help with boundary convergence, we only adopted a simple threshold learning strategy by consider time cost. In fact, if we learn the threshold of each pixel individually, rather than using only one threshold to control the selection of all pixels, the dice score and HD distance will be better. In the experiment, when CMT Block is used to extract image pyramid features, there is a large redundancy calculation, and perhaps feature fusion should be carried out at a deeper level instead of each layer. So, how to make the module better serve the target characteristics still needs to be further explored.

5   Conclusion

In this paper, we proposed the a pipline for tooth segmentation. In pipline, the possible boundary evolution surface equation is predicted for each image, and a simple network structure is used to control the evolution process of the level set, which helps the model control the boundary details in the final segmentation result.

1. In the encoders, we use Convolution block and group mult head self attention block extract potential high frequency and low frequency features respectively. we propose to use SK model for feature fusion of different distributed feature data.

2. In order to control the precision convergence of the model on the boundary, We propose a method to predict the level sets function and map DDPM complex noise reduction process to a simple boundary-expanding process.

Finally, the experimental results clearly show that our method can effectively fuse the data features of different distributions, and the boundary module realizes fine boundary control.

Acknowledgements.. The authors of this paper declare that the segmentation method they implemented for participation in the STS 2023 challenge has not used any pre-trained models nor additional datasets other than those provided by the organizers. The proposed solution is fully automatic without any manual intervention. We thank all the data owners for making the X-ray images and CT scans publicly available and Alibaba Cloud for hosting the challenge platform.

References

1. A fully automatic ai system for tooth and alveolar bone segmentation from cone-beam ct images. Nat. Commun
2. Kunzo, T., Kocur, V., Gajdošech, L., Madaras, M.: Processing and segmentation of human teeth from 2d images using weakly supervised learning. In: 2023 World Symposium on Digital Intelligence for Systems and Machines (DISA). IEEE (Sep 2023). https://doi.org/10.1109/disa59116.2023.10308924
3. Li, X., Wang, W., Hu, X., Yang, J.: Selective kernel networks. CoRR abs/ arXiv: 1903.06586 (2019)

4. Li, Y., et al.: GT u-net: a u-net like group transformer network for tooth root segmentation. CoRR abs/ arXiv:2109.14813 (2021)
5. Ma, J., et al.: Loss odyssey in medical image segmentation. Med. Image Anal. **71**, 102035 (2021)
6. Ronneberger, O., Fischer, P., Brox, T.: U-net: Convolutional networks for biomedical image segmentation. In: International Conference on Medical Image Computing and Computer-assisted Intervention, pp. 234–241 (2015)
7. Song, J., Meng, C., Ermon, S.: Denoising diffusion implicit models. In: 9th International Conference on Learning Representations, ICLR 2021, Virtual Event, Austria, 3-7 May 2021. OpenReview.net (2021).https://openreview.net/forum?id=St1giarCHLP
8. Wang, W., et al.: Pyramid vision transformer: A versatile backbone for dense prediction without convolutions. CoRR abs/ arXiv: 2102.12122 (2021)
9. Zhang, Y., et al.: Children's dental panoramic radiographs dataset for caries segmentation and dental disease detection. Scientific Data **10**(1), 380 (2023)

Semi-supervised 3D Tooth Segmentation Using nn-UNet with Axial Attention and Positional Correction

Qiupu Chen[1,2], Yimou Wang[1,2], Jun Xu[1,2], and Qiankun Li[1,2(✉)]

[1] HFIPS, Chinese Academy of Sciences, Hefei, Anhui, China
[2] University of Science and Technology of China, Hefei, China
qklee@mail.ustc.edu.cn

Abstract. Accurate 3D tooth segmentation plays a pivotal role in the realm of computer-aided dental diagnosis and treatment. Despite its significance, the scarcity of labeled 3D tooth data poses a substantial challenge. This paper details our contribution to the MICCAI 2023 semi-supervised teeth segmentation challenge, aimed at enhancing the precision of tooth segmentation through the application of deep learning within a semi-supervised learning framework. Our approach leverages the nn-UNet architecture, incorporating innovative modifications to improve segmentation performance. Notably, we introduce two novel components: an axial attention mechanism module and a positional correction module. The axial attention mechanism enhances the model's ability to capture contextual information in axial slices, contributing to improved segmentation accuracy. Simultaneously, the positional correction module solves the problem of incorrect segmentation of bony structures similar to tooth morphology and density. In the context of semi-supervised learning, where labeled data is limited, we propose a robust selection methodology for pseudo labels. This methodology considers the stability of pseudo labels across re-training iterations, ensuring the reliability of the learning process. The integration of these components and methodologies collectively enhances the model's adaptability to the challenges posed by limited labeled data. The proposed model ranked fifth in the final ranking on unseen test data, with a score of 81.47%. The code is available at https://github.com/qpuchen/nnUNet_att_position_correction.

Keywords: Tooth segmentation · Image segmentation · Semi-supervised learning · Deep learning · CBCT image

1 Introduction

Offering a low radiation dose coupled with high-definition imagery, the cone beam computed tomography (CBCT) has established itself as the gold standard in visualizing teeth conditions before surgical interventions [4]. The advent

---

Q. Chen and Y. Wang—Equal contributions.

Y. Wang et al. (Eds.): STS 2023, LNCS 14623, pp. 96–109, 2025.
https://doi.org/10.1007/978-3-031-72396-4_9

of three-dimensional (3D) tooth segmentation from CBCT images is now not only a possibility but a pre-requisite for precision-driven orthodontic surgeries, as it enables the accurate reconstruction of 3D tooth models [3] [2]. This practice, however, remains ensnared by challenges - especially when traditional semi-automatic segmentation techniques are employed. While these methods rely on voxel selection across consecutive slices, they often necessitate time-intensive manual corrections due to frequent under or over-segmentation - a process that is not only laborious but also operator-dependent and potentially compromised by artifacts, especially from metallic restorations [11]. Previous attempts to refine this process, such as employing graph cut methods for individual tooth segmentation from CBCT scans, have shown promise but still suffer from modifications induced in the foreground during iterations [1].

The landscape of tooth segmentation has been reshaped by the advent of deep learning approaches, aimed to overcome semi-automatic segmentation limitation. Jang et al. [8] developed a hierarchical multi-step model for fully automated segmentation and identification for individual teeth and jaws from CBCT images. Wang et al. [15] proposed the use of a multi-task 3D fully convolutional network and marker-controlled watershed transform to segment individual tooth. Meanwhile, the method based on nnU-Net has become a top tier solution for many challenges in medical image segmentation in recent years [10] [6]. Despite its state-of-the-art performance in fully supervised learning, nnU-Net presents limitations, notably its lack of native support for semi-supervised training and the difficulty in differentiating teeth from nearby bony structures of similar morphological and density profiles. This similarity may lead to significant segmentation errors [13], as shown in Fig. 1.

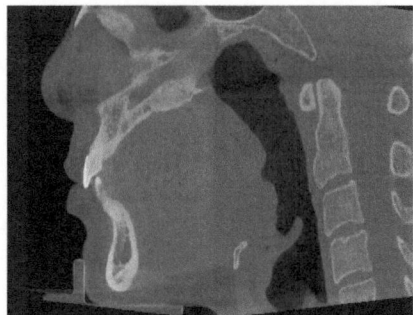 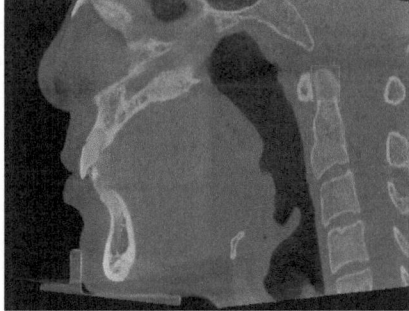

(a) Tooth image in the sagittal plane   (b) The odontoid process is incorrectly segmented

Fig. 1. The nnU-Net model misinterprets the odontoid process as teeth to be segmented.

The MICCAI 2023 Semi-supervised Teeth Segmentation Challenge (STS 2023) is a competition aimed at enabling researchers to accurately segment tooth regions using deep learning methods. This challenge endeavors to advance the precision of tooth segmentation using deep learning within a semi-supervised learning (SSL) framework. Due to the prohibitive costs-both financial and temporal-associated with exhaustive pixel-wise annotations, it is very reasonable to choose SSL, which is divided into two main strategies: consistency-regularization and pseudo-label-based methods. Our research adopts the latter approach for its inherent simplicity and integrates it with the nnU-Net framework.

We introduce a modification of the 3D nnU-Net framework to generate and utilize high-quality pseudo labels effectively. This entails an iteratively refined process of pseudo labeling over a dataset of 300 unlabeled images, augmented by two novel components: an axial attention mechanism and a positional correction module, both tailored to address the intricate challenges presented by tooth segmentation. Additionally, we introduce a selection methodology for pseudo labels based on their stability across re-training iterations, further ensuring the reliability of the semi-supervised learning process. Our contributions, delineated in this article, are threefold:

We introduce an axial attention mechanism tailored to enhance model sensitivity to the intricate details within tooth structures.

We design a positional correction module, specifically designed to adjust and correct segmentation errors, especially those resulting from the misidentification of non-tooth structures.

We establish a pseudo label selection process predicated on the robustness and stability of pseudo labels, ensuring an iterative refinement that enhances the overall segmentation accuracy.

2   Method

This section introduces the data processing, elaborates on the proposed modifications to the nnU-Net architecture, and details the post-processing steps of the segmentation outcomes.

2.1   Preprocessing

Preprocessing is the first critical step in our method, serving as the foundational work that paves the way for the successful application of deep learning models. We incorporate the preprocessing of nnU-Net to standardize and enhance the quality of the input data, which is essential for the consistent performance of our model. The preprocessing consists of resampling for resolution uniformity, intensity normalization to address the variability among scanning protocols, and cropping and padding to adapt the images to the requirements of the neural network.

2.2   Proposed Method

We propose an innovative method based on **nnUNet** that integrates the **A**xial **A**ttention mechanism and **P**ositional **C**orrection module (nnUNet-AA-PC), specifically for the segmentation of tooth structures in three-dimensional CBCT images. The overall architecture of the model is shown in Fig. 2.

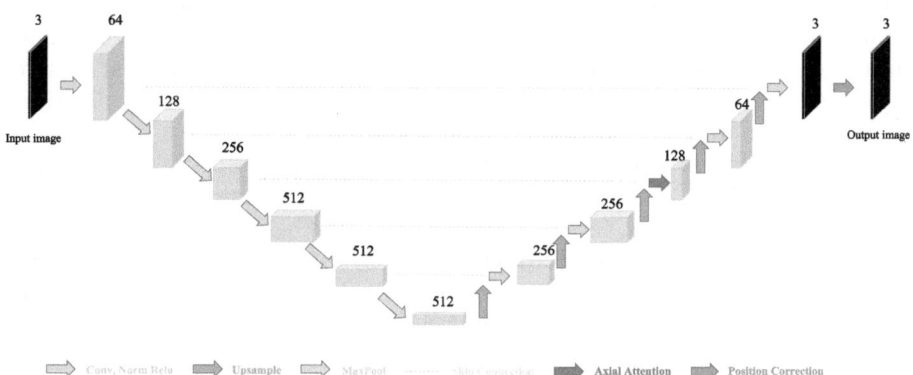

Fig. 2. Architecture diagram of the proposed nnUNet-AA-PC. After the given 3D CBCT image is downsampled by nnUNet, the axial attention mechanism is used in the third layer of the decoder to enhance the model's detail-oriented processing capabilities o for dental structure. After the segmentation is completed, the problem of incorrect segmentation of bone structures is solved through the positional correction module.

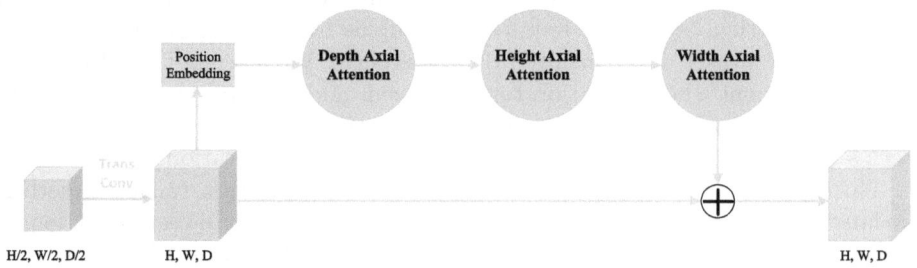

Fig. 3. Upsampling illustration showcasing the integration of Axial attention with residual connections, enhancing representation while boosting gradient flow.

Axial Attention Mechanism Module. The axial attention mechanism [5] is an enhancement to our model's ability to parse through the horizontal and vertical planes within the images, which is paramount in 3D tooth segmentation tasks. It improves the precision of the segmentation process by allowing the model to process feature maps along individual axes, thereby lowering computational demands and focusing on local dependencies crucial for tooth imagery, as depicted in Fig. 3. Considering the network's ability to capture more complex and abstract feature representations at deeper levels of feature mapping, which are crucial for the final accuracy of segmentation [17], and also considering the impact of feature dimensionality on computational complexity, we have implemented the attention mechanism in the third layer of the decoder. This targeted enhancement is not only expected to improve the model's overall performance but also to avoid blindly or unnecessarily increasing the computational complexity across the entire network. For an input image with dimensions (D, H, W, C), the algorithm iteratively processes as follows:

1. **Axis Selection and Slice Extraction**: We begin by selecting an axis (e.g., the depth axis, D). All slices on this axis are then extracted, each being a 2D tensor of shape (H, W, C).

2. **Attention Weight Calculation**: For each 2D tensor slice, the conventional multi-head attention mechanism [14] calculates the Query (Q), Key (K), and Value (V) matrices. The attention weights are determined using:

$$\text{Attention}(Q,\ K,\ V)\ =\ \text{softmax}\left(\frac{QK^T}{\sqrt{d_k}}\right)V \tag{1}$$

3. **Feature Map Update**: Using the calculated attention weights, the representation of each 2D tensor slice is updated.

4. **Axis Merging**: After completing attention computation for one axis, the updated slices are recombined to form a new 3D tensor.

5. Steps 1–3 are reiterated for other axes.

Positional Correction Module. The specific scanning range of 3D CBCT images is a critical issue that requires meticulous handling in our research. We analyzed the dataset and consulted dental experts. We learned that during CT scans, the patient's head position remains fixed, and the non-tooth bony structures are typically located farther from the teeth. Accurately demarcating the teeth's boundary is crucial for excluding erroneous segmentation items.

Through statistical analysis, we studied the segmentation range of teeth in the labeled dataset. In the training set, the maximum width of teeth (i.e., length in the x-axis direction) was observed to be 305 units. Consulting with dentists revealed individual variances in tooth size. To be conservative, we set the detection width w of the teeth to 320 units and the length l (i.e., length in the y-axis direction) as 0.8 times the width, equating to 256 units. To address the mis-segmentation issue, we meticulously crafted a positional correction module. This module encompasses the following four pivotal steps to ensure more accurate and trustworthy segmentation results:

1. **Determination of Points A and B**: Initially, in the transverse section images, we ascertain the location of the segmented tooth structure. In the image, the leftmost point A (coordinates: (x_0, y_0, z)) and the topmost point B (coordinates: (x_1, y_1, z)) are identified, as demonstrated in Fig. 4.

2. **Computation of Point C**: Next, point C is computed to rectify the position of the tooth accurately. Point C is the intersection of lines from points

A and B, where line A extends upwards, and line B stretches to the left. The coordinates of point C, typically (x_0, y_1, z), can be derived from points A and B.

3. **Constructing the Dental Region Box**: Using our predefined dental width and length parameters, starting from Point C, we create a dental region box along the x and y axes. This box accurately defines the dental range.

4. **Data Filtering**: The final step retains segmentation data within the tooth area frame and discards data outside of it. This step ensures only genuine tooth structure data is retained, effectively mitigating mis-segmentation issues.

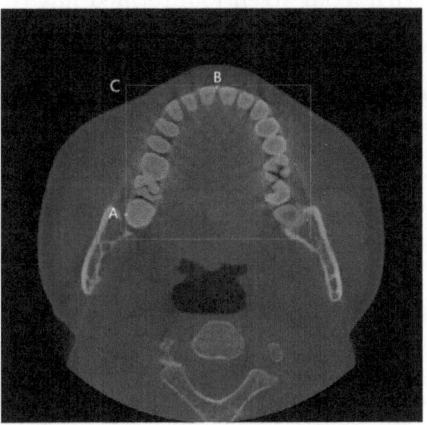

Fig. 4. Constructed dental region box depiction.

This comprehensive positional correction module, considering the unique characteristics of tooth structures, ensures our segmentation model accurately locates and segments teeth, simultaneously negating the possibility of incorrect non-tooth structure segmentation.

Pseudo-Labeling Method. To maximize the utilization of unlabeled data for model training, we adopted a sophisticated yet efficient pseudo-label generation strategy ensuring high-quality pseudo-labels and enhanced model performance. The detailed steps of our pseudo-labeling strategy are as follows:

1. **5-Fold Cross-Validation Training**: Initially, labeled data undergoes 5-fold cross-validation to train five independent nnU-Net models, ensuring model diversity.

2. **High-Quality Pseudo-label Generation**: During this phase, our meticulously crafted 5-fold nnU-Net ensemble is used for precise inference settings, predicting a pseudo-label on the unlabeled data. This step guarantees high-quality and accuracy of pseudo-labels.

3. **Iterative Training and Pseudo-label Updating**: We subsequently iteratively train an nnU-Net model on the union of labeled data with pseudo-labels and unlabeled data, generating a new pseudo-label post each training

round. This process continually refines pseudo-label quality and model performance.

4. **Pseudo-label Stability Selection**: As the generation process evolves, pseudo-label stability over various training epochs acts as our yardstick. The more stable a pseudo-label remains across different iterations, the higher its chances of selection.

5. **Final Model Training with Axial Attention**: Culminating our strategy, we integrate both the labeled dataset and the selectively pseudo-labeled unlabeled data to train the final model. Notably, this iteration employs an nnUNet incorporated with axial attention, termed nnUNet-AA. The purpose of introducing this axial attention mechanism is to adeptly differentiate and mitigate any interference from the pseudo-labels, ensuring impeccable tooth structure segmentation in the final model evaluations.

Loss Function. For the optimization objective, we employ a combination of binary cross-entropy and dice loss functions, utilizing a batch dice approach for stability and consistency across various sample sizes within the training set.

2.3   Post-processing

In the final phase of our method, post-processing includes test-time augmentation techniques to ensure robustness against possible orientation biases in the segmentation predictions and the application of our positional correction module to refine the segmentation outcomes. These steps are critical to guarantee the clinical applicability of our model by enhancing its accuracy and reliability.

3   Experiments

3.1   Dataset

The training set included 12 labeled CBCT scans where each tooth's structure was meticulously annotated, serving as the ground truth for supervised learning. Alongside, an additional 300 unlabeled CBCT scans were provided to explore semi-supervised learning techniques. These unlabeled scans were of paramount significance as they substantially increased the volume of data available for model training and were instrumental in evaluating the efficacy of the pseudo-labeling strategy we employed. The test set comprised 50 CT scans. The labels for these scans were retained by the competition organizers to serve as a blind test set, ensuring an unbiased evaluation of our models' generalizability and predictive performance. Participants were required to submit their segmentation predictions on this set for final scoring.

3.2   Evaluation Metrics

The evaluation of segmentation models was based on a composite score derived from three primary metrics, chosen for their relevance to the quality of segmentation in medical imaging:

Dice Coefficient: A statistical tool that measures the overlap between the predicted segmentation and the ground truth.

$$Dice = \frac{2 * |A \cap B|}{|A| + |B|} \tag{2}$$

Intersection over Union (IoU) : This metric calculates the overlap between two sets as the size of their intersection divided by the size of their union. It is given by:

$$IoU = \frac{|A \cap B|}{|A \cup B|} \tag{3}$$

where, A in the formula represents the mask predicted by the model, and B represents the benchmark mask for group truth.

Hausdorff Distance: A measure of the largest distance from a point in one set to the closest point in the other set, it is especially useful for capturing the worst-case scenario in segmentation tasks. It is calculated as:

$$H(d) = min(|x_1 - x_2| + |y_1 - y_2| + |z_1 - z_2|) \tag{4}$$

where, (x_1, y_1, z_1) and (x_2, y_2, z_2) represent the coordinates of the two voxels, while $|x_1 - x_2|$, $|y_1 - y_2|$, and $|z_1 - z_2|$ represent the distance on the corresponding coordinate axis.

The composite score for the competition, which integrates these three metrics, is formulated as:

$$score = 0.4 * Dice + 0.3 * IOU + 0.3 * (1 - H(d)) \tag{5}$$

This scoring method ensures a balanced assessment of the segmentation models, rewarding those that perform well across all three dimensions of accuracy.

3.3   Implementation Details

Environment Settings. To ensure reproducibility and maintain a standard benchmark, we adhered to a specific set of development environment requirements listed in Table 1.

Training Protocols. The nnU-Net framework was utilized as our core architecture for segmentation due to its state-of-the-art performance in a wide range of segmentation tasks. Table 2 presents our training protocols in detail. In addition, we included the following protocols during the experiment:

Table 1. Development environments and requirements.

System	Ubuntu 20.04.2 LTS
CPU	Intel(R) Xeon(R) Silver 4210 CPU @ 2.20 GHz
RAM	104×32 GB; 2400 MT/s
GPU (number and type)	2×NVIDIA V100 32 GB
CUDA version	11.4
Programming language	Python 3.9.16
Deep learning framework	torch 1.11.0, torchvision 0.12.0
Specific dependencies	nnU-Net 1.7.1
Code	https://github.com/qpuchen/nnUNet_att_position_correction

- We adopted 5-fold cross-validation to train our models. This technique mitigates overfitting and improves the robustness of the model by ensuring that
  each instance of the dataset has the opportunity to be in both the training
  and validation set.
- Data augmentation strategies were employed to artificially expand the diversity of the dataset, which included on-the-fly augmentations such as random
  rotations, scaling, elastic deformations, and mirroring.
- We applied the axial attention mechanism and positional correction modules to modify the U-Net architecture specifically for our nnUNet-AA and
  nnUNet-AA-PC models. These modifications aimed to enhance the model's
  ability to focus on relevant features and understand positional relationships
  in 3D space.
- For the unlabeled dataset, pseudo-labeling was utilized. This semi-supervised
  learning technique involved using our model to predict labels on the unlabeled data, then including these predictions as part of the training data in a
  subsequent training phase.

4   Results and Discussion

4.1   Quantitative Evaluation Results

In our experiments, we have developed and compared the leading medical image
segmentation methods. The results are shown in Table 3.

1. **Swin UNETR** [12]: It utilizes a Swin Transformer-based [9] encoder for
superior performance across various medical tasks.

2. **nnUNet-base** [7]: This represents the vanilla nnUNet model without any
specific modifications or enhancements.

3. **nnFormer** [16]: This model combines interleaved convolution with self-
attention operations. It also leverages both local and global volume-based self-
attention to learn representations from volumetric data.

Table 2. Training protocols.

Network initialization	
Batch size	8
Patch size	112×160×128
Total epochs	3000
Optimizer	SGD with nesterov momentum ($\mu = 0.99$)
Initial learning rate (lr)	0.01
Lr decay schedule	Poly learning rate policy: $(1 - epoch/3000)^{0.9}$
Training time	416 h
Loss function	Dice loss and cross entropy loss
Number of model parameters	87.4M
Number of flops	776G
CO_2eq	34.01 Kg

4. **nnUNet-AA**: Building upon the nnUNet-base, this model integrates a pseudo-label generation approach. Furthermore, an axial attention mechanism is incorporated after the second layer of the nnUNet's decoder. The training for this model is carried out on a union of labeled data and a selected subset of unlabeled data possessing pseudo-labels.

4. **nnUNet-AA-PC**: This model extends the capabilities of nnUNet-AA. It introduces an additional positional correction module, geared towards rectifying any anomalous points in the segmentation predictions.

Table 3. Comparative predictive performance of different models for 3D tooth segmentation

Method	Online Validation			
	Dice (%)	IoU (%)	HD (mm)	Scoree(%)
nnFormer [16]	58.42	70.46	29.72	65.59
Swin UNETR [12]	61.60	72.15	29.40	67.47
nnUNet-base [7]	66.69	74.97	29.21	70.41
nnUNet-AA	75.56	80.45	25.21	76.80
nnUNet-AA-PC	**79.32**	**82.90**	**17.08**	**81.47**

In the 3D tooth segmentation task, our proposed nnU-Net-centric models exhibited distinct performance advantages, significantly outperforming nnFormer and Swin UNETR. The nnUNet-base provided a fundamental benchmark with a Dice coefficient of 0.6669, an IOU of 0.7497, and a Hausdorff distance of 0.2921, resulting in a composite score of 0.7041. However, the addition of an axial attention mechanism and pseudo-labeling in the nnUNet-AA model marked a considerable improvement, raising the Dice coefficient to 0.7556 and the IOU to 0.8045, while decreasing the Hausdorff distance to 0.2521, culminating in a score of 0.768.

Most notably, the nnUNet-AA-PC model, which introduced a positional correction module, achieved the highest marks across all metrics: a Dice coefficient of 0.7932, an IOU of 0.8290, a reduced Hausdorff distance of 0.1708, and an overall score of 0.8147. Compared with the nnUNet-AA model, Dice Score, IOU and Hausdorff distance are relatively improved by 3.76%, 2.45% and 8.13% respectively, highlighting the effectiveness of the positional correction module. These metrics not only demonstrate the robustness of our models but also underscore the significance of integrating innovative techniques like axial attention and positional corrections in improving model accuracy for complex segmentation tasks.

4.2 Qualitative Evaluation Results

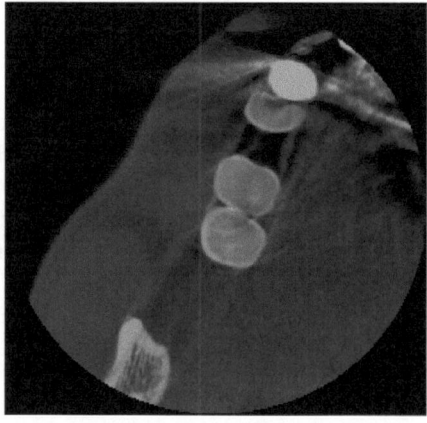

Fig. 5. Example of generating pseudo-label for unlabeled data

Good Segmentation Cases. The detailed steps of the pseudo-labeling strategy, designed to optimize the use of unlabeled data to bolster model performance. To significantly increase the training samples, we pseudo-label the unlabeled data provided by the competition. This augmentation is crucial for delineating tooth contours, textures, and shapes. Figure 5 shows an example of our model generating a pseudo-label from unlabeled data. With sufficient pseudo-label data with clear anatomical boundaries, our models, especially nnUNet-AA and nnUNet-AA-PC, show excellent performance in segmenting unknown teeth.

Failure Case Analysis. Our models, such as nnUNet-base and nnUNet-AA, face the challenge of distinguishing anatomical structures similar to tooth density from teeth. The similarity of these structures leads to incorrect segmentations.

The model incorporating the positional correction module, nnUNet-AA-PC, has been shown to help mitigate these issues, as illustrated in the comparison results before and after using the positional correction module (Fig. 6). The improvement highlights the module's utility in refining the model's predictions.

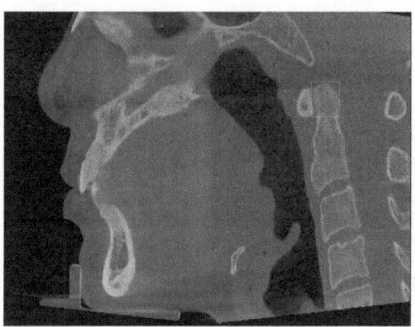
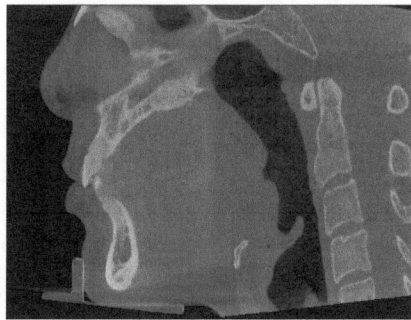

(a) Segmentation example before using the positional correction module

(b) Segmentation example after using the positional correction module

Fig. 6. Comparative illustration before and after the implementation of the positional correction module

4.3   Limitation and Future Work

Our study, while successful, is not without limitations. The models were optimized for tooth CBCT scans, and their performance on other medical imaging modalities remains untested. Furthermore, the potential introduction of noise through pseudo-labeling necessitates future refinement to ensure the consistency and reliability of semi-supervised learning approaches. Future research will aim to generalize the model to a broader range of medical images and enhance the pseudo-labeling methodology to reduce the risk of incorporating noisy data during training.

5   Conclusion

The integration of axial attention mechanisms and positional correction modules into our nnU-Net-based framework has demonstrated significant potential in 3D tooth segmentation. This study shows that the use of unlabeled data, when properly managed with sophisticated techniques like pseudo-labeling and attention mechanisms, can substantially enhance model performance. The nnUNet-AA-PC model, in particular, has shown how targeted corrections can rectify specific segmentation challenges, pointing to the value of continued innovation in model architecture. As a result, our approach not only sets a new precedent for semi-supervised learning in tooth CT segmentation but also opens avenues for its application to other medical imaging tasks.

Acknowledgements. The authors of this paper declare that the segmentation method they implemented for participation in the STS 2023 challenge has not used any pre-trained models nor additional datasets other than those provided by the organizers. The proposed solution is fully automatic without any manual intervention. We thank all the data owners for making the X-ray images and CT scans publicly available and Alibaba Cloud for hosting the challenge platform.

References

1. Chen, Y., et al.: Automatic segmentation of individual tooth in dental CBCT images from tooth surface map by a multi-task FCN. IEEE Access **8**, 97296–97309 (2020)
2. Cui, W et al.: Ctooth+: a large-scale dental cone beam computed tomography dataset and benchmark for tooth volume segmentation. In: MICCAI Workshop on Data Augmentation, Labelling, and Imperfections, pp. 64–73. Springer (2022). https://doi.org/10.1007/978-3-031-17027-0_7
3. Cui, W., et al.: Ctooth: a fully annotated 3d dataset and benchmark for tooth volume segmentation on cone beam computed tomography images. In: International Conference on Intelligent Robotics and Applications, pp. 191–200. Springer (2022). https://doi.org/10.1007/978-3-031-13841-6_18
4. Hao, J., et al.: Ai-enabled automatic multimodal fusion of cone-beam ct and intraoral scans for intelligent 3d tooth-bone reconstruction and clinical applications. arXiv preprint arXiv:2203.05784 (2022)
5. Ho, J., Kalchbrenner, N., Weissenborn, D., Salimans, T.: Axial attention in multi-dimensional transformers. arXiv preprint arXiv:1912.12180 (2019)
6. Huang, Z., et al.: Revisiting nnu-net for iterative pseudo labeling and efficient sliding window inference. In: MICCAI Challenge on Fast and Low-Resource Semi-supervised Abdominal Organ Segmentation, pp. 178–189. Springer (2022). https://doi.org/10.1007/978-3-031-13841-6_18
7. Isensee, F., Jaeger, P.F., Kohl, S.A., Petersen, J., Maier-Hein, K.H.: nnu-net: a self-configuring method for deep learning-based biomedical image segmentation. Nat. Methods **18**(2), 203–211 (2021)
8. Jang, T.J., Kim, K.C., Cho, H.C., Seo, J.K.: A fully automated method for 3d individual tooth identification and segmentation in dental cbct. IEEE Trans. Pattern Anal. Mach. Intell. **44**(10), 6562–6568 (2021)
9. Liu, Z., et al.: Swin transformer: Hierarchical vision transformer using shifted windows. In: Proceedings of the IEEE/CVF International Conference on Computer Vision, pp. 10012–10022 (2021)
10. Luu, H.M., Park, S.H.: Extending nn-unet for brain tumor segmentation. In: International MICCAI Brainlesion Workshop, pp. 173–186. Springer (2021). https://doi.org/10.1007/978-3-031-09002-8_16
11. Polizzi, A., et al.: Tooth automatic segmentation from cbct images: a systematic review. Clin. Oral Investi., 1–16 (2023)
12. Tang, Y., et al.: Self-supervised pre-training of swin transformers for 3d medical image analysis. In: Proceedings of the IEEE/CVF Conference on Computer Vision and Pattern Recognition, pp. 20730–20740 (2022)
13. Uthman, A., Salman, B., Aldeen, H.S., Marei, H., Al-Bayati, S.F., Al-Rawi, N.H.: Morphometric analysis of odontoid process among arab population: a retrospective cone beam ct study. PeerJ **11**, e15411 (2023)

14. Vaswani, A., et al.: Attention is all you need. Adv. Neural Inform. Process. Syst. **30** (2017)
15. Wang, H., Minnema, J., Batenburg, K.J., Forouzanfar, T., Hu, F.J., Wu, G.: Multiclass cbct image segmentation for orthodontics with deep learning. J. Dent. Res. **100**(9), 943–949 (2021)
16. Zhou, H.Y., Guo, J., Zhang, Y., Yu, L., Wang, L., Yu, Y.: nnformer: Interleaved transformer for volumetric segmentation. arXiv preprint arXiv:2109.03201 (2021)
17. Zhou, Z., Rahman Siddiquee, M.M., Tajbakhsh, N., Liang, J.: UNet++: a nested U-Net architecture for medical image segmentation. In: Stoyanov, D., et al. (eds.) DLMIA/ML-CDS -2018. LNCS, vol. 11045, pp. 3–11. Springer, Cham (2018). https://doi.org/10.1007/978-3-030-00889-5_1

Boundary Feature Fusion Network for Tooth Image Segmentation

Dongping Zhang[1], Zheng Li[1($\boxtimes$)], Fangao Zeng[2], and Yutong Wei[3]

[1] College of Information Engineering, China Jiliang University, Hangzhou, China
s22030810012@cjlu.edu.cn
[2] College of Optoelectronics, China Jiliang University, Hangzhou, China
[3] College of Computer and Control Engineering, Qiqihar University, Qiqihar, China

Abstract. Tooth segmentation is a critical technology in the field of medical image segmentation, with applications ranging from orthodontic treatment to human body identification and dental pathology assessment. Despite the development of numerous tooth image segmentation models by researchers, a common shortcoming is the failure to account for the challenges of blurred tooth boundaries. Dental diagnostics require precise delineation of tooth boundaries. This paper introduces an innovative tooth segmentation network that integrates boundary information to address the issue of indistinct boundaries between teeth and adjacent tissues. This network's core is its boundary feature extraction module, which is designed to extract detailed boundary information from high-level features. Concurrently, the feature cross-fusion module merges detailed boundary and global semantic information in a synergistic way, allowing for stepwise layer transfer of feature information. This method results in precise tooth segmentation. In the most recent STS Data Challenge, our methodology was rigorously tested and received a commendable overall score of 0.91. When compared to other existing approaches, this score demonstrates our method's significant superiority in segmenting tooth boundaries.

Keywords: Tooth segmentation · Boundary information · Boundary feature extraction · Feature cross-fusion

1 Introduction

With the continuous advancement in medical technology, the field of medical image processing has garnered increasing interest, especially in the critical domain of oral medical imaging. At the heart of dental imaging, tooth image segmentation plays a pivotal role in applications ranging from disease detection [13], gender determination [1], to human body identification [3]. The goal of tooth image segmentation is to precisely identify and isolate areas of interest, thereby providing dentists with a robust foundation for diagnosis. However, the intricate anatomical structure of teeth, encompassing various components like enamel, dentin, pulp, among others, presents a challenge. The indistinct boundaries among these components [8] significantly complicate the task of image segmentation. Moreover, the oral environment is fraught with numerous interfering elements such as saliva and reflections, further compromising tooth image quality and exacerbating the segmentation challenge.

In recent years, a plethora of image segmentation techniques have been investigated. These include the automatic segmentation of CBCT dental images using the Otsu threshold and boundary tracking methods [9], segmentation based on three-dimensional region merging and histogram thresholds [7], and tooth segmentation employing least squares SVM and the mean shift algorithm [11], among others. While these traditional methods have proven effective, they tend to be subjective and labor-intensive, particularly when processing large image datasets. Consequently, there has been a shift towards deep learning-based approaches, such as the utilization of the enhanced AlexNet network model for tooth segmentation [10], the adoption of the U-Net network for tooth image segmentation [15], and automatic tooth segmentation using a two-dimensional coupled shape model in conjunction with the U-Net network [18].

However, these methodologies often overlook the crucial aspect of integrating detailed tooth boundary information within the network. This paper addresses this oversight and makes the following contributions:

- We propose a Boundary Feature Fusion Network aimed at achieving precise segmentation of dental panoramic images.
- We introduce a Boundary Feature Extraction module based on a reverse attention mechanism, specifically tailored to extract nuanced details of tooth boundaries.
- We design a Feature Cross-Fusion module to amalgamate boundary detail information with high-level semantic information, thereby facilitating the layered synthesis of a more accurate tooth mask.

2   Method

This paper introduces a novel boundary feature fusion network, BFFNet, to address the challenges posed by the intricate neural tissue surrounding teeth and the resulting fuzzy boundary segmentation issues. BFFNet is mainly composed of a coding network (E1-E5), a boundary feature extraction module and a feature cross-fusion module. Figure 1 depicts the overall framework of our tooth image segmentation model. The sections that follow provide an in-depth examination of both the overall architecture and the model's critical elements.

Faced with the complexity of nerve tissue around teeth and the resulting blurred boundary segmentation problem, this research proposes the BFFNet, an innovative boundary feature fusion network. This network's design core is divided into two parts: the boundary feature extraction module and the feature cross-fusion module. Figure 1 depicts the overall structure of the tooth image segmentation model. The model's overall architecture and key components are then detailed.

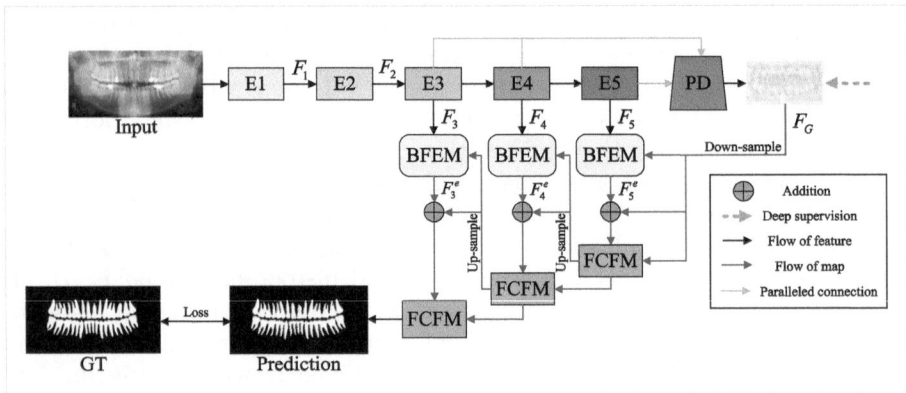

Fig. 1. Overview of the proposed BFFNet architecture. It mainly consists of three boundary feature extraction modules and three feature cross-fusion modules.

2.1 Proposed Method

In this paper, we propose an advanced segmentation network based on the fusion of tooth boundary features. Specifically, the network takes a tooth image I of size h×w as input and uses the backbone network based on the ResNet [6] architecture to extract five types of features F_i (i = 1,...,5) at different levels. These output features F_i are further subdivided into two categories: low-level features (F_1, F_2) and high-level features (F_3, F_4, and F_5). It is worth noting that we process high-level features through parallel connections and apply the partial decoder (PD) technology proposed in [19] to obtain the global mapping feature F_G.

Then, the global mapping features are fed into the first boundary feature extraction module (BFEM) designed by us to extract preliminary boundary information. Subsequently, the extracted boundary information and global mapping features are additively fused to enhance the interaction between details and global information. Thereafter, the fused information is input into the first feature cross-fusion module (FCFM) together with the original global mapping features to achieve deep cross-fusion between multiple features. Subsequent BFEM and FCFM modules follow similar processing flows. In particular, we take the output of the last FCFM as the final tooth mask prediction result.

This novel structural framework enables our network to address the issue of boundary blurring in dental pictures more effectively, providing a more effective and precise tool for oral medical image analysis.

2.2 Boundary Feature Extraction Module

In clinical dentistry, dentists must first determine the tooth area before marking the teeth based on information such as position and shape. As mentioned in Sect. 2.1, the global mapping feature F_G obtained through the output of the last layer of the convolutional neural network mainly contains coarse semantic information of dental tissue but lacks fine local details. To address this issue, our research introduces a boundary feature extraction module based on the reverse attention mechanism [4], which aims to extract more refined boundary information from high-level features and effectively transfer this information to promote a more accurate Generation of segmentation masks. Specifically, this module extracts boundary features by multiplying high-level features F_i (i=3,4,5) and reverse attention weights W_i. Formula 1 describes this process, and the specific expression of the reverse attention weight W_i is shown in formula 2.

$$F_i^e = (F_i \otimes W_i) \oplus F_i \tag{1}$$
$$W_i = E - (\varepsilon (U_p (S_{i+1}))) \tag{2}$$

$U_p(\cdot)$ represents the upsampling operation, $\varepsilon(\cdot)$ represents the Sigmoid function, E is the all-1 matrix, $\otimes$ represents the element-wise multiplication operation, and $\oplus$ represents the element-by-element addition operation. Figure 2 shows the details of the entire process.

With this module design, we can improve the detail capture of tooth boundaries while retaining global information, significantly improving the accuracy and detail richness of tooth image segmentation, and providing clinicians with more reliable diagnostic assistance.

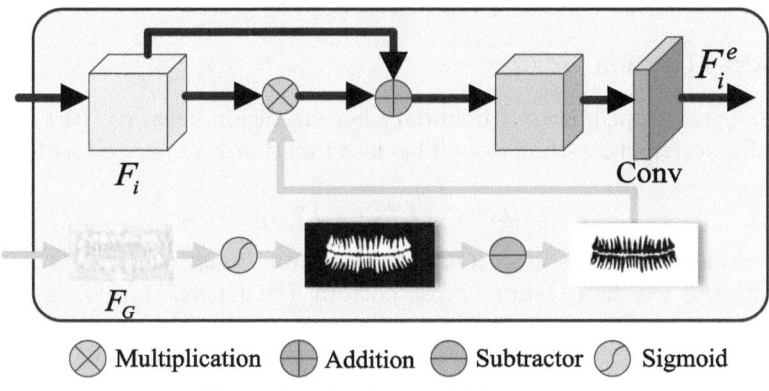

Fig. 2. Internal structure of BFEM.

2.3   Feature Cross-fusion Module

To more efficaciously integrate boundary detail features and realize precise mask prediction, we have designed a feature cross-fusion module (FCFM). The primary aim of this module is to excavate and amalgamate more nuanced semantic information. The architectural details of FCFM are depicted in Fig. 3. Within this module, a cross-fusion strategy is employed. The process unfolds as follows: initially, a concatenation operation merges two distinct features, followed by processing the merged features through a branch named 'Local Att.' This step is aimed at deriving features focused on local attention. The computational mechanics of this phase are detailed in formula 3 and formula 4.

$$F_{j,j+1}^{local} = Conv_3(F_{j,j+1}) \otimes W_{local} \oplus Conv_3(F_{j,j+1}) \tag{3}$$

$$W_{local} = \varepsilon(P - Conv_2(\delta(P - Conv_1(Conv_3(F_{j,j+1}))))) \tag{4}$$

$$F_{j,j+1}^{u} = Conv_3(Concat(F_{j,j+1}^{local}, Conv_3(F_{j,j+1}))) \tag{5}$$

$Conv_3$ represents a 3×3 convolution operation, W_{local} represents the local attention weight, where $P\text{-}Conv_i$ represents point-wise convolution, the kernel sizes of P-Conv$_1$ and P-Conv$_2$ are K/t×K×1×1 and K×K/t×1×1 respectively, and T represents the channel reduction rate, K represents the channel size. In addition, $\epsilon(\cdot)$ and $\delta(\cdot)$ represent the Sigmoid and ReLU activation functions respectively.

Following that, the local attention branch features are spliced with another set of features to finally generate fused features. The process is expressed by formula 5, where Concat represents the concatenation operation.

The FCFM as a whole is intended to improve the model's ability to capture detailed information in tooth images via fine feature processing and fusion, resulting in higher precision results for tooth segmentation and further improving the efficiency and accuracy of tooth image analysis.

2.4   Loss Function

In this paper, we optimize our boundary feature fusion network (BFFNet) using a specially designed loss function. This loss function is expressed as follows:

$$Loss = L_{IOU}^{w} + L_{BCE}^{w} \tag{6}$$

L_{IOU}^{w} represents the weighted IOU loss based on global constraints and L_{BCE}^{w} represents the weighted binary cross entropy (BCE) loss based on local constraints.

These loss function definitions are consistent with those found in the literature [14,17]. It is worth noting that we adopt a deep supervision method for the output of three FCFMs (i.e.: F_3^s, F_4^s, F_5^s) and the global map F_G . The global map obtains the same size as the ground truth map G through an upsampling operation. Therefore, the overall loss function of BFFNet can be expressed as:

$$L_{total} = L\left(G, F_G^{up}\right) + L\left(G, F_3^{s-up}\right) + L\left(G, F_4^{s-up}\right) + L\left(G, F_5^{s-up}\right) \tag{7}$$

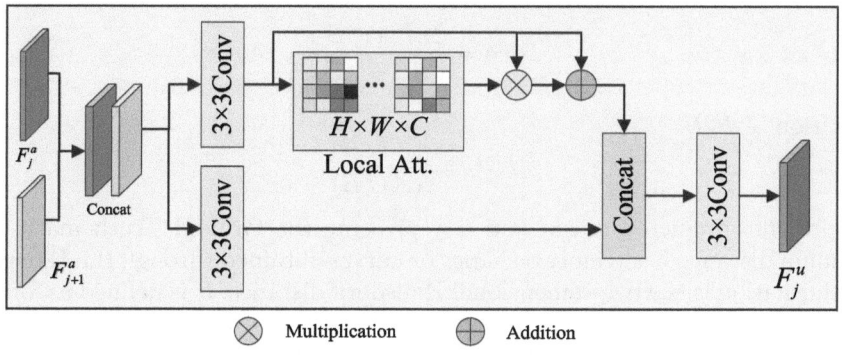

Fig. 3. Internal structure of FCFM.

3   Experiments

3.1   Datasets and Comparative Models

Our experimental study utilizes the STS (Tooth Segmentation Task Based on 2D Panoramic Image) dataset, which was introduced by Zhang et al. [21] as part of the MICCAI 2023 Challenges. This unique dataset comprises dental panoramic photographs from 106 pediatric patients, ranging in age from 2 to 13 years. It stands as the world's first panoramic photo dataset specifically tailored for pediatric dentistry. The dataset's annotations were meticulously crafted using the efficient interactive segmentation annotation software EISeg and the image annotation software LabelMe. These annotations are primarily geared towards research in caries segmentation and dental disease detection. Additionally, the dataset encompasses dental panoramas from 93 other pediatric patients, as well as 2692 images sourced from three international adult dental datasets. It is important to note that our research utilized only 2000 data entries from the preliminary phase of the STS Data Challenge.

Furthermore, to evaluate the efficacy and superiority of our proposed method, we compared the proposed method with four other leading medical image segmentation methods, including U-Net [16], UNet++ [22], LDNet [20], and CCBANet [12].

3.2   Evaluation Metrics

To evaluate the model's performance in the experiment, we used the official evaluation indicators of the MICCAI 2023 Challenge, which are the *Dice* coefficient, *IOU*, Hausdorff distance, and a comprehensive score Score. The specific formula is as follows:

Definition of dice coefficient:

$$Dice = \frac{2* \mid A \cap B \mid}{\mid A \mid + \mid B \mid} \tag{8}$$

Definition of IOU:

$$IOU = \frac{(A \cap B)}{(A \cup B)} \tag{9}$$

A represents predicted mask, and B represents the Ground Truth mask. The minimum distance between two shapes or curves obtained through the Hausdorff transformation is the two-dimensional Hausdorff distance. It is defined as follows:

$$H(d) = \min(\mid x_1 - x_2 \mid + \mid y_1 - y_2 \mid) \tag{10}$$

(x_1, y_1) and (x_2, y_2) represent the coordinates of two-pixel points, $\mid x_1 - x_2 \mid$ and $\mid y_1 - y_2 \mid$ represent the distance on the corresponding coordinate axis.

The model's performance is primarily determined by the three scoring indicators listed above. The official established a comprehensive score Score to facilitate the observation of the model's performance. Specifically defined as follows:

$$Score = w_1 * Dice + w_2 * IOU + w_3 * (1 - H(d)) \tag{11}$$

w_1, w_2 and w_3 represent the weight coefficients, which are 0.4, 0.4, and 0.3 respectively.

3.3   Implementation Details

Environment Settings. In this study, we built a specialized development environment, whose detailed configuration is shown in Table 1. We chose the Windows 10 operating system as the primary platform. The core processing unit (CPU) uses Intel(R) Core(TM) i7-8700K, with a clock speed of 3.70 GHz. The system memory is 16 GB RAM, distributed in two 8 GB modules. To handle complex image segmentation tasks, we are equipped with an NVIDIA GeForce RTX 2080 SUPER 8G graphics card. The CUDA version installed in the system is 11.6, which is a key component for deep learning calculations. On the software side, we chose Python 3.7 as the primary programming language. In terms of deep learning frameworks, we used Torch 1.8 and Torch-vision 0.9.

Training Protocols. In this study, the training hyperparameters are set as shown in Table 2. The framework is implemented based on PyTorch and trained on an NVIDIA GeForce RTX 2080 SUPER graphics card equipped with 8G video memory. To optimize the overall parameters of the network, we adopted the Adam optimization algorithm and set the learning rate to 10^{-4}. All input images are uniformly resized to 320×640 pixels. To enhance the robustness of the model, we use three different scales $\{0.75, 1, 1.25\}$ to train the model. The entire network adopts an end-to-end training method, and the batch size is set to 4. The entire training process lasts for 300 epochs. In selecting the optimal

Table 1. Development environments and requirements.

System	Windows 10
CPU	Intel(R) Core(TM) i7-8700K CPU @ 3.70GHz
RAM	16GB
GPU version	NVIDIA GeForce RTX 2080 SUPER 8G
CUDA version	11.6
Programming language	Python 3.7
Deep learning framework	torch 1.8, torchvision 0.9

model, we determine the best model based on the principle of minimum loss. It is important to emphasize that we did not use any unlabeled data during the entire training process to ensure the high quality and consistency of the training set.

Table 2. Training protocols.

Batch size	4
Train size	320×640
Total epochs	300
Optimizer	Adam
Initial learning rate (lr)	0.0001
Lr decay schedule	50
Training time	48 h
Number of model parameters	32.55M

3.4 Ablation Study

In this section, we conduct ablation experimental studies on each small component designed to evaluate their specific contribution to the performance of the proposed model. Through these experiments, we aim to reveal the impact of individual components on the overall performance of the model. Table 3 shows the detailed experimental results of the model using various module combinations. Figure 4 provides a thorough box plot analysis, visually representing the impact of different module integrations on model performance.

Table 3. Results of ablation experiments on various BFFNet components. The best outcomes are highlighted. ↑ indicates that the higher the value, the better the performance, whereas ↓ indicates that the lower the value, the better the performance.

Settings	Dice (↑)	IOU (↑)	HD (↓)	Score (↑)
Backbone	0.6868	0.8515	0.2097	0.7673
Backbone+BFEM	0.7175	0.8902	0.0395	0.8422
Backbone+FCFM	0.7212	0.8944	0.0269	0.8487
Backbone+BFEM+FCFM	**0.7911**	**0.9848**	**0.0174**	**0.9061**

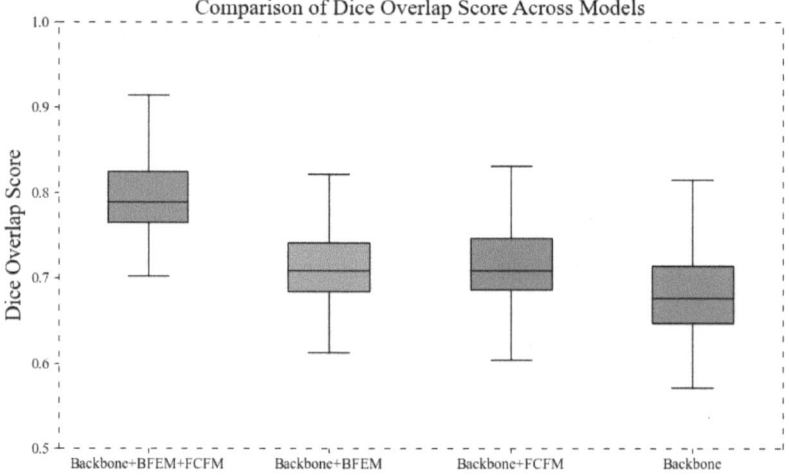

Fig. 4. Box plot under different module combinations.

BFEM of Effectiveness. We study the importance of the boundary feature extraction module. By comparing the data in the second and third rows in Table 3, we find that the performance of the model is significantly improved after integrating BFEM in the backbone network. Specifically, the *Dice* coefficient increased from 0.6868 to 0.7175, the *IOU* increased from 0.8515 to 0.8902, and the overall score (Score) increased from 0.7673 to 0.8422. These results clearly show that BFEM plays a key role in improving model performance.

FCFM of Effectiveness. Further, we studied the impact of FCFM on model performance. By comparing the experimental data in the second and fourth rows in Table 3, we can find that the performance of the model has also been significantly improved after integrating FCFM: the *Dice* coefficient increased to 0.7212, the *IOU* increased to 0.8944, and the total score increased to 0.8487. These experimental results fully demonstrate the importance of FCFM in improving model performance.

Table 4. Model Comparison Results.

Settings	Dice (↑)	IOU (↑)	HD (↓)	Score (↑)
UNet	0.5832	0.7232	0.2428	0.6774
UNet++	0.5939	0.7365	0.2429	0.6857
LDNet	0.6951	0.8564	0.2202	0.7689
CCBANet	0.7273	0.9023	0.0599	0.8436
BFFNet(Our)	**0.7911**	**0.9848**	**0.0174**	**0.9061**

BFEM and FCFM of Effectiveness. To verify the effectiveness of the combination of BFEM and FCFM, we studied the performance of the combined model. Compare the experimental data in the fifth row and the second to fourth rows in Table 3. We can find that the performance of the model has been significantly improved after adding the two modules, especially the two evaluation indicators of *Dice* and *IOU* have been improved by 7% and 9% respectively, and *HD* has reached the lowest value. Further, the boxplot in Fig. 4 reveals that the model incorporating both BFEM and FCFM components yields the highest median *Dice* Overlap Score. This suggests that the synergistic interaction of these components significantly bolsters the model's segmentation performance. Additionally, the model's interquartile range being relatively narrow indicates consistent and stable performance. Consequently, it can be inferred that the model integrating both BFEM and FCFM outperforms all other configurations.

4   Results and Discussion

BFFNet is a novel automatic segmentation model for tooth images that we created. The experimental results will be analyzed and discussed further below.

4.1   Quantitative Results

In evaluating and comparing model performance, we consider several key factors in segmentation tasks, including important aspects such as accuracy, consistency, and shape matching. Table 4 shows the quantitative comparison results between our proposed method and the other four methods on four key evaluation indicators.

Figure 5 clearly shows that our model achieves significant improvements in segmentation performance due to the use of high-performance components. In addition, the precision-recall curve of BFFNet covers the curves of other segmentation models, which not only highlights its excellent performance but also further verifies the superiority of our proposed tooth segmentation model in various performance indicators.

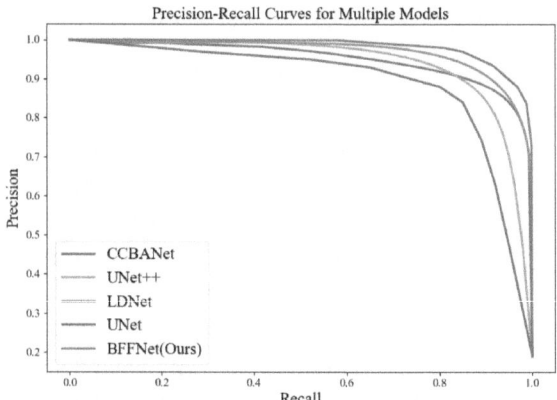

Fig. 5. Precision-Recall curves of BFFNet and other four models.

4.2   Qualitative Results

The segmentation results of BFFNet and its four models are output and displayed. The detailed comparison results are shown in Fig. 6 below. Examining the visualization results reveals that our proposed model has significant advantages in performing boundary segmentation, as well as a robust anti-interference capability against background noise. This level of performance not only highlights the model's ability to discern fine details but also demonstrates its formidable ability to maintain the image's overall stability. Such characteristics highlight the model's effectiveness and dependability in complex image-processing scenarios.

In addition, we find that the four compared models can complete effective segmentation and the BFFNet proposed in this paper achieves the best performance, especially in boundary segmentation, where our model is more advantageous. However, we find that UNet has the worst segmentation results, which is mainly attributed to our limited hardware resources, and through repeated experiments, the results show that the UNet model has never been able to achieve considerable results.

4.3   Limitation and Future Work

This paper mainly employs dental images to develop a fully supervised model. However, we did not consider the potential impact of label inaccuracies in the data on model prediction results. In future research, we will consider more about developing tooth image segmentation models based on weak supervision or unsupervised learning.

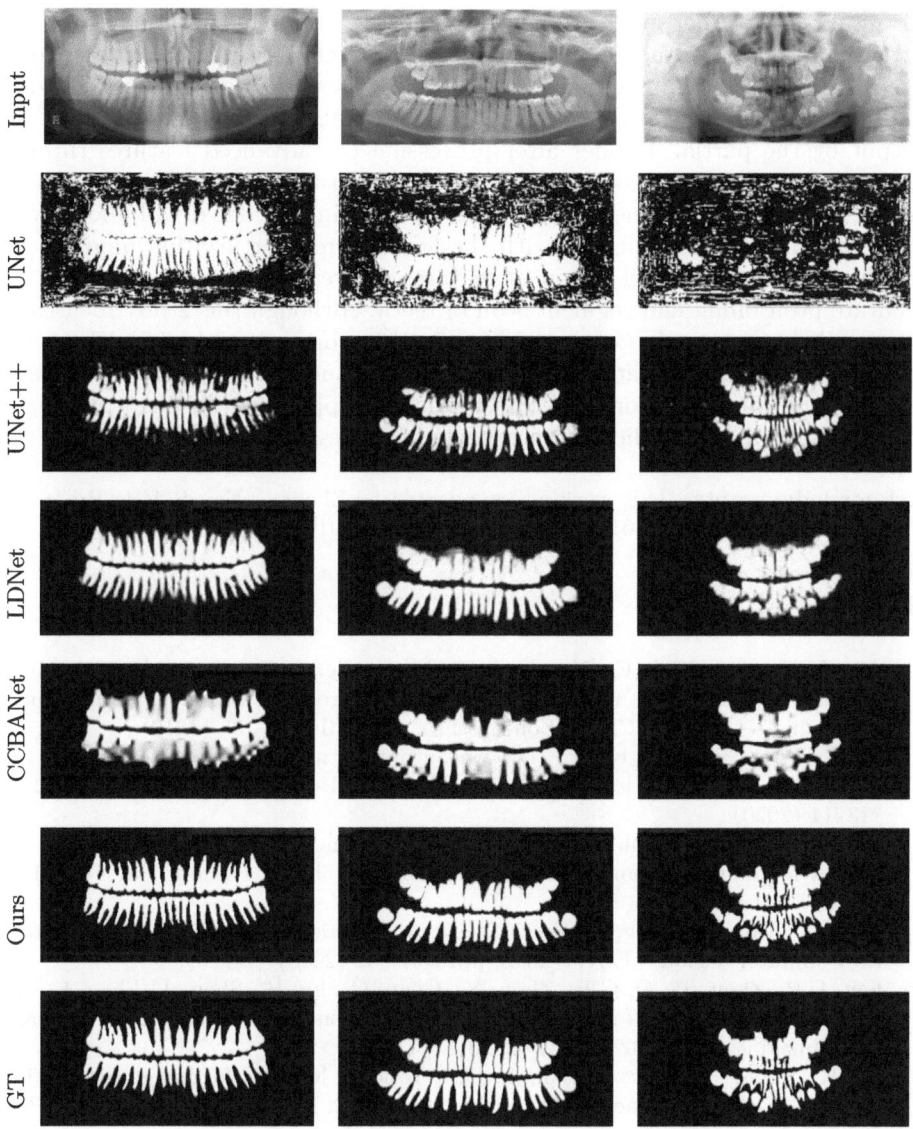

Fig. 6. Qualitative results of different methods.

5   Conclusion

In this paper, we address the problem of boundary blur in tooth images and propose an innovative **B**oundary **F**eature **F**usion **N**etwork (***BFFNet***) that can be used to accurately segment teeth on panoramic X-rays. This method performed admirably in the preliminary competition of MICCAI 2023 Challenges. The experimental results fully demonstrate the proposed method's significant advantages over other medical image segmentation technologies, and it has the potential to become an important tool to assist clinicians in rapid diagnosis. Specifically, the tooth images are first processed by the coding network (E1-E5) to obtain features at different scales, and then the global mapping features are output by the partial decoder after processing the advanced features through parallel concatenation. Secondly, the boundary feature extraction module based on the inverse attention mechanism is used to obtain the edge detail information of the teeth. Finally, combined with the feature cross-fertilization module, the effective transmission and fusion of features are realized, so as to achieve the accurate positioning and segmentation of teeth. Although this study focuses on the detailed segmentation of dental images, the proposed method also has wide applicability in other related fields, such as cell nucleus segmentation [2], segmentation of lung infection [5], etc., showing its application in medical images. Broad potential and application prospects in processing fields.

Acknowledgements. This work was supported by Zhejiang Key R & D Project of China (2024C01102, 2024C01108, 2023C01030, 2022C01082).

References

1. Avuçlu, E., Başçiftçi, F.: Novel approaches to determine age and gender from dental x-ray images by using multiplayer perceptron neural networks and image processing techniques. Chaos, Solitons Fractals **120**, 127–138 (2019)
2. Banik, P.P., Saha, R., Kim, K.D.: An automatic nucleus segmentation and cnn model based classification method of white blood cell. Expert Syst. Appl. **149**, 113211 (2020)
3. Bozkurt, M.H., Karagol, S.: Jaw and teeth segmentation on the panoramic x-ray images for dental human identification. Chaos, Solitons Fractals **33**, 1410–1427 (2020)
4. Chen, S., Tan, X., Wang, B., Hu, X.: Reverse attention for salient object detection. In: Computer Vision – ECCV 2018, pp. 236–252 (2018)
5. Fan, D.P., Zhou, T., Ji, G.P., Zhou, Y., Chen, G., Fu, H., Shen, J., Shao, L.: Infnet: automatic covid-19 lung infection segmentation from ct images. IEEE Trans. Med. Imaging **39**(8), 2626–2637 (2020)
6. He, K., Zhang, X., Ren, S., Sun, J.: Deep residual learning for image recognition. In: 2016 IEEE Conference on Computer Vision and Pattern Recognition (CVPR), pp. 770–778 (2016)
7. Indraswari, R., Kurita, T., Arifin, A.Z., Suciati, N., Astuti, E.R., Navastara, D.A.: 3d region merging for segmentation of teeth on cone-beam computed tomography images. In: 2018 Joint 10th International Conference on Soft Computing and Intelligent Systems (SCIS) and 19th International Symposium on Advanced Intelligent Systems (ISIS), pp. 341–345 (2018)
8. Li, S., Fevens, T., Krzyżak, A., Jin, C., Li, S.: Semi-automatic computer aided lesion detection in dental x-rays using variational level set. Pattern Recogn. **40**(10), 2861–2873 (2007)
9. Lin, P., Huang, P., Huang, P., Hsu, H., Chen, C.: Teeth segmentation of dental periapical radiographs based on local singularity analysis. Comput. Methods Programs Biomed. **113**(2), 433–445 (2014)

10. Miki, Y., Muramatsu, C., Hayashi, T., Zhou, X., Hara, T., Katsumata, A., Fujita, H.: Classification of teeth in cone-beam ct using deep convolutional neural network. Comput. Biol. Med. **80**, 24–29 (2017)

11. Mortaheb, P., Rezaeian, M.: Metal artifact reduction and segmentation of dental computerized tomography images using least square support vector machine and mean shift algorithm. J. Med. Signals Sensors **6**(1), 1–11 (2016)

12. Nguyen, T.-C., Nguyen, T.-P., Diep, G.-H., Tran-Dinh, A.-H., Nguyen, T.V., Tran, M.-T.: CCBANet: cascading context and balancing attention for polyp segmentation. In: de Bruijne, M., Cattin, P.C., Cotin, S., Padoy, N., Speidel, S., Zheng, Y., Essert, C. (eds.) MICCAI 2021. LNCS, vol. 12901, pp. 633–643. Springer, Cham (2021). https://doi.org/10.1007/978-3-030-87193-2_60

13. Park, K.J., Kwak, K.C.: A trends analysis of dental image processing. In: 2019 17th International Conference on ICT and Knowledge Engineering (ICT&KE), pp. 1–5 (2019)

14. Qin, X., Zhang, Z., Huang, C., Gao, C., Dehghan, M., Jagersand, M.: Basnet: boundary-aware salient object detection. In: 2019 IEEE/CVF Conference on Computer Vision and Pattern Recognition (CVPR), pp. 7471–7481 (2019)

15. Ronneberger, O., Fischer, P., Brox, T.: Dental x-ray image segmentation using a u-shaped deep convolutional network. In: International Symposium on Biomedical Imaging, pp. 1–13 (2015)

16. Ronneberger, O., Fischer, P., Brox, T.: U-Net: convolutional networks for biomedical image segmentation. In: Navab, N., Hornegger, J., Wells, W.M., Frangi, A.F. (eds.) MICCAI 2015. LNCS, vol. 9351, pp. 234–241. Springer, Cham (2015). https://doi.org/10.1007/978-3-319-24574-4_28

17. Wei, J., Wang, S., Huang, Q.: F3net: Fusion, feedback and focus for salient object detection. In: AAAI (2020)

18. Wirtz, A., Mirashi, S.G., Wesarg, S.: Automatic teeth segmentation in panoramic X-Ray images using a coupled shape model in combination with a neural network. In: Frangi, A.F., Schnabel, J.A., Davatzikos, C., Alberola-López, C., Fichtinger, G. (eds.) MICCAI 2018. LNCS, vol. 11073, pp. 712–719. Springer, Cham (2018). https://doi.org/10.1007/978-3-030-00937-3_81

19. Wu, Z., Su, L., Huang, Q.: Cascaded partial decoder for fast and accurate salient object detection. In: 2019 IEEE/CVF Conference on Computer Vision and Pattern Recognition (CVPR), pp. 3902–3911 (2019)

20. Zhang, R., et al.: Lesion-aware dynamic kernel for polyp segmentation. In: Wang, L., Dou, Q., Fletcher, P.T., Speidel, S., Li, S. (eds.) MICCAI 2022. LNCS, vol. 13433, pp. 99–109. Springer, Cham (2022). https://doi.org/10.1007/978-3-031-16437-8_10

21. Zhang, Y., et al.: Children's dental panoramic radiographs dataset for caries segmentation and dental disease detection. Sci. Data **10**(1), 380 (2023)

22. Zhou, Z., Rahman Siddiquee, M.M., Tajbakhsh, N., Liang, J.: Unet++: a nested u-net architecture for medical image segmentation. In: Deep Learning in Medical Image Analysis and Multimodal Learning for Clinical Decision Support, pp. 3–11 (2018)

Self-training Based Semi-Supervised Learning and U-Net with Denoiser for Teeth Segmentation in X-Ray Image

Zhouhao Lin, Yibo Yang, Anrui Huang, Zeyang Shou, and Qizhong Zhang$^{(\boxtimes)}$

Hangzhou Dianzi University, Hangzhou, China
zqz@hdu.edu.cn

Abstract. Segmentation of X-ray images of teeth plays an important role in dental diagnosis. However, the labeling information is expensive, and it is of great significance to effectively use the unlabeled images to improve the segmentation performance. In order to make full use of unlabeled data, in this paper, we design a three-stage pseudo-label training framework based on self-training to improve the pseudo-label quality in a progressive way. Hard data augmentation is introduced to act on the pseudo-labels to mitigate the model overfitting to the noise in the pseudo-labels. In addition, we designed segmentation model with denoiser to improve the segmentation result while reducing the noise in pseudo-labels by removing the noise from the segmentation map generated by the segmentation model. Our method achieved an Dice score of 93.15%, an IoU score of 98.03% and HD score of 97.68% for the teeth segmentation on the validation set using a NVIDIA GeForce RTX 3090. The average training time was 2 h.

Keywords: Semi-supervised learning · Teeth segmentation · Denoiser · Hard augmentation

1 Introduction

Dental diseases are not only oral problems, but also increase the risk of other diseases, according to a large number of studies patients suffering from periodontitis, dental caries and other dental diseases have a significantly increased risk of coronary heart disease, myocardial infarction, cerebrovascular disease (e.g., stroke), and higher risk of ischemic and hemorrhagic stroke and cerebral ischemia [7]. Currently, the diagnosis and treatment of dental diseases rely heavily on doctors' diagnosis of patients' X-rays and on-site observation; however, the contradiction between the rapid increase of patients and the relative scarcity of specialized dentists is a serious constraint to the timely diagnosis and treatment of dental problems [7]. Therefore, it is important to design an algorithm for automatic diagnosis and recognition of dental diseases, which will greatly simplify the consultation process of doctors and improve the efficiency of medical diagnosis. However, manually labeling teeth in X-ray images is time-consuming and

Y. Wang et al. (Eds.): STS 2023, LNCS 14623, pp. 124–132, 2025.
https://doi.org/10.1007/978-3-031-72396-4_11

expensive. Therefore, it is usually not possible to obtain a large number of labeled X-ray images. At present, semi-supervised medical segmentation has attracted more and more attention. It aims to use a small number of labeled samples and a large number of unlabeled samples to train the model, so as to obtain useful information from the unlabeled samples. The organizers of STS2023 provided a dataset of X-ray images of children and adults with 900 labeled and 2,100 unlabeled images. The challenge is to exploit the large amount of unlabeled data to develop semi-supervised algorithms to improve segmentation performance.

Self-training is the most common semi-supervised algorithm, and its simple pseudo-label iterative training makes it widely used. ST++ [4] improves self-training by introducing Strong Data Augmentation (SDA) and filtering mechanism, and achieves strong performance. In addition, there are many semi-supervised algorithms trained end-to-end such as Mean Teachers [3] that guide the student model by obtaining pseudo-labels from the teacher model. Fixmatch [2] introduces consistency regularization to perform strong data augmentation and weak data augmentation on unlabeled images respectively, and uses weak data augmentation as a pseudo-label to supervise the prediction of strong data augmented images.

Inspired by ST++, we employ a pseudo-label filtering mechanism to select the easy samples from the pseudo-labels generated by the fully supervised trained model and add them for retraining. We further extend SDA by introducing hard data enhancements such as Mixup [6] and Cutmix [5], as well as using TTA post-processing to prevent the model from overfitting to pseudo-labels. Additionally we designed a denoiser for the segmentation model to reduce the noise in the segmentation maps predicted by the model while improving the quality of the pseudo-labels. In the end, our method achieved the 7th place.

2 Method

As shown in the Fig. 1, we train the model using the paradigm of self-training, and our proposed method has three steps. The easy samples from the unlabeled samples are filtered and co-trained with the labeled samples in the second stage. The pseudo-labels are regenerated for the remaining difficult samples, and finally the hard samples are added to the training to obtain the final high-performance model.

2.1 Preprocessing

Since the images in the dataset are all of size (640, 320) and are multiples of 32, they meet the requirements for downsampling. Therefore we keep the size of input images and perform Z-score normalization on the images. Since the value of the label is between (0, 255), we normalize it to be between (0, 1)

2.2 Method Detail

Our proposed segmentation model with denoiser is shown in Fig. 2, where the first **U-Net** uses efficientnet-b7 as the backbone and the denoiser is also a

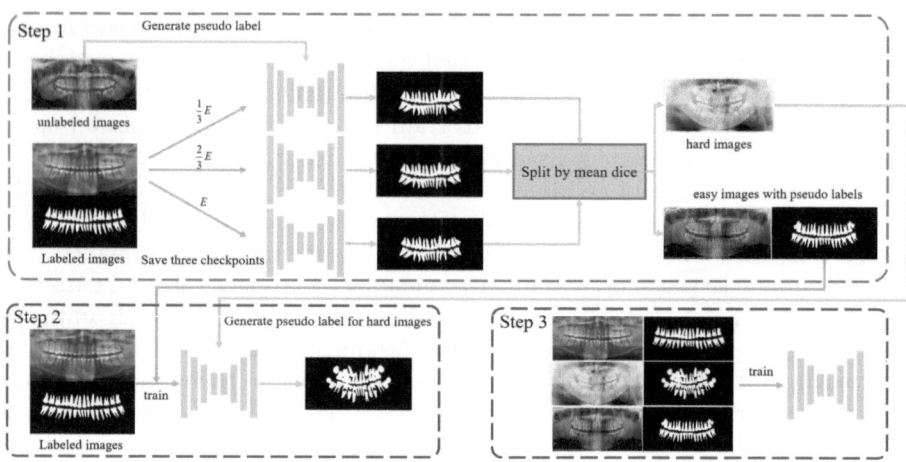

Fig. 1. Overview of our proposed three step semi-supervised framework.

U-Net architecture with a backbone of resnet-10t. The denoiser takes the first Unet generated segmentation map as input to predict the noise in it, and then subtract the noise from the segmentation map to obtain the final clean mask.

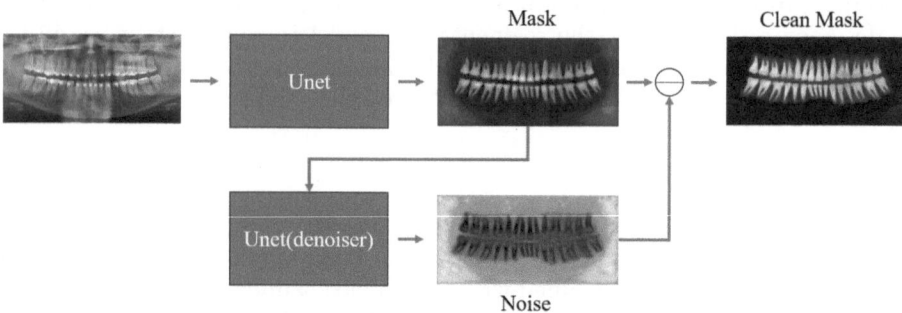

Fig. 2. The architecture of our segmentation model.

Loss function: we use the summation between Dice loss and cross-entropy loss because compound loss functions have been proven to be robust in various medical image segmentation tasks [1].

Our three-stage training framework consists of fully supervised training, mixed training with easy and labeled samples, and mixed training with hard and easy samples and labeled samples.

For fully supervised training, we used Mixup and Cutmix combination augmentation to improve the generalization ability of the model and Test-Time

Augmentation(TTA) to improve the quality of pseudo-labels when generating pseudo-labels. The checkpoints are saved at three epoch nodes E/3,2E/3,E and these three checkpoints are used to generate three sets of pseudo-labels, denoted as M_1 ,M_2 ,M_3 respectively. Then the average Dice of M_1 ,M_2 and M_3 are calculated separately with the following equations:

$$MeanDice = \frac{Dice(M_1, M_3) + Dice(M_2, M_3)}{2} \tag{1}$$

These three sets of pseudo-labels represent the prediction of unlabeled samples in the early, middle, and late stages of model training, respectively. If the MeanDice score of the pseudo-labels for a particular sample is higher, it means that the model predicts the sample well at an earlier stage of training, and the sample is recognized as an easy sample, denoted as X_{easy}. For those samples with low MeanDice, they are considered hard samples, denoted as X_{hard}. We sort the unlabeled data according to the MeanDice value from high to low, and then divide the unlabeled data into easy and hard samples according to the 3:1 ratio. Use M_3 as the final pseudo-label.

In the second stage, since the amount of unlabeled data is approximately two times that of labeled data, to ensure that the model receives enough correct supervisory signals, we oversample the labeled data to ensure that there is the same amount of labeled data as unlabeled data in each batch. The strategy of oversampling is very simple. After completing the traversal of labeled data, the pseudo labeled data has not yet been fully traversed. We traverse the labeled data again until the pseudo labeled data is traversed. In addition, to prevent the model from overfitting pseudo-labeled noise, we apply strong data augmentation and hard data augmentation to the unlabeled data. Meanwhile, only weak data augmentation is applied to labeled data to ensure that the model learns the correct labels more easily and prevent the model from being biased by pseudo-labels. Finally, in order to fully utilize the remaining hard samples, the pseudo-labels are re-generated using the model trained in the second stage, where the noise in the pseudo-labels will be reduced compared to the first stage.

In the third stage, we added labeled data to the training along with all unlabeled data, using a similar oversampling and hard data augmentation strategy as in the second stage. It is worth noting that we only used a single model and did not use model integration methods.

2.3   Post-processing

For the threshold of the segmentation result, we simply choose 0.5. In order to improve the robustness of the segmentation results, we perform TTA on the segmentation results. Since the dimensions are rectangular, we use the flip TTA

3   Experiments

3.1   Dataset

The STS2023-2D dataset [7] contains 2D dental panoramic radiographic images of adults and children, the children's data were obtained from Hangzhou Xiasha District Dental Hospital, and the images were annotated using the EISeg tool. The adult data were obtained from three public datasets, Dataset and code, Panoramic radiography Database, and Archive, where the training set contains 900 labeled dental panoramic radiography images and 2100 unlabeled dental panoramic radiography images. The test set contains 1000 dental panoramic radiography images. The resolution of 2D dental panoramic images is (640, 320) and the number of channels is 3.

3.2   Evaluation Metrics

The final evaluation score consists of three different evaluation metrics: the Dice score, the Iou score, and the hausdorff score. The final ranking score can be calculated by the formula:

$$Score = 0.4 * Dice + 0.3 * IOU + 0.3 * (1 - H(d)) \qquad (2)$$

where $H(d)$ is formulated as:

$$H(d) = min(|x1 - x2| + |y1 - y2|) \qquad (3)$$

3.3   Implementation Details

Environment Settings. The development environments and requirements are presented in Table 1. The system is running Windows 10 as the operating system. The CPU in use is an Intel(R) Core(R) Gold 5317 CPU with a clock speed of 3.00GHz. The system has a total of 64 GB RAM, divided into 16 modules of 4 GB each, operating at a speed of 2.67 MT/s. The system is equipped with four NVIDIA 3090 24G GPUs. The CUDA version installed on the system is 11.8. The programming language used for development is Python 3.9. The deep learning framework employed includes torch 2.0.1, torchvision 0.15.2, and monai 1.2.0. These specifications provide insight into the hardware and software setup used for the development of a specific project or application.

Training Protocols. Our training protocols is shown in Table 2.
1. Processing of the unlabeled images
   In the first stage of our training framework, after all the generated pseudo-labels are sorted according to MeanDice, the top 75% of the samples are selected as easy samples and the remaining as hard samples.
2. Data augmentation
   The data augmentation we use contains three parts: weak data augmentation, strong data augmentation, hard data augmentation. Weak data augmentation

Table 1. Development environments and requirements.

System	Windows 10
CPU	Intel(R) Core(TM) i9-7900X CPU@3.30 GHz
RAM	16×4GB; 2.67MT/s
GPU (number and type)	One NVIDIA 3090 24G
CUDA version	11.0
Programming language	Python 3.9
Deep learning framework	torch 2.0.1, torchvision 0.15.2, monai 1.2.0

Table 2. Training protocols.

Network initialization	"He" normal initialization
Batch size	16
Patch size	640×320
Total epochs	50
Optimizer	AdamW
Initial learning rate (lr)	0.0001
Lr decay schedule	Cosine Annealing Policy
Training time	2 h
Loss function	Dice+BCE
Number of model parameters	280.48M[a]
Number of flops	45.08G[b]
CO_2eq	43 Kg[c]

[a]https://github.com/sksq96/pytorch-summary
[b]https://github.com/facebookresearch/fvcore
[c]https://github.com/lfwa/carbontracker/

contains: flip, rotation. Strong data augmentation contains: flip, rotate, elastic transformation, Gaussian blur, Gaussian noise, Gaussian sharpening, Intensity transformation. Hard data augmentation is the combination of Mixup and Cut-Mix. Specifically, we set the probability value $p = 0.6$ and $p_{cutmix} = 0.84$, which means that there is a probability of 0.6 to use Hard data augmentation, and there is a probability of 0.84 to use CutMix and 0.16 to use Mixup.

3. Patch sampling strategy

Instead of using patch sampling strategy, we directly use the original image size (640, 320) as input.

4. Optimal model selection criteria

We divided 20% of the training set as the validation set, and each epoch computes the evaluation metrics on the validation set, and the epoch with the highest score is selected as the final model.

Table 3. Quantitative evaluation results.

Method	Internal Validation			Online Validation		
	Dice(%)	IoU(%)	HD(mm)	Dice(%)	IoU(%)	HD (mm)
Baseline	93.97 ± 0.02	88.72 ± 0.04	98.31± 0.01	92.67	97.90	97.47
full pseudo	95.02 ± 0.01	90.66 ± 0.03	98.52± 0.001	92.89	97.96	97.61
+easy sample	95.00 ± 0.002	90.63 ± 0.001	**98.52** ± 0.012	92.96	97.98	**97.70**
ours	**95.09** ± 0.001	**90.78** ± 0.003	98.51 ± 0.001	**93.15**	**98.03**	97.68

4   Results and Discussion

4.1   Quantitative Results on Validation Set

The quantitative results on the validation set are shown in the "internal val-idation" column of Table 3. Baseline represents the results of fully supervised training, and our method is shown in the fourth row. Compared with Baseline, our method achieves 1.12%, 2.06%, and 0.2% performance improvement in Dice, IoU, and HD metrics, respectively. In addition, we also conducted ablation exper-iments to demonstrate the effectiveness of the method. Full pseudo indicates that all pseudo-labels generated in the first stage are used to join the training, and "+easy sample" means that only the top 75% of the filtered pseudo-labels with MeanDice scores are used for training with labeled data. Using only easy sam-ples is better than "full pseudo" in "Online Validation" and performs similarly to "full pseudo" in "Internal Validation". Overall, It can be seen that using only easy sample for training can achieve better performance than "full pseudo", which indicates that the quality of pseudo-labels is more important than the quantity of pseudo-labels. Low-quality pseudo-labels may cause the model to learn incorrect knowledge and deteriorate the model performance.

4.2   Qualitative Results on Validation Set

Figure 3 demonstrates two good segmentation results of our method. Our method can segment the overall structure of the tooth well and improve the bad segmen-tation of Baseline at some tooth roots. Figure 4 shows two bad segmentation results of our method. It can be seen that the teeth are stuck together in many places, and it is difficult to match the thickness of the roots with the ground truth. And the segmentation results of Baseline also show similar results, which indicates that the addition of pseudo labels to training may not be sufficient to solve this boundary problem. The model itself struggles to deal with fuzzy boundaries and is easily misled by artifacts.

4.3   Results on Final Testing Set

The results on the test set are shown in the "Online validation" column in Table 3. Our method ultimately scores 93.15%, 98.03%, and 97.68% on Dice, Iou,

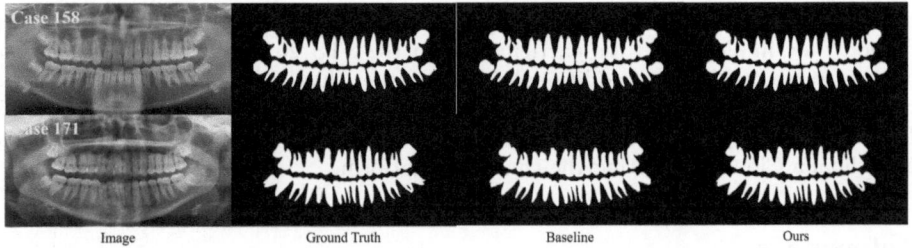

Fig. 3. Qualitative results on two good cases.

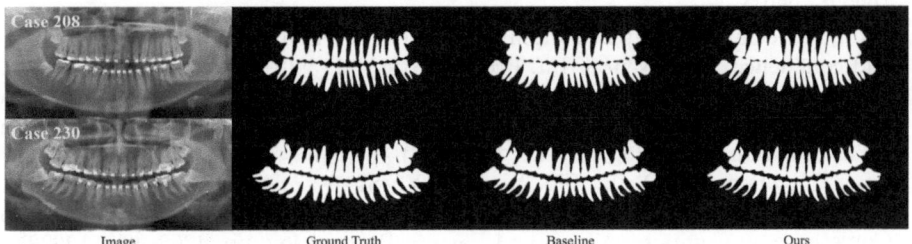

Fig. 4. Qualitative results on two bad cases.

and HD, respectively. Compared with Baseline, it achieves 0.48%, 0.13%, and 0.21% improvement, respectively. This shows that our method can effectively utilize unlabeled data. And it achieves better performance than full pseudo, which proves the effectiveness of re-generating pseudo labels.

4.4   Limitation and Future Work

The limitation of our approach is the need to train the model multiple times, which will consume more computational resources. End-to-end semi-supervised algorithms can be explored in the future. Deep supervision can also be tried on the model side to improve performance, as well as distillation and pruning to reduce the number of model parameters and improve inference efficiency.

5   Conclusion

In this paper, we design U-Net with denoiser to improve segmentation quality and reduce noise in pseudo-labeling. And a three-stage pseudo-label training framework is proposed to efficiently utilize unlabeled data for training. Compared with fully supervised training, our method achieves an improvement. We believe that our method can provide a good baseline for semi-supervised medical segmentation.

Acknowledgements. The authors of this paper declare that the segmentation method they implemented for participation in the STS 2023 challenge has not used any pre-trained models nor additional datasets other than those provided by the organizers. The proposed solution is fully automatic without any manual intervention. We thank all the data owners for making the X-ray images and CT scans publicly available and Alibaba Cloud for hosting the challenge platform.

References

1. Ma, J., et al.: Loss odyssey in medical image segmentation. Med. Image Anal. **71**, 102035 (2021)
2. Sohn, K., et al.: Fixmatch: simplifying semi-supervised learning with consistency and confidence. Adv. Neural. Inf. Process. Syst. **33**, 596–608 (2020)
3. Tarvainen, A., Valpola, H.: Mean teachers are better role models: weight-averaged consistency targets improve semi-supervised deep learning results. Advances in neural information processing systems **30** (2017)
4. Yang, L., Zhuo, W., Qi, L., Shi, Y., Gao, Y.: St++: make self-training work better for semi-supervised semantic segmentation. In: Proceedings of the IEEE/CVF Conference on Computer Vision and Pattern Recognition, pp. 4268–4277 (2022)
5. Yun, S., Han, D., Oh, S.J., Chun, S., Choe, J., Yoo, Y.: Cutmix: regularization strategy to train strong classifiers with localizable features. In: Proceedings of the IEEE/CVF International Conference on Computer Vision, pp. 6023–6032 (2019)
6. Zhang, H., Cisse, M., Dauphin, Y.N., Lopez-Paz, D.: mixup: beyond empirical risk minimization. arXiv preprint arXiv:1710.09412 (2017)
7. Zhang, Y., et al.: Children's dental panoramic radiographs dataset for caries segmentation and dental disease detection. Scientific Data **10**(1), 380 (2023)

UX-CNet: Effective Edge Information Acquisition for Teeth Image Segmentation

Hao Leng[1(✉)] and Lianghuang Huang[2]

[1] University of Shanghai for Science and Technology, Shanghai, China
242619365@qq.com
[2] Jiangxi Normal University, Nanchang, China

Abstract. Currently, the dataset of children's teeth suffers from the problems of less data, expensive annotation, poor segmentation of the edges of the teeth, and difficulty in accurately segmenting the detailed information of the edges of the teeth. In this paper, we design a deep learning algorithm named **UX-CNet** that can effectively segment teeth and solve the problem of poor effect of teeth edge segmentation. In the experiment, data augmentation was performed on the children's teeth image dataset to improve the learning ability of the model, followed by training the data with UX-CNet to improve the model in terms of overall segmentation and detail segmentation. Our method achieved an average DSC score of 95.64% and an average HD error of 0.03 for the teeth segmentation on the validation. The experiments show that UX-CNet has a great improvement over the baseline algorithm and other algorithms, proving the effectiveness of the method.

Keywords: Tooth segmentation · UX-CNet · Data augmentation · Deep learning

1 Introduction

With the development of computer-aided design (CAD) technology, as well as being influenced by many factors such as rising economic levels and the trend of an aging population, the development of dentistry is showing increasing importance and urgency. Dental diseases not only cause serious oral problems, but also have adverse effects on other organs. Numerous studies have shown that patients suffering from periodontitis, dental caries and other dental diseases have a significantly increased risk of coronary artery disease, myocardial infarction, cerebrovascular and other diseases [?]. Nearly 3.5 billion people worldwide suffer from oral diseases, with dental caries being the most prevalent in permanent teeth. Dental caries is one of the most common chronic diseases and everyone is at risk of developing this dental disease. This disease develops in the crown and root and in early childhood may manifest with aggressive teeth decay [8]. Early childhood caries may lead to a more severe caries experience in adulthood. Globally, about 520 million children suffer from dental caries in their milk

Y. Wang et al. (Eds.): STS 2023, LNCS 14623, pp. 133–144, 2025.
https://doi.org/10.1007/978-3-031-72396-4_12

teeth and the situation of caries in children is increasing every year. Therefore, proper prevention and treatment of early childhood caries is of great medical importance.

At present, the treatment of children's teeth largely depends on the on-site diagnosis of doctors, who will combine panoramic X-rays to diagnose the patient's dental disease, so as to give the correct treatment plan. Most children exhibit multiple dental diseases and cross-diseases, which poses an even greater challenge for the doctor to identify lesions and plan treatment. In addition, existing public datasets on adult teeth are not only different from children's teeth in physiological structure, but also unsuitable for caries segmentation and disease detection. The datasets about children's teeth are less, expensive to annotate, and less effective for edge segmentation of teeth, making it difficult to accurately segment the edge detail information of teeth. Designing a deep learning algorithm that effectively segments teeth and automatically analyzes diseases can greatly simplify the diagnostic process for doctors, reduce the misclassification and miss rate, and thus improve the efficiency of medical work.

Existing methods for teeth image segmentation are mainly categorized into two types, one is based on supervised learning and the other is based on semi-supervised methods. The supervised learning methods for teeth segmentation are mainly based on U-Net [7], which consists of a symmetric Encoder-Decoder with skip connections. In the encoder, a series of Convolutional layers and continuous down-sampling layers are used to extract deep features with large receptive fields. Then, the decoder upsamples the extracted deep features Then, the decoder upsamples the extracted deep features to the input resolution for pixel-level semantic prediction, and the high-resolution features of different scales from the encoder are fused with skip connections to alleviate the loss of spatial information caused by down-sampling.

The simplicity of the structure has allowed U-Net to achieve great success in various medical imaging applications. Currently there are two types of improvements to U-Net, CNN-based methods like Res-UNet [14] and Transformer-based methods like Swin-UNet [1], both of which have achieved good results in medical image segmentation. Semi-supervised methods extract knowledge from labeled data in a supervised manner and from unlabeled data in an unsupervised manner, thus reducing the labeling work required in fully supervised scenarios and obtaining better results than unsupervised scenarios. There are five main categories of semi-supervised methods, the first category is GAN-like structure and adversarial training between two networks, one acting as a generator and the other as a discriminator. The second category is consistency regularization methods. These methods include a regularization term in the loss function to minimize the differences between different predictions of the same image, which are obtained by applying perturbations to the image or the model in question. The third category is pseudo-labeling methods. Pseudo-labeling of unlabeled images is generated based on predictions made by models previously trained on labeled data. Then, the labeled dataset is extended using these new pairs of images and pseudo-labels, and a new model is trained on this new dataset. The fourth category is the comparison-based learning approach. This learning paradigm groups similar elements and separates them from different elements in a particular representation space. The last category is hybrid methods, i.e., consisting of a combination of consistency regularization, pseudo-labeling, and contrastive learning.

In this paper, we summarize the techniques used in the competition and propose an effective method for solving the problem of poor edge segmentation of teeth. The dataset we use is the dataset of children's teeth provided by Zhang et al. [16]. The following is a brief overview of our solution:

- Effective data augmentations strategies.
- A UX-CNet for teeth segmentation.
- Model fusion and post-processing methods of test time augmentation (TTA).

2 Method

2.1 Preprocessing

The preliminary training set provides 2000 panoramic images of teeth and the test set provides 500 panoramic images of teeth. The training set includes the original images as well as the corresponding masks, and the test set provides only the original images. By analyzing the dataset, it was found that the resolution size of the preliminary data images were 320*640, the training set images were grayscale images, and the masks were binary images. Since the teeth segmentation dataset was small, a data augmentation strategy was used.

Data augmentation is an effective way to increase the diversity of training images. It can increase the data diversity, generalization ability and robustness, and improve the performance and effect of deep learning models. The commonly used data augmentation are HorizontalFlip, VerticalFlip, RandomRotate, RandomCrop, RandomBrightnessContrast, ShiftScaleRotate, ColorJitter, noise augmentation are GaussianBlur, GaussNoise, MotionBlur, and distortion augmentation are GridDistortion, OpticalDistortion, ElasticTransform, CoarseDropout, etc. Since the image is a grayscale image there is no need for color augmentation, and the shape and size of the segmented teeth and the location are relatively fixed, the use of VerticalFlip and Rotate will destroy the original position, affecting the effect of the segmentation, ShiftScaleRotate is mainly to translate, scale and rotate the image, a small degree of rotation in the case of not affecting the image of the original position, can improve the effect of model prediction. Through experimental analysis, HorizontalFlip, RandomCrop and ShiftScaleRotate are found to have better results.

2.2 Proposed Method

ConvNext [5] is based on ResNet50, following the idea of Swin Transformer [4] for one-to-one reduction, and finally reverses Swin Transformer in a variety of effects. In terms of macroscopic design, it is the same as Swin Transformer, with 4 Stages, the ratio of the number of Blocks in each Stage is consistent with Swin Transformer, and a 4*4 convolutional layer is used for 4-fold downsampling. In

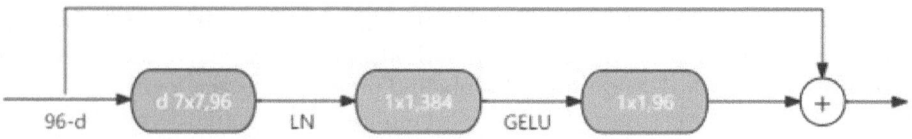

Fig. 1. ConvNext block.

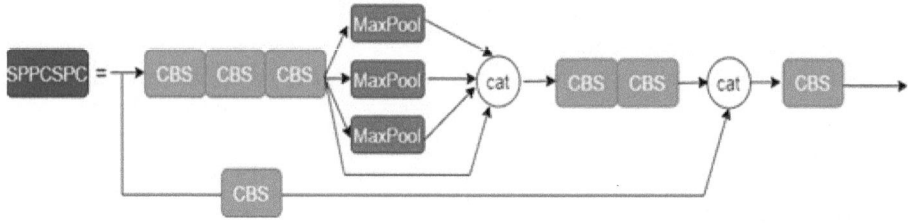

Fig. 2. SPPCSPC module.

the micro-design, the following strategies are mainly used: (1) Replace the ReLU activation function with the GELU activation function. (2) Employing fewer activation functions instead of adding activation functions after each layer. (3) Use fewer regularization layers. (4) Replace batch normalization (BN) with layer normalization (LN). The specific ConvNext Block is shown in Fig. 1 below.

The SPPCSPC module was proposed by Alex et al. in YOLOv7 [12] and improved on the basis of the SPPNet module [2], the role of the SPPNet layer is to increase the receptive field, so that the algorithm can be adapted to images of different resolutions. One branch of the SPPCSPC module carries out a number of parallel Max Pooling operations after a number of convolutions, which are at different scales of Max Pooling has four kinds of receptive field, mainly used to distinguish between objects with different targets, another branch carries out ordinary convolution processing, and finally these two branches are merged, which not only reduces the amount of computation, but also increases the receptive field to avoid image distortion caused by the operation on the image. The specific results are shown in Fig. 2 below.

The difficulty in segmenting children's teeth lies in the segmentation of the edges of the teeth, which makes it difficult to accurately segment the edge detail information of the teeth. A large number of methods work well for overall segmentation, but are not good enough for segmentation of edge detail information. Therefore, we propose a UX-CNet method, which combines modules such as ConvNext, U-Net, and SPPCSPC to realize the accurate segmentation of teeth. The specific structure is shown in Fig. 3 below. UX-CNet uses U-Net as our base-architecture, and the Encoder uses ConvNext as the backbone, where each ConvNext Block corresponds to the Block of each stage of ConvNext. After 32-fold down-sampling, the SPPCSPC module was used, mainly to increase the

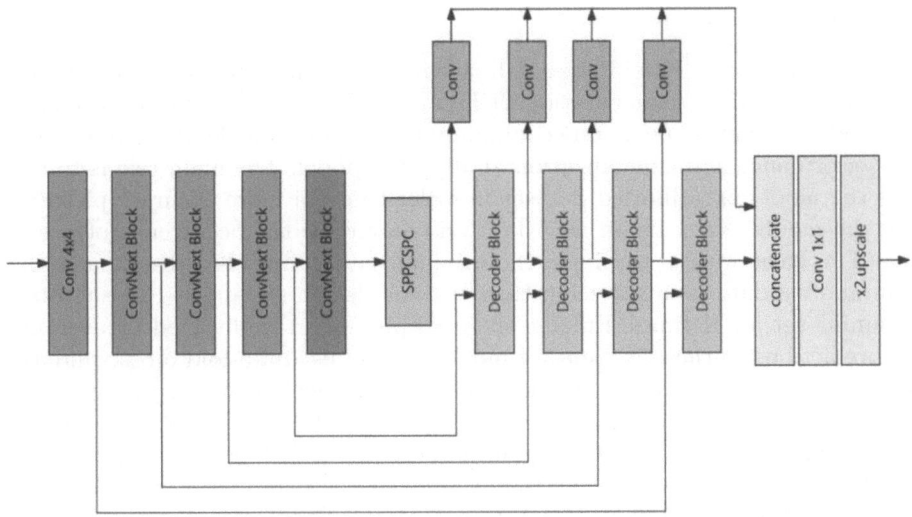

Fig. 3. The architecture of UX-CNet, which is composed of encoder, bottleneck, decoder and skip connections.

receptive field and to fuse features at different scales so as to have a more accurate segmentation of the whole. The structure of Pixel Shuffle [9] and FPN are used in Decoder. Pixel Shuffle is used for upsamples, which effectively amplifies the reduced feature map, and effectively guarantees the stability of the quality of the image. The FPN's structure passes the deep semantic information to the shallow layer, effectively fuses the deep semantic information with the shallow positional information, and improves the accurate segmentation of the edge detail information of the teeth.

For the loss function, a combination of SoftBCEWithLogits Loss and Dice Loss was used. Cross entropy Loss for binary classification was used because teeth images have only 1 category and only foreground and background need to be distinguished and Sigmoid is more friendly to edge effects compared to Softmax. Dice is the calculation of similarity between predicted segmented image and real segmented image to optimize the model. The combination of SoftBCEWithLogits Loss and Dice Loss is used, because compound loss functions have been proven to be robust in various medical image segmentation tasks.

Pseudo-label training is a very effective training method. The model trained on labels is used to make predictions on the image data without labels, and the predicted masks and the image data without labels are added to continue the training, so as to help the model to obtain better convergence characteristics. In this competition, we used the method of pseudo-label for training, and found that the effect improvement was not obvious.

2.3   Post-processing

For post-processing, K-fold cross validation, model ensemble, threshold adjustment, and test time augmentation (TTA) [?] were used. K-fold cross-validation is a model evaluation technique commonly used in machine learning to estimate the performance and generalization ability of a model. The main role is to evaluate the model on a limited dataset in order to get a more accurate picture of how the model performs on new data and to reduce the occurrence of overfitting. The basic idea is to divide the original dataset into K subsets, and then train and validate each subset in turn as a validation set and it K-1 subsets as a training set for K times. Finally, the final prediction is obtained by averaging the predictions of these K times of modeling. We used a 5-fold cross-validation for one experiment. Model ensemble is also an effective way to reduce overfitting by integrating the results of multiple models and finally obtaining the fused results. Commonly used fusion methods are Stacking and simple averaging. The simple multi-model averaging used in the competition uses U-Net as our base-architecture, EfficientNetV2-L [11], ResNeSt-200 [15], RegNetX-300 [6], RegNetY-300 [6], EfficientNetB7 [10], and ConvNextV2 [13] as backbone.

TTA [?] has HorizontalFlip, VerticalFlip, Rotate, and Scale, since Rotate and VerticalFlip would destroy the original position of the teeth in the image, they were not used, and only a simple strategy of HorizontalFlip was used. Good results were also achieved by adjusting the threshold.

3   Experiments

3.1   Dataset

The dataset used for STS competition is a dataset of children's teeth images collected by Zhang [16] et al. The preliminary training set provides 2000 panoramic images of teeth and the test set provides 500 panoramic images of teeth. The training set includes the original images as well as the corresponding masks, and the test set provides only the original images. The training set for the final round provides 4000 panoramic images of teeth and the test set provides 1000 panoramic images of teeth. The training set consisted of images containing 2000 labeled teeth (original images as well as corresponding masks were provided) and 2000 unlabeled panoramic images of teeth. The test set provides only the original images without mask. The data of the preliminary and final rounds are different. In the preliminary round, 500 panoramic images of teeth will be provided as the test set, and 1000 images of teeth will be provided as the test set in the final round. All the original images are grayscale images, masks are binary images, and the resolution size is 320*640. This experiment uses the data from the preliminary round. Some sample images are shown in Fig. 4 below.

3.2   Evaluation Metrics

IoU is one of the important metrics to measure the performance of segmentation models, and the degree of overlap between the predicted segmentation results

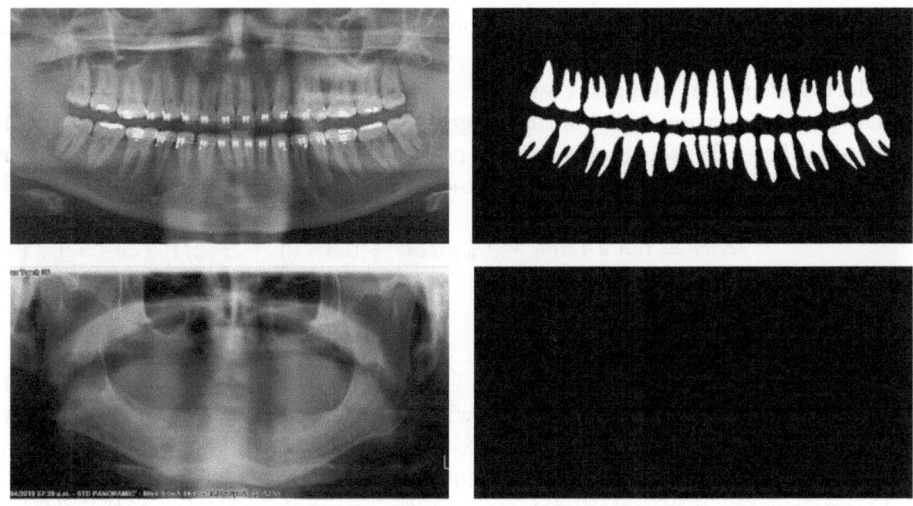

Fig. 4. Two different images and masks are shown in the training set.

and the real segmentation results are measured by calculating the intersection ratio between the two. The specific representation can be formulated as:

$$IoU = \frac{A \cap B}{A \cup B} \tag{1}$$

The value range of IoU is [0,1], where A in Eq. 1 denotes the mask predicted by the model and B denotes the baseline mask of Ground Truth. Larger values indicate higher overlap between the predicted segmentation results and the true segmentation results.

Dice coefficient is also a commonly used metric for calculating segmentation models, which focuses on calculating the similarity between two samples. The similarity between the predicted segmentation result and the real mask is measured by calculating the ratio of the overlap between the two in terms of the overall number of pixels in both. Dice is computed as follows:

$$Dice = \frac{2 * |A \cap B|}{|A| + |B|} \tag{2}$$

The value of Dice is in the range of [0,1], where A denotes the predicted mask and B denotes the baseline mask of Groud Truth in Eq. 2.

The two-dimensional Hausdorff distance (HD) is the minimum distance between two shapes or curves obtained by Hausdorff transformation [3], it can be formulated as:

$$HD(A, B) = \min(|x_1 - x_2| + |y_1 - y_2|) \tag{3}$$

where (x_1, y_1) and (x_2, y_2) denote the coordinates of the two pixel points and $|x_1 - x_2|$ and $|y_1 - y_2|$ denote the distances on the corresponding axes. This formula represents the sum of the absolute distances between two pixel points on the horizontal and vertical axes in a two-dimensional medical image, i.e., the Hausdorff distance at the pixel level.

The final evaluation index is the weighted average of Dice, IoU and Hausdorff distance. Where Hausdorff distance is normalized so that its value is between 0–1. The final rating formula is computed as follows:

$$Score = 0.4 * Dice + 0.3 * IoU + 0.3 * (1 - H(d)) \tag{4}$$

3.3   Implementation Details

The experiment is achieved based on Python 3.8 and Pytorch 1.11.0. We train our model on a Nvidia A5000 GPU with 24 GB memory. The system used is Ubuntu 20.04. The weights pretrained on ImageNet are used to initialize the model parameters. The specific environment settings are shown in Table 1 below.

During the training period, data augmentations such as HorizontalFlip, RandomCrop and ShiftScaleRotate are used to increase data diversity. We add 500 images from the test set as pseudo-labeled data to the training, the input image size are set as 320×640. The batch size is 16 and the popular AdamW optimizer with momentum 0.9 and weight decay 5e-4 is used to optimize our model. The specific settings are shown in Table 2 below.

Table 1. Development environments and requirements.

System	Ubuntu 20.04
CPU	AMD EPYC 7371 16-Core Processor
RAM	28GB
GPU(number and type)	One RTX A5000 24G
CUDA version	11.3
Programming language	Python 3.8
Deep learning framework	torch 1.11.0, torchvision 0.12.0
Other packages	timm, segmentations_models_pytorch

4   Results and Discussion

4.1   Results on Final Testing Set

In the competition, our baseline used U-Net as our base-architecture and ResNet50 as backbone, comparing the effects of UX-CNet and U-Net based on different backbone and SwinUnet on the preliminary dataset. The experimental results are shown in Table 3 below. Combining the post-processing and the data augmentation experiments, the final submitted experimental results are shown

Table 2. Training protocols.

Network initialization	The weights pretrained on ImageNet
Batch size	16
Image size	320×640
Total epochs	20
K fold	5
Optimizer	AdamW with momentum=0.9
Initial learning rate (lr)	1e-4
Lr decay schedule	5e-4
Lr scheduler	CosineAnnealingLR
Training time	About 4 h for one fold
Loss function	0.5*Dice + 0.5*SoftBCEWithLogitss

Table 3. Segmentation accuracy of different methods on the Online Validation.

Methods	Dice (%)	IoU (%)	1 - HD (%)	Score (%)
U-Net(ResNet50)	91.11	95.44	92.25	92.75
U-Net(ResNet101)	89.65	95.50	95.38	93.12
U-Net(EfficientNetB7)	90.57	95.92	95.56	93.67
U-Net(ResNeSt101)	90.62	95.91	95.64	93.71
U-Net(ConvNext)	90.63	95.70	96.27	93.84
SwinUnet	90.50	95.81	96.23	93.81
UX-CNet	90.94	96.00	96.98	94.27

in Table 4. From Table 3, it can be seen that UX-CNet has a large improvement compared to both baseline and other algorithms, although there is not much improvement in Dice, but it improves 4.7% in HD, and the final Score reaches 94.27%. From Table 4, it can be seen that data augmentation and model ensemble bring great improvement, effective data augmentation can increase the learning ability of the model, the specific ablation experiments are shown in the following Table 5. Model ensemble can merge the effect of different models to get better results. Among them, the choice of threshold also brings considerable effect.

Data augmentation is a very effective strategy, Table 5 gives the data enhancement methods that worked well in this competition, and it can be seen that the effect enhancement is obvious after using data augmentation. Among them, RandomCrop brings the biggest enhancement. TTA only uses HorizontalFlip, but the enhancement is not obvious. Pseudo-labelings were trained using the test dataset from the preliminary round, and the prediction mask that scored the highest on the list was added to the training as the Ground Truth, but the results obtained were less satisfactory.

Table 4. The final results on the Online Validation.

Methods	Dice (%)	IoU (%)	1 - HD (%)	Score (%)
ResU-Net (baseline)	91.11	95.44	92.25	92.75
UX-CNet	90.94	96.00	96.98	94.27
+ Augmentations	92.48	96.60	96.96	95.06
+ Threshold (0.32)	93.08	96.78	96.91	95.34
+ K Fold	93.25	96.86	96.96	95.45
+ Ensemble Models	93.61	96.99	96.99	95.63
+ TTA	93.62	96.98	97.00	95.64

Table 5. Ablation study on data augmentation. HFlip stands for HorizontalFlip; RCrop stands for RandomCrop.

RCrop	HFlip	ShiftScaleRotate	Dice (%)	IoU (%)	1 - HD (%)	Score (%)
✓			91.78	96.25	96.98	94.68
✓	✓		92.01	96.40	96.85	94.78
✓	✓	✓	92.48	96.60	96.96	95.06

4.2   Limitation and Future Work

In the competition, although we proposed that UX-CNet improved the edge details of the teeth in children's teeth segmentation, it was difficult to divide the edge information of the teeth in some unclear images, and the segmented edges were not smooth enough and there were adhesion problems between the teeth. We will improve this problem in the future. In addition, semi-supervised segmentation is a very effective method and will be investigated in the future.

5   Conclusion

In this paper, we summarize the techniques used in the competition in terms of data augmentation, model improvement, and post-processing. For data augmentation, we adopted some effective data augmentation based on the characteristics of the dataset itself. After using data augmentation, the prediction effect is greatly improved. In terms of modeling, we proposed UX-CNet for solving the problem of poor edge segmentation of teeth and improving the model's effectiveness in overall segmentation and detail segmentation. Finally, in post-processing, we used model ensemble and K Fold with some adjustments to the threshold, and finally achieved a score of 95.64%.

Acknowledgements. The authors of this paper declare that the segmentation method they implemented for participation in the STS 2023 challenge has not used any pre-trained models nor additional datasets other than those provided by the organizers. The proposed solution is fully automatic without any manual intervention. We thank all the data owners for making the X-ray images and CT scans publicly available and Alibaba Cloud for hosting the challenge platform.

References

1. Cao, H., et al.: Swin-unet: Unet-like pure transformer for medical image segmentation. In: ECCV 2022. LNCS, pp. 205–218. Springer (2022). https://doi.org/10.1007/978-3-031-25066-8_9
2. He, K., Zhang, X., Ren, S., Sun, J.: Spatial pyramid pooling in deep convolutional networks for visual recognition. IEEE Trans. Pattern Anal. Mach. Intell. **37**(9), 1904–1916 (2015)
3. Huttenlocher, D.P., Klanderman, G.A., Rucklidge, W.J.: Comparing images using the hausdorff distance. IEEE Trans. Pattern Anal. Mach. Intell. **15**(9), 850–863 (1993)
4. Liu, Z., et al.: Swin transformer: hierarchical vision transformer using shifted windows. In: Proceedings of the IEEE/CVF International Conference on Computer Vision, pp. 10012–10022 (2021)
5. Liu, Z., Mao, H., Wu, C.Y., Feichtenhofer, C., Darrell, T., Xie, S.: A convnet for the 2020s. In: Proceedings of the IEEE/CVF Conference on Computer Vision and Pattern Recognition, pp. 11976–11986 (2022)
6. Radosavovic, I., Kosaraju, R.P., Girshick, R., He, K., Dollár, P.: Designing network design spaces. In: Proceedings of the IEEE/CVF Conference on Computer Vision and Pattern Recognition, pp. 10428–10436 (2020)
7. Ronneberger, O., Fischer, P., Brox, T.: U-Net: convolutional networks for biomedical image segmentation. In: Navab, N., Hornegger, J., Wells, W.M., Frangi, A.F. (eds.) MICCAI 2015. LNCS, vol. 9351, pp. 234–241. Springer, Cham (2015). https://doi.org/10.1007/978-3-319-24574-4_28
8. Selwitz, R.H., Ismail, A.I., Pitts, N.B.: Dental caries. The Lancet **369**(9555), 51–59 (2007)
9. Shi, W., et al.: Real-time single image and video super-resolution using an efficient sub-pixel convolutional neural network. In: Proceedings of the IEEE Conference on Computer Vision and Pattern Recognition, pp. 1874–1883 (2016)
10. Tan, M., Le, Q.: Efficientnet: rethinking model scaling for convolutional neural networks. In: International Conference on Machine Learning, pp. 6105–6114. PMLR (2019)
11. Tan, M., Le, Q.: Efficientnetv2: smaller models and faster training. In: International Conference on Machine Learning, pp. 10096–10106. PMLR (2021)
12. Wang, C.Y., Bochkovskiy, A., Liao, H.Y.M.: Yolov7: trainable bag-of-freebies sets new state-of-the-art for real-time object detectors. In: Proceedings of the IEEE/CVF Conference on Computer Vision and Pattern Recognition, pp. 7464–7475 (2023)
13. Woo, S., et al.: Convnext v2: co-designing and scaling convnets with masked autoencoders. In: Proceedings of the IEEE/CVF Conference on Computer Vision and Pattern Recognition, pp. 16133–16142 (2023)

14. Xiao, X., Lian, S., Luo, Z., Li, S.: Weighted res-unet for high-quality retina vessel segmentation. In: 2018 9th International Conference on Information Technology in Medicine and Education (ITME), pp. 327–331. IEEE (2018)
15. Zhang, H., et al.: Resnest: split-attention networks. In: Proceedings of the IEEE/CVF Conference on Computer Vision and Pattern Recognition, pp. 2736–2746 (2022)
16. Zhang, Y., et al.: Children's dental panoramic radiographs dataset for caries segmentation and dental disease detection. Sci. Data **10**(1), 380 (2023)

2D Teeth Segmentation Base on Half-Image Approach and VCMix-Net+

Mengzhuo Shen[1], Haocheng Li[1], Qing Li[1], Shidong Zhang[1], Tairong Xing[2], and Zhenzhen Wan[1(✉)]

[1] Key Laboratory of Digital Medical Engineering of Hebei Province, College of Electronic and Information Engineering, Hebei University, Baoding 071002, China
wanzhenzhen@126.com
[2] School of Nursing, Shanxi Medical University, Taiyuan 030001, China

Abstract. Teeth image segmentation has significant implications for various aspects of dental medicine, forensic odontology identification, scientific research, and education. However, the annotations made by radiologists may be subjective, and manual annotation requires a considerable amount of time and labor costs. In this paper, we propose deep-learning model VCMix-Net+ to achieve high-quality segmentation of 2D teeth images. Our VCMix-Net+ performs parallel operations of convolution and a multi-layer perceptron with class attention at multiple scales, simultaneously capturing both local and local-global information. Additionally, we have successfully reduced the annotation cost by employing a self-training semi-supervised approach. Our contribution lies in introducing a dedicated pseudo-label filtering network during the pseudo-label generation phase of semi-supervised training. This filtering network helps in selecting high-quality pseudo-labels, thereby reducing the risk of error accumulation in the self-training process. Meanwhile, we propose the concept of half-image training, which effectively improves the segmentation evaluation metrics. Finally, the average Score of our method's predicted results on the online test set is 92.89.

Keywords: Teeth segmentation · Half-image · VCMix-Net+

1 Introduction

High-quality teeth segmentation holds significant importance in the field of oral medicine, guiding clinical diagnoses and formulating appropriate surgical plans [1]. Furthermore, in the realm of forensic odontology, teeth segmentation is crucial for utilizing anatomical structures to identify dental records in criminal investigations [2–4]. However, teeth segmentation is primarily carried out through manual or semi-automatic interactive segmentation by dentists, which is a laborious task heavily reliant on the prior knowledge of dental professionals.

M. Shen and H. Li—Contributed equally to this work.

Y. Wang et al. (Eds.): STS 2023, LNCS 14623, pp. 145–155, 2025.
https://doi.org/10.1007/978-3-031-72396-4_13

To aid dentists in teeth segmentation more effectively, the MICCAI 2023 Semi-supervised Teeth Segmentation Challenge provided a dataset of teeth images based on 2D panoramic X-rays, aiming for accurate and automated teeth area segmentation through deep learning methods [5].

Nevertheless, achieving precise automated teeth segmentation poses challenges. There is a considerable amount of unlabeled data in teeth imaging datasets, and labeling the data requires a significant amount of time from dental experts. In situations where there is a scarcity of labeled data and a substantial amount of unlabeled data, semi-supervised learning methods prove to be more effective in leveraging data and reducing annotation costs.

Considering the challenges posed by a large amount of unlabeled data, this paper adopts a self-training-based semi-supervised training method. The idea can be summarized in the following stages:

1. Initial Training: Train an initial segmentation network using labeled data.
2. Prediction: Use this segmentation network to predict unlabeled data.
3. Pseudo-label Generation: Based on the confidence of the predictions, select samples with high confidence as pseudo-labels.
4. Data Augmentation: Incorporate the pseudo-labels into the labeled data.
5. Re-training: Retrain the segmentation network using the augmented data. Repeat the above process until convergence, which is called self-training.

However, self-training algorithms have obvious drawbacks. Firstly, the quality of the initial segmentation network has a significant impact on the final results. If the initial network has poor segmentation capabilities, it may propagate incorrect pseudo-labels in the self-training process, leading to a decline in model performance. We use VCMix-Net+ as the segmentation network in our self-training approach, which has excellent segmentation capabilities to improve the quality of pseudo-labels and alleviate the accumulation of errors. VCMix-Net+ is an improvement over VCMix-Net [6], enhancing the network's ability to extract local features and long-range correlations at multiple scales, based on the outstanding local and local-global feature extraction capabilities of VCMix-Net.

Secondly, the method of selecting pseudo-labels based on confidence in the pseudo-label generation stage also has certain issues. Samples with high confidence usually indicate that the self-training model has high confidence in its predictions and are considered as an indication of label quality. However, the iterative process of a single model can easily form erroneous cycles, leading to error accumulation. To address this issue, we introduce a Res-Net50 as a pseudo-label filter in the pseudo-label generation stage to select high-quality pseudo-labels.

Human teeth possess a biological characteristic of approximate left-right symmetry, which is prominently reflected in 2D panoramic X-ray teeth images. To capitalize on this characteristic, we propose a half-image training method to train a half-image expert model. The half-image method is based on the half-image dataset proposed in this paper. Creating the half-image dataset can expand the size of the dataset. Half-image dataset allowing for training of smaller models without information loss caused by image resizing. The half-image model, when

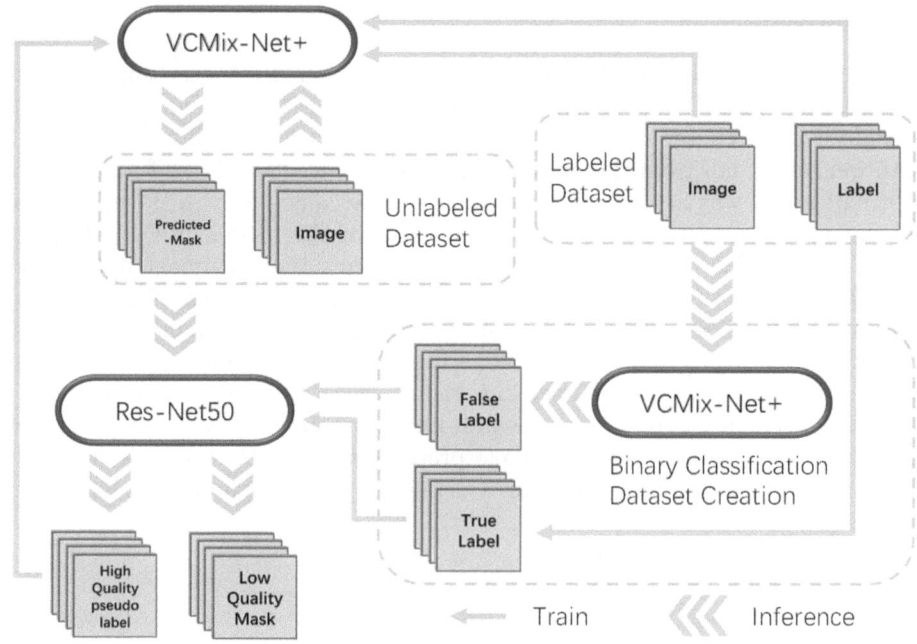

Fig. 1. Semi-supervised training process.

predicting the complete 2D image mask, predicts the left and right half-image separately and then reassembles them into a complete mask.

The primary contributions of this work are as follows:

1. We propose a half-image cut training method based on the approximate left-right symmetric characteristics of 2D images.
2. We employ pseudo-label-based semi-supervised learning to utilize a large amount of unlabeled data.
3. We specifically develop a pseudo-label filtering model to select high-quality pseudo-labels.
4. We introduce the VCMix-Net+ network for accurate segmentation of two-dimensional panoramic X-ray teeth images.

2   Method

In this paper, we conducted supervised training and semi-supervised training based on VCMix-Net+. Our semi-supervised training framework is illustrated in the Fig. 1. In the supervised training experiments, we evaluated the segmentation performance of VCMix-Net+ and the improvement in teeth segmentation achieved by the half-image approach. In the semi-supervised training experiments, we tested the application capability of our semi-supervised framework on unlabeled data.

2.1   Preprocessing

Half-Image Preprocess. Official 2D Dataset is provided by the official source [5]. Each 2D image in dataset is in PNG format with dimensions of 640*320. Considering the characteristics of the teeth image, we vertically sliced the 2D teeth images in half from the middle, resulting in two 320*320 half-images. The right half-image was horizontally flipped to ensure consistency in the orientation of left and right teeth images. We aimed to train the model into a half-image expert model using the half-image dataset. Creating the half-image dataset can expand the size of the dataset. Half-image dataset allowing for training of smaller models without information loss caused by image resizing. The half-image model, when predicting the complete 2D image mask, predicts the left and right half-image separately and then reassembles them into a complete mask. The Fig. 2 illustrates a schematic diagram of the half-image prediction process. In the paper, the dataset that underwent half-image preprocessing is referred to as the half-image dataset, and the model trained using the half-image dataset is called a half-image model.

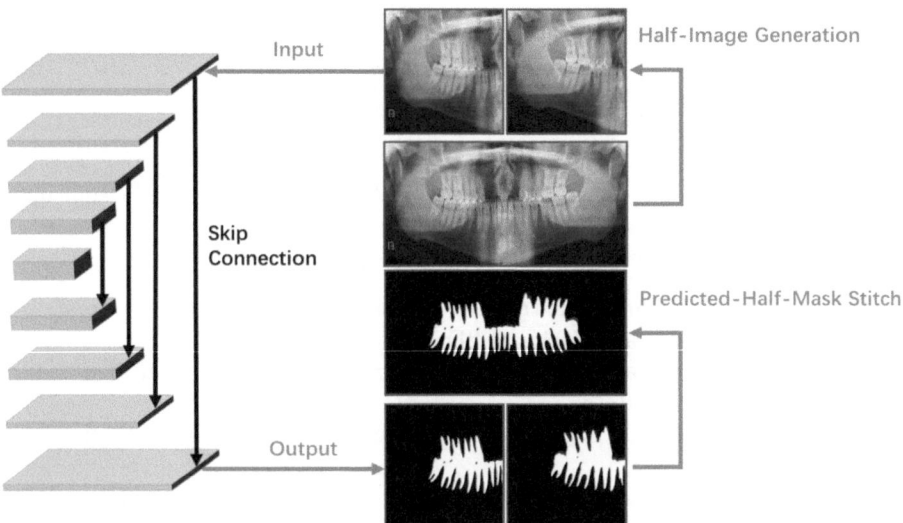

Fig. 2. Schematic diagram of half-image prediction.

2.2   Proposed Method

VCMix-Net+. VCMix-Net is a segmentation network for medical images, proposed by Zhao and others [6]. The overall structure of VCMix-Net is based on U-Net [7], with the addition of the VCMix module at the bottleneck layer to obtain richer feature information. This approach not only captures information about the local receptive field of the convolutional part but also captures the long-range correlation of the multi-layer perceptron in class attention. This provides more feature information from the original feature map during the up-sampling process, resulting in improved segmentation results.

To obtain multi-scale feature information, we introduced the VCMix module at the skip connections of the third and fourth layers in VCMix-Net, resulting in VCMix-Net+. This enhanced version is illustrated in Fig. 3.

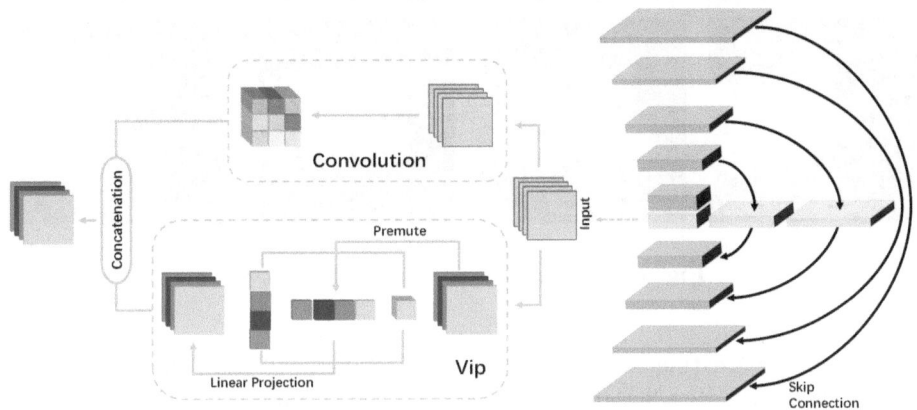

Fig. 3. Structure of VCMix-Net+.

By incorporating the VCMix module at specific layers, VCMix-Net+ aimed to enhance its ability to capture and utilize multi-scale feature information, contributing to improved segmentation performance.

Supervised Training. We divided the data into training, validation, and test sets. We performed training, validation, and testing on three models: U-Net, VCMix-Net, and VCMix-Net+. U-Net is a classic medical image segmentation network, VCMix-Net is a newly proposed medical image segmentation network in 2023, and VCMix-Net+ is the segmentation network proposed in this paper. For each model, we trained them separately using both the full-image dataset and the half-image dataset.

Semi-supervised Training. The overall architecture of this method is illustrated in the Fig. 1. The VCMix-Net+ on the left side of the figure is the self-training segmentation model used for semi-supervised. It serves as the initial model during the initial training phase, predicts unlabeled data for the pseudo-label generation phase, and is used for final predictions after semi-supervised training is completed. The ensemble model, consisting of four sub-initial models, is used in the first round to predict masks for unlabeled data. These four sub-models are trained using four-fold cross-validation with labeled data. During the re-training phase, an augmented dataset is used, which is randomly split into a training set and a validation set in a 3:1 ratio. The VCMix-Net+ on the right

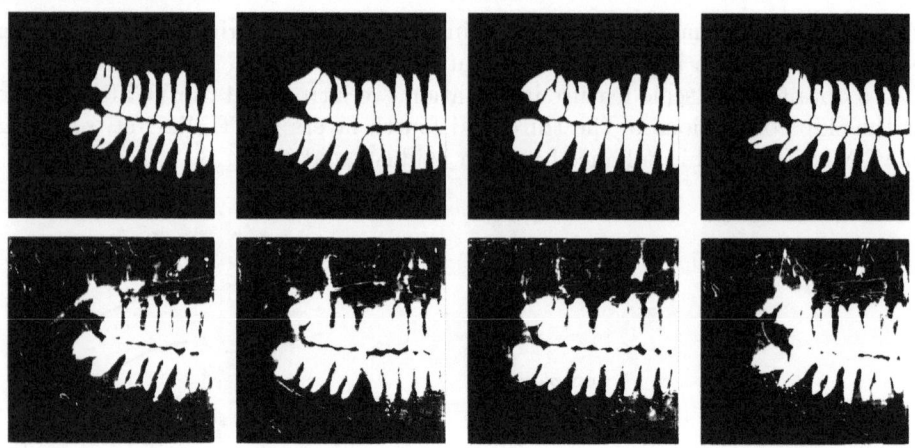

Fig. 4. The training dataset for Res-Net50.

side is used for creating a binary classification dataset to train the pseudo-label filtering network. Res-Net50 is employed as the filtering network to filter out high-quality pseudo-labels.

Pseudo-label generation: We performed four-fold cross-training using the labeled half-image data, training four sub-models. The ensemble model of these sub-models was used to make predictions on the unlabeled data. The predicted results were filtered using Res-Net50 to obtain high-quality pseudo-labels. The training of Res-Net50 was based on a binary classification dataset created from the labeled half-image dataset of the final round. The binary classification dataset included "high-quality masks" and "low-quality masks". The process involved labeling labeled half-image masks as "high-quality masks". To obtain "low-quality masks", we loaded early-stage weights in VCMix-Net+ and lowered the segmentation threshold for mask generation. We input labeled data into this model to obtain the "low-quality masks". The binary classification dataset, as shown in Fig. 4, contains different quality labels for masks of the same patient.

By incorporating pseudo-labels and refining the training process, the semi-supervised training method aims to leverage unlabeled data effectively and improve the model's segmentation performance.

2.3   Post-processing

In the post-processing stage, we filled in some segmentation areas near the mask boundaries and filled in small holes with a perimeter less than 85. For the majority of the experimental results in this study, post-processing was not applied. Only a set of post-processing controls was added as a comparison in the final online validation.

3 Experiments

3.1 Dataset

The official dataset is divided into a preliminary round dataset and a final round dataset. The preliminary round dataset consists of 2000 labeled images. The final round dataset comprises 900 labeled images and 2100 unlabeled images. After data preprocessing, the datasets used in this paper include the following:

1. Preliminary round full-image dataset, is equivalent to the preliminary round dataset.
2. Preliminary round half-image dataset, obtained by applying half-image preprocessing to the preliminary round dataset.
3. Final round half-image dataset, obtained by applying half-image preprocessing to the final round dataset.

In addition to these, an official final round online test dataset was included. The term "preliminary round full-image dataset" is equivalent to the "preliminary round dataset". In order to contrast it with the half-image approach, we referred to it as the "preliminary round full-image dataset" in the paper. We conducted supervised training using the preliminary round full-round dataset and the preliminary round half-image dataset. For supervised training, the preliminary round full-round dataset and the preliminary round half-image dataset were split into training, validation, and test sets following the official naming order with a ratio of 6:2:2. The evaluation metrics for supervised training in the paper are based on the test set obtained from this split.

The final round half-image dataset consists of labeled and unlabeled data. These data were used for semi-supervised training. The final test set for semi-supervised training used the official final round online test dataset.

3.2 Evaluation Measures

We used four metrics: Dice coefficient, Intersection over Union (IoU), Hausdorff distance (HD), and Score.

The Dice coefficient is used to assess the similarity between two sets, and its formula is as follows:

$$Dice = \frac{2 \times |A \cap B|}{|A| \cup |B|} \tag{1}$$

where A and B represent two sets, $|A|$ and $|B|$ denote the number of elements in each set, and $|A \cap B|$ represents the number of elements in their intersection.

Table 1. Development environments and requirements.

CPU	14 vCPU Intel(R) Xeon(R) Gold 6330 CPU @ 2.00GHz
GPU (number and type)	1 NVIDIA GeForce RTX 3090(24G)
CUDA version	11.8
Programming language	Python 3.8
Deep learning framework	Pytorch (Torch 2.0.0)

Besides, IoU (Intersection over Union) can be calculated as follows:

$$IoU = \frac{|A \cap B|}{|A \cup B|} \tag{2}$$

The two-dimensional HD is the minimum distance between two shapes or curves obtained through the Hausdorff transformation. The formula can be written as:

$$HD(A, B) = \min(|x_1 - x_2| + |y_1 - y_2|) \tag{3}$$

where (x_1, y_1) and (x_2, y_2) denote the coordinates of the two pixel points and $|x_1 - x_2|$ and $|y_1 - y_2|$ denote the distances on the corresponding axes. This formula represents the sum of the absolute distances between two pixel points on the horizontal and vertical axes in a two-dimensional medical image, i.e., the Hausdorff distance at the pixel level.

Model evaluation is primarily based on the three aforementioned scoring metrics. To facilitate scoring, the Hausdorff distance is normalized to ensure its values fall within the range of 0 to 1. The final Score is calculated as the weighted average of the three metrics, with the specific scoring formula being:

$$Score = 0.4 * Dice + 0.3 * IoU + 0.3 * (1 - H(d)) \tag{4}$$

3.3   Implementation Details

Environment Settings. For this experiment, we rented cloud servers and primarily used NVIDIA GeForce RTX 3090 GPU (Table 1).

Training Protocols. Unlabeled images were used to generate pseudo-labels, which were used to augment the dataset during the semi-supervised training data augmentation phase without any additional data augmentation operations. In our training process, the images were resized to 512×512 before being input into the model. After each epoch, we calculated the dice coefficient on the validation set to determine and retain the best model. In supervised training, the total number of epochs was 80, while in semi-supervised training, the total number of epochs was 100. Table 2 displays our training protocols.

Table 2. Training protocols.

Batch size	10
Patch size	512×512
Optimizer	Adam
Initial learning rate	0.0001
Lr decay schedule	No
Loss function	Binary Cross Entropy Loss
Number of model parameters	42.21M

4 Results and Discussion

4.1 Quantitative Results on Preliminary Round Data

Table 3 shows that the metrics of the half-image model on the internal test set are better than those of the full-image model. VCMix-Net+ achieves better metrics on the internal test set compared to U-Net and VCMix-Net.

Table 3. Internal validation on the preliminary round data.

Models	datasets	Dice(%)	IoU(%)	HD(mm)	Score
U-Net	Full-image dataset	87.10	88.26	11.92	87.74
	Half-image dataset	86.85	87.78	6.93	89.00
VCMix-Net	Full-image dataset	87.56	86.91	15.11	86.56
	Half-image dataset	88.16	90.89	8.11	90.10
VCMix-Net+	Full-image dataset	86.80	84.78	6.71	88.14
	Half-image dataset	88.24	90.67	4.96	91.01

4.2 Qualitative Results on Preliminary Round Data

In Fig. 5, a, b, c and d refer to the half-image, half-label and half-predict-label of the train-22, train-262, train-642 and train-110 images (train-22, train-262, train-642, and train-110 are the official names given to the images). Among them, a and b show good segmentation results, while c and d show bad segmentation results. c indicates that the model tends to segment the background as teeth, whereas d shows that the model struggles to individually segment each tooth.

4.3 Quantitative Results on Final Test Set

Table 4 presents the validation metrics for the online test set of the final round. The three sets of validation metrics in the table include:

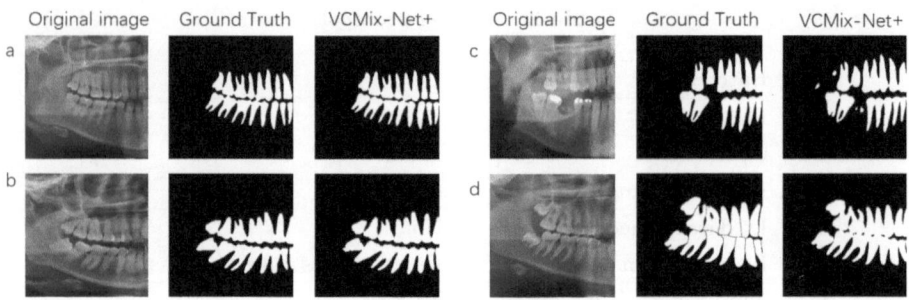

Fig. 5. Good and bad segmentation results.

Table 4. Online validation on the final round data.

Methods	Online Validation			
	Dice(%)	IoU(%)	HD(mm)	Score
Initial Model	85.76	95.53	7.39	90.75
Retrained Model	88.81	96.61	5.39	92.89
Retrained Model (Post-Processing)	89.02	96.70	4.60	93.24

1. Online metrics of the initial model trained using labeled data for initial training in semi-supervised training.
2. Online metrics of the retrained model obtained after re-training with an augmented dataset.
3. Online metrics of the retrained model with post-processing applied.

The semi-supervised results in the table are solely based on one round of pseudolabel filtering and one round of mixed training.

4.4   Limitation and Future Work

We did not use any data augmentation methods, except for the data augmentation phase where pseudo-labels were used to expand the data in semi-supervised training. In the future, we will explore various data augmentation techniques to determine which ones are beneficial for tooth segmentation.

5   Conclusion

In this paper, we created a half-image dataset to train the half-image expert model. Experimental results demonstrated that the segmentation capability of the half-image expert model is superior to the full-image model. We improved VCMix-Net, and the new VCMix-Net+ has the ability to extract local features from multiple scales and capture long-range relationships. We performed semi-supervised training based on VCMix-Net+ to leverage a substantial amount of unlabeled data, thereby effectively addressing the issue of limited labeled data of teeth images and significantly enhancing the predictive capacity of our model. We specifically created a binary classification dataset to train a Res-Net50 classification network, which is used to select high-quality pseudo-labels and optimize the effectiveness of semi-supervised training. The Dice, IoU, H(d), and Score obtained by our proposed method in the online validation were 88.81, 96.61, 5.39, and 92.89, respectively, which fully demonstrated the effectiveness of our approach at that time.

Acknowledgements. The authors of this paper declare that the segmentation method they implemented for participation in the STS 2023 challenge has not used any pre-trained models nor additional datasets other than those provided by the organizers. The proposed solution is fully automatic without any manual intervention. We thank all the data owners for making the X-ray images and CT scans publicly available and Alibaba Cloud for hosting the challenge platform.

References

1. Zhao, Y., et al.: Tsasnet: tooth segmentation on dental panoramic x-ray images by two-stage attention segmentation network. Knowl.-Based Syst. **206**, 106338 (2020)
2. Abdel-Mottaleb, M., Nomir, O., Nassar, D.E.., Fahmy, G., Ammar, H.H.: Challenges of developing an automated dental identification system. In: 2003 46th Midwest Symposium on Circuits and Systems, vol. 1, pp. 411–414. IEEE (2003)
3. Oktay, A.B.: Tooth detection with convolutional neural networks. In: 2017 Medical Technologies National Congress (TIPTEKNO), pp. 1–4. IEEE (2017)
4. Said, E.H., Nassar, D.E.M., Fahmy, G., Ammar, H.H.: Teeth segmentation in digitized dental x-ray films using mathematical morphology. IEEE Trans. Inf. Forensics Secur. **1**(2), 178–189 (2006)
5. Zhang, Y., et al.: Children's dental panoramic radiographs dataset for caries segmentation and dental disease detection. Sci. Data **10**(1), 380 (2023)
6. Zhao, H., Wang, G., Yanlin, W., Wang, H., Li, Y.: Vcmix-net: a hybrid network for medical image segmentation. Biomed. Signal Process. Control **86**, 105241 (2023)
7. Ronneberger, O., Fischer, P., Brox, T.: U-Net: convolutional networks for biomedical image segmentation. In: Navab, N., Hornegger, J., Wells, W.M., Frangi, A.F. (eds.) MICCAI 2015. LNCS, vol. 9351, pp. 234–241. Springer, Cham (2015). https://doi.org/10.1007/978-3-319-24574-4_28

Automated Dental CBCT Segmentation Using Pseudo Labeling Method

Weiyan Feng[✉][iD]

South China Normal University, Guangzhou, China
weifguna@foxmail.com

Abstract. The significance of 3D medical image segmentation in contemporary artificial intelligence-assisted diagnosis is growing. Accurate
teeth segmentation can provide strong evidence for disease diagnosis.
However, the annotation cost of medical images such as cone beam computed tomography (CBCT) is relatively high, and many unlabeled data
have not been fully utilized. In this paper, we propose a training strategy
for the 3D CBCT segmentation task and design a semi-supervised learning method to optimize the model using unlabeled data. Our method
achieved an average score of 0.7743, an average Dice coefficient of 0.7750,
and an average Intersection over Union (IoU) of 0.8167 for teeth segmentation on the validation set of CTooth+.

Keywords: Medical segmentation · Pseudo Labeling method · 3D
segmentation

1 Introduction

The rapid development and outstanding performance of deep learning have been
successfully demonstrated in medical image analysis [6,10], with one crucial
branch being medical segmentation. Medical segmentation tasks are essential
in the fields of medical image processing and computer vision. They aim to
precisely segment or label structures or regions within medical images. These
medical images may include X-rays, computed tomography (CT), magnetic res-
onance imaging (MRI), ultrasound images, tissue section images, 3D Cone Beam
Computed Tomography, and others. The primary objective of medical segmentation tasks is to automatically or semi-automatically identify and label relevant
biological structures, organ tissues, or pathological areas within the images. This
assists doctors in diagnosis, treatment planning, and disease monitoring.

3D Cone Beam Computed Tomography (CBCT) is a medical imaging technology used to obtain high-resolution images of the three-dimensional head, neck,
and maxillofacial regions. CBCT is a specialized imaging technique for oral and
craniofacial imaging, distinct from traditional medical CT scans, and it possesses
the following features.

Y. Wang et al. (Eds.): STS 2023, LNCS 14623, pp. 156–168, 2025.
https://doi.org/10.1007/978-3-031-72396-4_14

- CBCT employs a cone-shaped X-ray beam, whereas traditional CT uses a fan-shaped beam. The design of this cone beam makes CBCT imaging more suitable for oral and maxillofacial regions, providing higher resolution and lower radiation doses.
- CBCT images have high resolution, allowing for detailed visualization of structures in the oral, craniofacial, and maxillofacial regions, such as teeth, jawbones, sinuses, pulp cavities, and soft tissues.
- The images generated by CBCT are three-dimensional, meaning that doctors can examine the patient's oral and head-neck structures from different angles and planes. This aids in a better understanding of the three-dimensional relationships of anatomical structures.

The purpose of 3D CBCT tooth image segmentation in the field of dentistry is to precisely segment different parts or structures of teeth in order to achieve the following objectives.

- **Tooth analysis and diagnosis**: By segmenting tooth images, dental professionals can more accurately identify and analyze the structures of different teeth, including tooth crowns, roots, pulp chambers, and more. This helps in making more precise diagnoses of dental issues such as cavities, apical periodontitis, pulpitis, and others.
- **Orthodontics and implant surgery**: When performing orthodontic treatments or dental implant surgery, segmenting tooth images can assist oral surgeons in accurately determining the position, angle, and size of teeth, enabling the development of more precise treatment plans. This is crucial for ensuring the success of orthodontic procedures and dental implant surgery.
- **Monitoring tooth-related diseases and treatment planning**: By regularly analyzing the segmentation results from 3D CBCT images, clinicians can track the evolution of a patient's oral health status, especially concerning periodontal diseases, alveolar bone resorption, and other dental problems. This aids in treatment planning and monitoring the progression of diseases.

However, there are still many challenges when using CBCT for medical tasks. In the field of image segmentation task, 3D CBCT images typically have high resolution and contain a large number of voxels. This results in a massive data volume, requiring significant computational resources for processing and analysis. CBCT images may be affected by noise and artifacts, which can interfere with the performance of segmentation algorithms. Especially in oral and maxillofacial imaging, noise and artifacts can be introduced due to hard tissues, metallic objects, or motion artifacts. Structures in oral and maxillofacial regions can vary greatly in terms of shape and size across different individuals, increasing the complexity of the segmentation task. Partial volume effects may exist in CBCT images, where structures may span across multiple voxels. This can lead to partial occlusion and blurred regions in the images, adding to the segmentation challenges.

The acquisition of CBCT data also increases the challenge of the task to some extent. Acquiring appropriate labeled data, i.e., images annotated by experts for training supervised learning models, is often a challenging and time-consuming process. Such data requires the expertise of medical professionals for annotation, and the process demands high levels of skill.

The inspired challenge of data acquisition provides us with inspiration for utilizing unlabeled data. Due to the high cost of obtaining labeled samples and the relatively lower difficulty and cost of acquiring unlabeled samples, to reduce the cost of acquiring dataset and simultaneously enhance the utilization of unlabeled data, semi-supervised learning methods have been introduced into medical image segmentation tasks. These methods allow for the effective use of limited labeled data in the 3D CBCT tooth segmentation approach, while fully leveraging a substantial amount of unlabeled 3D CBCT data.

In this paper, we present a scheme for 3D CBCT image segmentation, along with data augmentation strategies tailored for a dental dataset. Additionally, we employ advanced semi-supervised methods to optimize the 3D segmentation model. Ultimately, we conduct testing and analysis of the model training on different GPU and deploy our model to an Ascend development board for offline inference applications, providing robust support for downstream segmentation tasks. Our contributions can be summarized as follows.

- We have introduced a 3D CBCT segmentation pipeline.
- We have proposed a semi-supervised learning strategy for 3D CBCT teeth segmentation task.
- We have evaluated model training on various GPU machines and deployed the model to an offline development board for offline applications support.

2   Related Work

2.1   2D Segmentation

In medical segmentation tasks, 2D segmentation is usually based on 2D medical images such as CT to obtain pixel-level segmentation masks of certain organs of patients for various downstream tasks. U-Net [5] is a classic 2D medical segmentation network, which consists of a contracting path to capture context and a symmetric expanding path for precise localization. It can be trained in few images and output high-quality segmentation masks. The proposal of U-Net has opened up a new paradigm for medical segmentation tasks, which also have been introduced to 3D medical segmentation.

2.2   3D Segmentation

After the introduction of U-Net, many well performing networks used U-shape structures for 3D medical segmentation tasks.

ToothNet [5] use a two-stage network to achieve automatic and accurate tooth instance segmentation, where in the first stage, an edge map is extracted from the input CBCT image to enhance image contrast along shape boundaries. In the second stage, a 3D region proposal network is used with a novel learned similarity matrix to efficiently remove redundant proposals and improve training speed and GPU memory usage.

UNEt TRansformers (UNETR) [7] addresses the limitation of fully convolutional neural networks in capturing long-range spatial dependencies by leveraging the success of transformers in natural language processing for long-range sequence learning, which combines "U-shaped" network design with transformer encoder.

nnFormer [12] combines interleaved convolution and self-attention operations and introduces local and global volume-based self-attention mechanisms to learn volume representations, as well as utilizes skip attention to replace traditional concatenation/summation operations in skip connections.

2.3   Semi-supervised Learning

The scope of semi supervised learning methods is very broad, and the commonly used methods in recent work can be divided into Consistency Regulation, Pseudo Labeling method and Transfer Learning.

Consistency normalization refers to the addition of disturbances to input data, which requires the network to have a basically consistent distribution of outputs for the disturbed input, i.e. output consistency. Temporal Ensembling [9] forms a consensus prediction of the unknown labels using the outputs of the network-in-training on different epochs and under different regularization and input augmentation conditions. Mean teachers [11] improves the performance of Temporal Ensembling by updating model weights instead of label predictions.

Pseudo labeling method means using networks trained on annotated data to annotate unlabeled data, and adding the newly annotated data to the training set for model training.

Transfer learning is the transfer of knowledge from one field to another, enabling better learning outcomes in the target field. Usually, transfer learning requires transferring the knowledge learned under sufficient data volume to a new environment with small data volume. SimCLR [2] proposes using powerful data augmentations, large batch sizes and more training steps to learn helpful representation.

3   Method

3.1   Preprocessing

Due to the substantial GPU memory occupation and prolonged inference time during network training and inference for 3D volume data, we partitioned the 3D CBCT data into distinct patches as inputs for 3D segmentation. Through statistical analysis of the 3D volume data from CTooth+ [3], we observed that the majority of data had a shape of [200, 266, 266]. Ultimately, we decided to use [112, 160, 128] as the input size for the segmentation network. In the data preprocessing phase, we initially applied padding to data with a volume

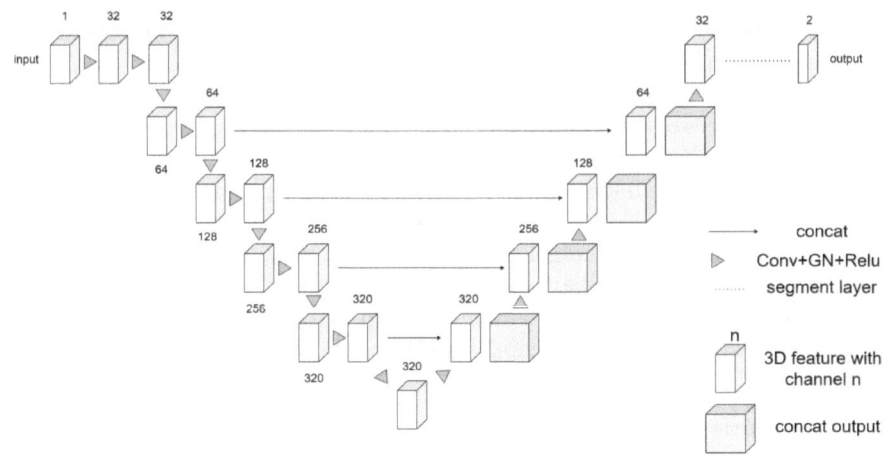

Fig. 1. The overview of the 3D U-Net network architecture

size smaller than the network input size. Subsequently, we employed a sliding window approach to segment the data into blocks, with the block size matching the network's input size. The step size and number of steps for the sliding window were determined based on the disparity between the input size and the corresponding dimensions of the network.

For data augmentation strategies, we employed random rotation to increase sample diversity while enhancing the model's robustness. Random cropping was not utilized, as cropped data may lead to the loss of critical information within the 3D volume. However, this scenario is typically not encountered in 3D medical segmentation tasks.

3.2   Network

For the 3D segmentation task in CTooth+ [3], we simply employ the classical 3D U-Net [1] architecture, making specific adjustments based on the CTooth+ [3] dataset. We set the network's input dimensions to [112,160,128] to ensure that our model does not excessively consume GPU memory while maintaining high-quality segmentation results. Additionally, we incorporate Group Normalization after each 3D convolution layer. Given that the batch size is generally small in medical segmentation tasks, using Batch Normalization in tasks with smaller batch sizes can lead to a decline in model performance. Group Normalization addresses this issue associated with small batch sizes. An overview of the entire network is illustrated in the Fig. 1.

3.3   Loss Function

Since the CTooth+ [3] dataset only requiring segmentation of tooth volume, we have chosen BCELoss and DiceLoss as our loss functions. As the CTooth+ [3]

dataset employs Dice, IoU, and three-dimensional Hausdorff distance as evaluation metrics with weights [0.4, 0.3, 0.3] respectively, we have assigned different weights to BCELoss and DiceLoss. The final representation of the loss function is as follows:

$$\mathcal{L}_{\text{total}} = \alpha\mathcal{L}_{\text{BCE}} + \beta\mathcal{L}_{\text{Dice}} \tag{1}$$

where α and β represent the weights of their corresponding loss functions. And we used [0.4, 0.6] in this task.

3.4   Post-processing

Inspired by the training strategy of nnU-Net [8], we introduce corresponding Gaussian filtering weights for volumes at different positions. Through visualization, we observe that the majority of teeth volumes that need segmentation are located at the center of the entire 3D volume. Therefore, we directly apply a Gaussian filter to process them, obtaining a Gaussian weight matrix of the same size as the input image. This weight matrix is multiplied with the network's output to serve as the final output, representing the segmentation confidence for each volume. Finally, we simply use softmax to perform binary classification on the output as the ultimate result of our segmentation task.

3.5   Pseudo Labeling Augmentation

Due to the fact that the original output of the network model is a confidence matrix processed by a Gaussian filtering matrix, we can extract the output separately before passing it through the activation function. This implies that even without real label data, we can assess the credibility of the segmentation results for unlabeled data by evaluating the confidence of the network model's output. By setting a confidence threshold as a criterion for correctly segmented volume in the segmentation results, we can then assess the uncertainty of the entire segmentation outcome based on this criterion. Through evaluating the uncertainty of a series of unlabeled teeth CBCT data, we can establish an uncertainty threshold to determine which unlabeled data can use the model's output, then through softmax, as its own train label, which can be introduced into the model for training later. Additionally, we can also directly set a number to determine how many unlabeled samples, after pseudo-labeling, will be used for training the model. Since we have a five-fold model in total, we can simultaneously utilize the pseudo-labeled data from all five folds for weighted averaging, aiming to enhance the stability and reliability of uncertainty. For the segmentation result in shape [X, Y, Z] with a confidence metrix $M \in \mathbb{R}^{X \times Y \times Z}$, the formula for computing uncertainty is as follows:

$$uncertainty = \sum_i -W_i \frac{\sum e_i \cdot \log(e_i)}{\sum(e_i > 0.5)} / |F| \tag{2}$$

where e represents each element in the confidence matrix, W_i represents the weight assigned to the i-th fold when calculating uncertainty and $|F|$ refers to the total number of folds.

The selection of the confidence threshold for pseudo-labeling is a challenging issue, closely tied not only to the performance of the model itself but also influenced by the distribution of unlabeled data. If the model demonstrates strong robustness and generalization capabilities, a higher confidence threshold can be chosen. Conversely, a poorly performing model is more prone to introducing erroneous segmentation results, leading to potentially incorrect pseudo-label data. In such cases, a lower confidence threshold should be adopted. Additionally, the distribution of unlabeled data significantly impacts the confidence threshold. If the distribution of unlabeled data deviates significantly from the training data, the resulting uncertainty naturally increases, resulting in fewer reliable pseudo-label data. Conversely, if the unlabeled data shares a similar distribution with the training data, the uncertainty will be smaller.

To select an appropriate confidence threshold, we treat it as a hyperparameter and dynamically adjust it during the training process. In the initial state, this parameter is determined through experiments to find the optimal value. After incorporating pseudo-label data for training, the uncertainty of unlabeled data is re-evaluated at each training stage. The confidence threshold hyperparameter is then adjusted to incorporate more or fewer pseudo-label data into the training process accordingly. The experiment results of hyperparameter initialization for the CTooth+ dataset will be presented in the Results and discussion section.

4   Experiments

4.1   Dataset

We use the CTooth+ [3] dataset as the training and testing data for our model. CTooth+ [3] consists entirely of Cone Beam Computed Tomography (CBCT) scans of teeth, which is an enriched and extended version of the CTooth [4] dataset. In the MICCAI 2023 Challenges STS, a total of 312 CBCT scans are provided as training data, with 12 labeled CBCT scans comprising approximately 2400 slices. The remaining 300 CBCT scans are unlabeled data, amounting to around 60,000 slices. The test set consists of 50 labeled CBCT scans, totaling approximately 10,000 slices. The test set data is retained by the authors and can not be used for model training; instead, it is utilized for the final evaluation of the model.

4.2   Evaluation Metrics

In the MICCAI 2023 Challenges STS, the evaluation metrics for the model include the Dice coefficient, Intersection over Union, and three-dimensional Hausdorff distance, with corresponding weights of [0.4, 0.3, 0.3]. The specific scoring rule is defined as follows:

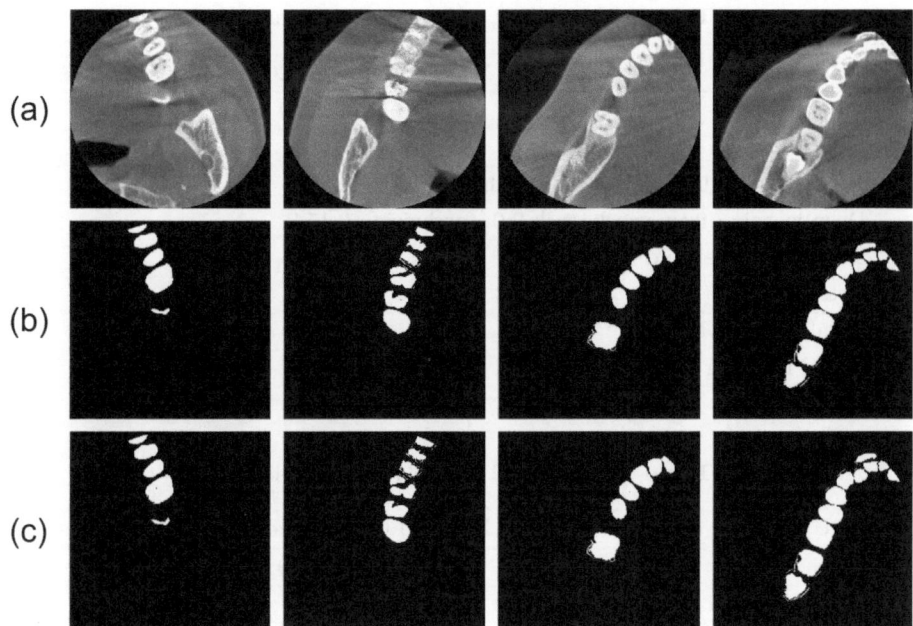

Fig. 2. Visualization results of (a) Raw data, (b) Pseudo-labeled data and (c) Labeled data. Please zoom in for clearer visualization.

$$S(X,Y) = W_1 \cdot \frac{2|X \cap Y|}{|X| + |Y|} + W_2 \cdot \frac{|X \cap Y|}{|X \cup Y|} + W_3 \cdot (1 - H(\mathrm{d})) \qquad (3)$$

where X is the predicted result and Y is the ground truth. W represents the weight of different evaluating indicator. $H(\mathrm{d})$ represents the three-dimensional Hausdorff distance in voxel level.

Voxel-based three-dimensional Hausdorff distance is a measure used to quantify the difference between two three-dimensional objects or volumes. In three-dimensional space, a voxel is the three-dimensional counterpart of a pixel, representing a volumetric element, which is a small cube in three-dimensional space. In this task, our specific formula for calculating the three-dimensional Hausdorff distance is as follows:

$$H(d) = \min \left(|x_1 - x_2| + |y_1 - y_2| + |z_1 - z_2| \right) \qquad (4)$$

where (x_1, y_1, z_1) and (x_2, y_2, z_2) represent the coordinates of two voxels.

4.3   Implementation Details

In this experiment, we utilized two separate machines to train our model, aiming to assess the differences in model training across different GPU. The hardware information for both machines, and the corresponding training parameters of the model and training time are presented in Table 1 and Table 2 respectively.

Table 1. Machine 1 and relative information.

CPU	Intel(R) Xeon(R) CPU E5-2683 v4 64G 32 cores
GPU	NVIDIA GeForce RTX 4090
CUDA version	11.7
Programming language	e.g., Python 3.8
Deep learning framework	torch 2.0, torchvision 0.15.2
Total epoch per fold	500
Total fold	5
Total training time(h)	93.75
Initial learning rate (lr)	1e-2
Weight decay	3e-5

Table 2. Machine 2 and relative information.

CPU	Intel(R) Xeon(R) CPU E5-2686 v4 32G 36 cores
GPU	NVIDIA GeForce RTX 4070 Ti
CUDA version	11.7
Programming language	e.g., Python 3.8
Deep learning framework	torch 2.0, torchvision 0.15.2
Total epoch per fold	500
Total fold	5
Total training time (h)	173.6
Initial learning rate (lr)	1e-2
Weight decay	3e-5

Table 3. Ascend Atlas 200I DK A2 device parameters and performance.

NPU	DaVinciV300 AI core 500MHz
CPU	four TAISHANV200M 1.0GHz
Batch size	1
Patch size	112×160×128
FP16 computational power	4 TFLOPS
INT8 computational power	8 TOPS
Inference time per slice (s)	330

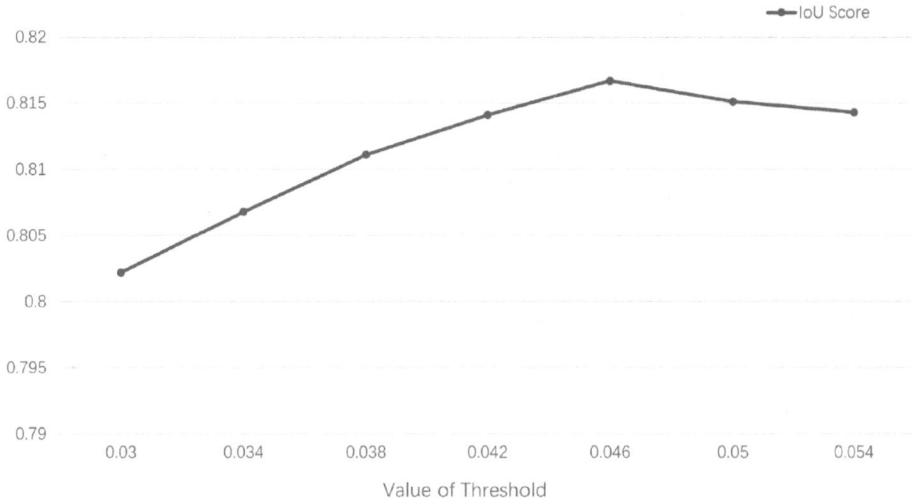

Fig. 3. Different confidence threshold selections and their corresponding IoU scores.

4.4 Deployment

To enable the segmentation model to be applied in practical medical scenarios, we performed embedded deployment of the model and conducted performance testing. The deployment was carried out on the Ascend Atlas 200I DK A2, coupled with compute architecture for neural networks (CANN) 6.2 for offline inference. The specific parameters of the device and the performance of offline inference are detailed in Table 3.

5   Results and Discussion

5.1   Choice of Pseudo Labeling Threshold

The choice of confidence threshold has a significant impact for pseudo-labels on the model's performance, setting a threshold that is too high may introduce incorrect data, while a threshold that is too low may fail to fully leverage unlabeled data. In order to determine an appropriate confidence threshold, we treat it as a hyperparameter during model training and conduct comparisons across multiple different confidence thresholds. The results of different confidence threshold selections and their corresponding IoU scores are presented in the Fig. 3.

We believe that, in this hyperparameter initialization experiment, the process of increasing the confidence threshold from 0.030 to 0.046 corresponds to introducing more and more effective pseudo-labeled data. However, beyond 0.046, the model gradually incorporates some incorrect pseudo-labels, leading to learning incorrect representations and a subsequent decrease in performance.

Table 4. Training protocols for the refine model.

Configurations	Before fine-tuning	After fine-tuning
IoU score	0.8022	0.8167
Dice score	0.7521	0.7750
Hausdorff score	0.2750	0.2690
Total score	0.7590	0.7743

5.2   The Effect of Using Unlabelled Cases

In the initial training phase, we used only 12 labeled CT scans to train the model. Through online evaluation, our model achieved promising scores on public leaderboard. Subsequently, we employed the model to generate pseudo-labels for 10 unlabeled CT scans. We selected the four data points with the lowest uncertainty along with their pseudo-labels and added them to the training data. The model was then fine-tuned using this new training data. We opted not to retrain the model because we believe that the pseudo-labeling approach, while improving model performance, might introduce erroneous information, leading the model to converge to local minima or learn irrelevant features. The evaluation results before and after fine-tuning with pseudo-labeled data are presented in Table 4.

5.3   Comparative Experiments

We conducted a comparative analysis by contrasting the performance of our method with the mainstream model nnU-Net [8] in different resolution. nnU-Net has three different processing modes, namely low resolution, full resolution, and 3D cascade. These modes involve segmenting data using different resolutions. Here, we conducted comparative experiments using low resolution and full resolution. The specific comparative results are presented in the Table 5.

Table 5. comparative result

Configurations	nnU-Net low-res	nnU-Net high-res	Ours
IoU score	0.7247	0.8022	0.8167
Dice score	0.6217	0.7521	0.7750
Hausdorff score	0.2948	0.2750	0.2690
Total score	0.6777	0.7590	0.7743

5.4   Visualization

To explicitly assess the performance of our pseudo-labels, we visualized the pseudo-labeled data and conducted a comparation with both the labeled data and the original input data. The results of the visualization are presented in the Fig. 2. The visualized data utilized in our study was randomly sampled. It is evident from our observations that the pseudo-labeled data exhibits a high degree of similarity to the ground truth. Consequently, it can be inferred that the pseudo-labels derived from our method are capable of facilitating effective pseudo-labeling training processes.

5.5   Evaluation and Future Work

Through visualizing the segmentation results, we observed that the model performs well on the segmentation of common adult CT scans. However, its segmentation performance is less satisfactory when dealing with CT scans containing fewer skeletal structures or incomplete teeth, which are less prevalent in the training data. The model is capable of meeting the demands of common dental CT segmentation tasks for various medical downstream applications.

We believe that future feasible work in this field can be divided into dataset expansion and the exploration of more effective combinations of semi-supervised learning methods with segmentation tasks. In order to enhance the robustness and richness of the models, training data must encompass a more diverse and extensive set of annotated data. CT scans from patients of different ages and with varying skeletal structures should be included in certain proportions. This includes CT scans with missing teeth and those without teeth, as models can learn more comprehensive information from such complex data.

Additionally, since most CT scans lack segmentation annotations, more powerful semi-supervised learning methods can efficiently leverage unlabeled data. For instance, when using pseudo-label data based on confidence, the model can be fine-tuned using high-confidence data while simultaneously utilizing low-confidence data for representation learning, thus fully exploiting the potential of unlabeled data.

6   Conclusion

In this paper, we propose a segmentation task strategy for CBCT and simultaneously provide a semi-supervised learning approach for this task. We achieved promising results on the CTooth+ [3] dataset. Additionally, we conducted tests and evaluations of the model's training time cost on multiple machines. We also assessed the inference efficiency of the model on an offline machine. The evaluation results and offline inference efficiency of the model confirm the effectiveness of our training strategy and its applicability to offline scenario tasks.

Acknowledgements. We thank all data owners for publicly disclosing X-ray images and CT scans, and Alibaba Cloud for hosting the challenge platform as well as Gpushare Cloud for providing access to different GPU machines.

References

1. Ahmed, S.F., Rahman, F.S., Tabassum, T., Bhuiyan, M.T.I.: 3d u-net: Fully convolutional neural network for automatic brain tumor segmentation. In: 2019 22nd International Conference on Computer and Information Technology (ICCIT), pp. 1–6 (2019). https://doi.org/10.1109/ICCIT48885.2019.9038237
2. Chen, T., Kornblith, S., Norouzi, M., Hinton, G.: A simple framework for contrastive learning of visual representations. In: III, H.D., Singh, A. (eds.) Proceedings of the 37th International Conference on Machine Learning. Proceedings of Machine Learning Research, vol. 119, pp. 1597–1607. PMLR (13–18 Jul 2020). https://proceedings.mlr.press/v119/chen20j.html
3. Cui, W., et al.: Ctooth+: a large-scale dental cone beam computed tomography dataset and benchmark for tooth volume segmentation. In: Nguyen, H.V., Huang, S.X., Xue, Y. (eds.) Data Augmentation, Labelling, and Imperfections, pp. 64–73. Springer, Cham (2022)
4. Cui, W., Wang, Y., Zhang, Q., Zhou, H., Song, D., Zuo, X., Jia, G., Zeng, L.: Ctooth: a fully annotated 3d dataset and benchmark for tooth volume segmentation on cone beam computed tomography images. In: Liu, H., Yin, Z., Liu, L., Jiang, L., Gu, G., Wu, X., Ren, W. (eds.) Intelligent Robotics and Applications, pp. 191–200. Springer, Cham (2022)
5. Cui, Z., Li, C., Wang, W.: Toothnet: automatic tooth instance segmentation and identification from cone beam ct images. In: 2019 IEEE/CVF Conference on Computer Vision and Pattern Recognition (CVPR), pp. 6361–6370 (2019). https://doi.org/10.1109/CVPR.2019.00653
6. Guan, H., Liu, M.: Domain adaptation for medical image analysis: a survey. IEEE Trans. Biomed. Eng. **69**(3), 1173–1185 (2022). https://doi.org/10.1109/TBME.2021.3117407
7. Hatamizadeh, A., Tang, Y., Nath, V., Yang, D., Myronenko, A., Landman, B., Roth, H.R., Xu, D.: Unetr: Transformers for 3d medical image segmentation. In: 2022 IEEE/CVF Winter Conference on Applications of Computer Vision (WACV), pp. 1748–1758 (2022). https://doi.org/10.1109/WACV51458.2022.00181
8. Isensee, F., Jaeger, P.F., Kohl, S.A., Petersen, J., Maier-Hein, K.H.: nnu-net: a self-configuring method for deep learning-based biomedical image segmentation. Nat. Methods **18**(2), 203–211 (2021)
9. Laine, S., Aila, T.: Temporal ensembling for semi-supervised learning (2017)
10. Litjens, G., Kooi, T., Bejnordi, B.E., Setio, A.A.A., Ciompi, F., Ghafoorian, M., van der Laak, J.A., van Ginneken, B., Sánchez, C.I.: A survey on deep learning in medical image analysis. Med. Image Anal. **42**, 60–88 (2017). https://doi.org/10.1016/j.media.2017.07.005. https://www.sciencedirect.com/science/article/pii/S1361841517301135
11. Tarvainen, A., Valpola, H.: Mean teachers are better role models: Weight-averaged consistency targets improve semi-supervised deep learning results (2018)
12. Zhou, H.Y., Guo, J., Zhang, Y., Han, X., Yu, L., Wang, L., Yu, Y.: nnformer: volumetric medical image segmentation via a 3d transformer. IEEE Trans. Image Process. **32**, 4036–4045 (2023). https://doi.org/10.1109/TIP.2023.3293771

Prior-Aware Cross Pseudo Supervision for Semi-supervised Tooth Segmentation

Tingyi Lin[1,3], Pengju Lyu[2,3], Junchen Xiong[3], Xiaodong Wang[3], Kehan Song[3], and Qiong Lou[1(✉)]

[1] School of Science, Zhejiang University of Science and Technology,
Hangzhou 310012, China
bearqiong@163.com
[2] City University of Macau, Macau, China
[3] Hanglok-Tech Co., Ltd., Hengqin 519000, China

Abstract. Automatic and precise tooth segmentation is crucial in computer aided dentistry, serving a pivotal role in various applications likes diagnosis and treatment planning. While prominent methods can attain satisfactory segmentation results, disproportion in the proportion of annotated images have an impact on model performance. In this paper, we present a cascade semi-supervised method named C-CPS for tooth segmentation, which designed for imbalanced datasets. C-CPS is built upon the idea that the model can acquire more essential information about uncertainty. It consists of two subtly different decoders and utilizes two distinct strategies for generating pseudo-labels. Particularly, one strategy aims at minimizing entropy and enhancing posterior probabilities, while the other constrains predictions by incorporating prior information. To boost the model training, we integrate the two generation strategies into a cycle supervision module. We evaluate C-CPS in MICCAI 2023 Challenge and respectively achieve 76.70% of Dice, 81.46% of IOU, and 16.42% normalized HD.

Keywords: Cross pseudo supervision · Cascade network · Consistency regularization · Prior constraint

1 Introduction

Accurate segmentation of teeth from Cone Beam Computed Tomography (CBCT) is a fundamental task in computer-aided dentistry. Prominent methods have achieved satisfactory results with extensive annotated CBCT images, most of which employing various segmentation network models for pixel-level segmentation of teeth. However, in the medical field, annotating medical images such as CBCT and CT for pixel-level is a time-consuming and costly task. Besides, segmentation model trained with limited annotated images probably get stuck in the mud of overfitting. Therefore, semi-supervised learning have introduced to address these challenge as mentioned above, which can incorporate unlabeled

Y. Wang et al. (Eds.): STS 2023, LNCS 14623, pp. 169–179, 2025.
https://doi.org/10.1007/978-3-031-72396-4_15

images into network training. Semi-supervised learning aims to exact additional information from images without annotations, which can be categorized in two paradigms: self-training [1, 12, 14] and consistency regularization [9, 10, 19].

Self-training is a prevalent method in semi-supervised learning, involving the generation of pseudo labels for unlabeled images, which are then combined with annotated images for model training. However, depending solely on a static confidence threshold may lead to the generation of inaccurate predictions. Consequently, it is imperative to implement sophisticated strategies to mitigate the risk of the model overfitting to these predictions. Yu et al. [16] designs a mean teacher model with exponential moving averaging (EMA) to produce pseudo labels of unannotated image, thereby improve the model's generalization performance. FixMatch [11] employs robust data augmentation techniques and consistency loss to enhance model training, and ultimately improving the model's generalization performance. Chen et al. [3] extract valuable information for images without annotation by using a two-branch network, which simultaneously encodes strong and pseudo-label representations.

Apart from establishing various confidence rules for unannotated images, some studies focus on leveraging prior information specific to medical images. For instance, Zheng et al. [18] pioneered the integration of a probabilistic atlas of four abdominal organs into the Bayesian framework, facilitating the segmentation of low-contrast organs. Dong et al. [4] proposes AtlasNet, which generates multiple atlases by employing multiple forward transformers and mapping the entire training data into a shared subspace to mitigate biological diversity.

Consistency regularization is founded on the principle that the model's predictions should remain stable even in the presence of data perturbations and geometric transformations. Mittal et al. [8] narrow the gap between low-level and high-level semantic information, thereby eliminate false positive in pseudo labels. Li et al. [6] incorporates a geometric shape prior information constraint into the segmentation process to improve discrimination on the left atrial boundary. MC-Net [13] implements a cyclic pseudo supervision strategy to regularize consistency between two predictions from two different decoders, achieving satisfied performance in left atrial segmentation. Most cross pseudo supervision methods [2, 15] primarily aim to enhance the similarity between the predictions with different generation rules, but neglect that Low-quality pseudo-labels can result in ineffective guidance and impact the subsequent training of the model. Lu et al. [7] proposes UPC, which utilizes the similarity of two predictions as an additional index to reflect the certainty of different predictions.

Therefore, we proposes a novel Cascade Cross Pseudo Supervision model (C-CPS) for semi-supervised tooth segmentation from CBCT images in Sec. 2. Specially, we not only crop region of interest (ROI) in whole CBCT images, but also produce Probabilistic Atlas Map (PA-map) from the prediction of the first cascade segmentation network. During model training, we pair both annotated and unanntotaed images into the second segmentation model for semi-supervised learning, whose architecture is similar with MC-Net. The primary distinction between our proposed method and MC-Net lies in the application of two distinct pseudo constraint rules for the two predictions, which encompass dynamic confidence threshold and pseudo PA-map shape regularization.

The contributions of our model include: (1) we explore uncertainty information by designing two distinct constraint rules to enhance model discrimination on uncertain regions. (2) we improve our segmentation results by connected components algorithm. (3) C-CPS have achieve satisfied performance in semi-supervised method on CTooth datasets with using both annotated and unannotated images.

2 Method

In this section, we describe our pre-processing strategy, including data augmentation and Houndfield Unit (HU) adjustment in Sect. 2.1. Secondary, we establish our novel cascade cross pseudo supervision model mathematically and give the overview of our method in Sect. 2.2. Finally, we introduce our designed loss function in details in Sect. 2.3.

2.1 Pre-processing

For different stages of the cascaded networks, we employ distinct preprocessing strategies. In the first phase of the cascade network, we initially adjust the window width to 1500 and window level to 500 for labeled images. After window adjustment, we apply various augmentation for these adjusted images, such as 3D rotation, flip, random Gaussian blur and add random noise. This augmentation process expands the 12 labeled images to a larger datasets. Subsequently, we perform 5-fold cross-validation on this batch of images based on nnU-Net [5]. Simultaneously, we generate coarse segmentation of 50 randomly selected unlabeled images.

In the second phase of the cascade network, we also adjust the same window width and window level for unlabeled images. But different with the first phase, we apply random crop in both labeled and unlabeled images of size $256 \times 256 \times 72$. It is noteworthy that we crop the unlabeled images based on their coarse segmentation, which guarantee the ratio of teeth achieve 2/3.

2.2 Model Architecture

Given a labeled images datasets $D_l = \{x_i, y_i\}_{i=1}^{N_l}$ and a unlabeled images datasets $D_u = \{x_i\}_{i=1}^{N_u}$. In the first phase of model training, we train a robust segmentation model based on D_l, and generate a coarse segmentation $\mathcal{P}_i^u$ for each unlabeled image x_i^u. Considering the coarse segmentation $\mathcal{P}_i^u$ contains statistical information referring to the spatial distribution of object in unlabeled images, we subsequently calculate the pseudo probabilistic atlas map based on pair of unlabeled images and coarse. In the second phase of model training, we take both of labeled and unlabeled datasets as input to train a semi-supervised tooth segmentation method, whose architecture is similar with cycle pseudo supervision methods (CPS). During the second model training, we apply two distinct constraint strategy to generate pseudo-labels and start pseudo supervision.

Cascade CPS Segmentation Model. In the 1st phase network, with a goal to precisely crop ROI and generate a skimp-noise coarse segmentation results, we choose nnU-Net as our first robust segment network. To obtain pseudo PA-map, we only average each $\mathcal{P}_i^u$ in the unlabeled datasets. However, it is obviously that there are some noise in the original pseudo PA-map, whose location is dissociate from the main object area. In order to eliminate these noise, we select the largest connected component and take it as the final pseudo PA-map (Fig. 1).

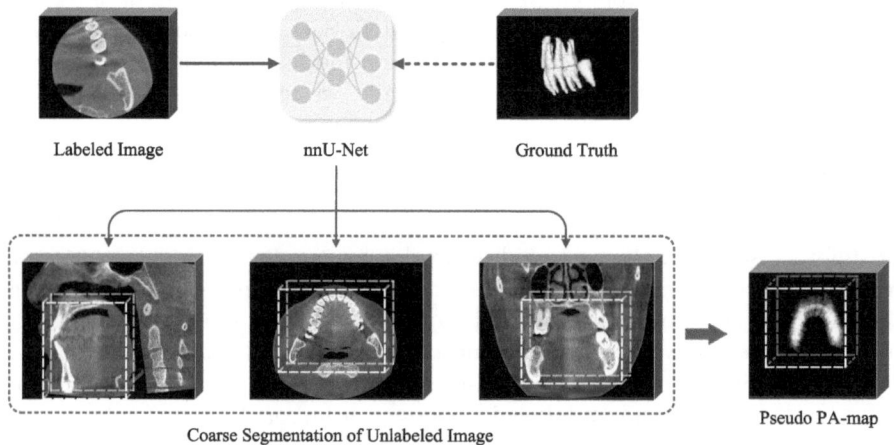

Labeled Image   nnU-Net   Ground Truth

Coarse Segmentation of Unlabeled Image

Pseudo PA-map

Fig. 1. Diagram of our Pseudo PA-map generation.

Most of CPS methods' architecture are comprise of one encoder and two decoders, whose purpose is capture the difference between two outputs from different decoders. Our 2nd phase segmentation model is building upon the typical model design. Therefore, two different decoder receive the same feature input from the single encoder, and then generate two slightly different SoftMax outputs P_A and P_B. Besides, following MC-Net, we set original transposed convolution for up-sampling in θ_A, and simultaneously set tri-linear interpolation as a up-sampling in θ_B. This process can be formulate as follows,

$$P_A = f_A(x;\ \theta_A),$$
$$P_B = f_B(x;\ \theta_B),$$

(1)

where $f_A(x;\ \theta_A)$ and $f_B(x;\ \theta_B)$ respectively represents the first pipeline with decoder θ_A and the second pipeline with decoder θ_B.

Instead of solely apply confidence threshold to select qualified pseudo labels, we design two distinct transform strategy to separately generate pseudo labels with different emphasis. Specially, we use dynamic confidence threshold to select high-certainty pixels in the first decoder θ_A, while apply prior constrain to eliminate high-confidence but unrealistic pixels in the second decoder θ_B (Fig. 2).

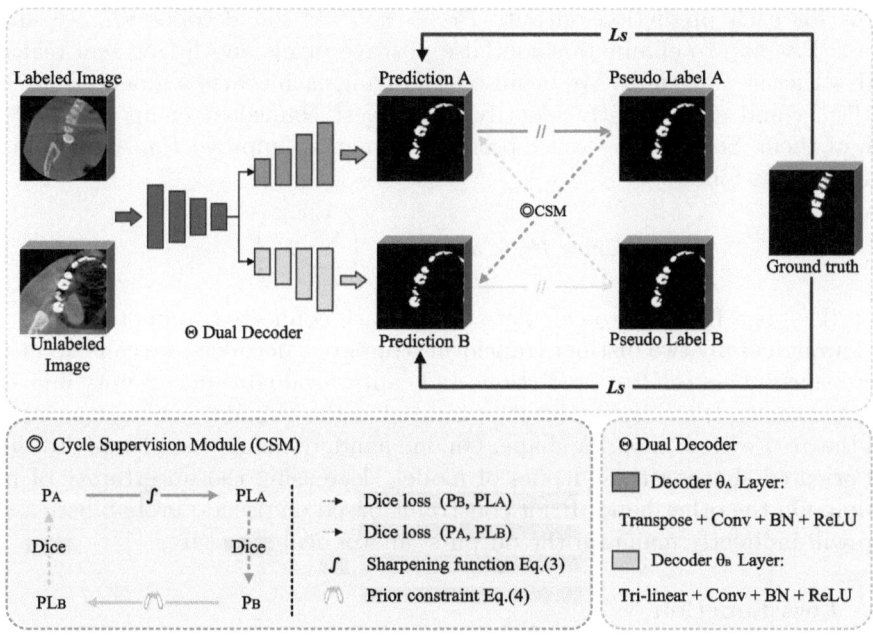

Fig. 2. Diagram of our second phase semi-supervised segmentation method.

Dual PL Generation Strategy. Solely set a fixed threshold obviously ignoring model performance generation. Therefore, it is of great necessity to find a suitable confidence threshold during model training. Inspired by [17], we design a dynamic confidence threshold based on two decoders' outputs to achieve entropy minimization. Specially, as for each prediction outputs $P_A \in \mathbb{R}^{2 \times H \times W}$ in decoder θ_A, we first transform these prediction outputs into certainty map $C_A \in \mathbb{R}^{1 \times H \times W}$, which can formulate as follows,

$$C_A = 1 - exp\left(1 - \frac{p_{max}}{p_{min}}\right), \tag{2}$$

where p_{max} and p_{min} respectively denotes the larger and the smaller value of prediction outputs P_A in each pixel. Obviously, pixels in C_A have larger value means the higher certainty, whose range is $[0, 1)$.

To reduce the impact from uncertain pixels, we multiply prediction outputs P_A with certainty map C_A, and then select the pixels, whose value beyond the 60th value of C_A, as pseudo labels PL_A. Finally, we define pseudo labels PL_A in decoder A θ_A as follows,

$$PL_A = \mathbb{K}\left[P_A \otimes C_A > \alpha_t\right], \tag{3}$$

where α_t represents the 60th certainty value of C_A.

As for each prediction outputs $P_B \in \mathbb{R}^{2 \times H \times W}$ in decoder θ_B, we apply pseudo PA-map to eliminate some false positive pixels and fitting real realistic teeth structure. Specially, We begin by averaging each coarse segmentation $\mathcal{P}_i \in \mathbb{R}^{1 \times H \times W}$, and subsequently identify the largest connected component within each of them. Secondary, we use pseudo PA-map to improve P_B, which can be formulated as follows,

$$PL_B = P_B \otimes \arg\max_{V} V\left(\sum_{i=1}^{N_u} \mathcal{P}_i\right), \tag{4}$$

where $V(\cdot)$ is a function to calculate size of each connected component.

Through apply two distinct transform strategy in decoders, we can extent the discrepancies between two predictions and capture valuable uncertainty information. Generally, these uncertainty are located in the boundary of segment object and the area with same prior shape. On one hand, dynamic confidence threshold will oriented sharpen the outputs of model, decreasing the uncertainty of prediction. On the other hand, Prior constraint based on pseudo probabilistic atlas map will indirectly maintain the outputs' anatomical structure.

2.3   Loss Function

As mentioned above, our goal is to minimize the sum of segmentation loss and consistency loss at each training epoch. Specially, as for each labeled image, we use Dice loss to minimize the dissimilarity between "Ground Truth" and both two predictions P_A and P_B from different decoders in Eq. 6. The processing of train unlabeled images is quite similar with labeled images', and difference between them are only optimizing model parameters. As for each unlabeled image, we correspondingly generate pseudo labels PL_A and PL_B for two predictions, and then use Dice loss to optimize the model parameters in Eq. 7. The total loss is as follows,

$$L = L_s + \lambda_u L_u, \tag{5}$$

where L_s and L_u respectively represents the supervised and unsupervised loss, λ_u is the weight of unsupervised loss, and set as 0.5 in our experiments. Both supervised and unsupervised loss are formulated as follows,

$$L_s = \frac{1}{2|D_l|} \sum_{(x_i, y_i) \in D_l} [Dice(P_A, y_i) + Dice(P_B, y_i)], \tag{6}$$

$$L_u = \frac{1}{2|D_u|} \sum_{(x_i) \in D_u} [Dice(P_B, PL_A) + Dice(P_A, PL_B)]. \tag{7}$$

Table 1. Development environments and requirements.

System	Ubuntu 20.04 LTS
CPU	Intel(R) Core(TM) i7-9700 CPU@3.30GHz
RAM	8×2GB
GPU (number and type)	Two NVIDIA 3090 16G
CUDA version	11.8
Programming language	Python 3.8.16
Deep learning framework	torch 2.0.0, torchvision 0.15.0

2.4   Post-processing

We use a connected components algorithm to group pixels in the segmentation results into different connected regions, representing various areas in the image. By sorting these connected regions based on pixel count, the largest connected region typically represents the primary target, while smaller connected regions may result from noise or minor structures. To better model the spatial relationships of smaller connected regions with respect to the main target, the module calculates the Euclidean distance between the centroid of each non-maximum connected region and the centroid of the largest connected region. This distance provides information about the relative positions of smaller connected components to the main target. We select 120 as the threshold and eliminate the connected components whose distance is bigger than 120.

3   Experiments

3.1   Dataset

We evaluate our proposed method on teeth segmentation datasets from the MIC-CAI 2023 Challenge, which consists of 362 CBCT images with 12 labeled images, 300 unlabeled images, and 50 test images. To prevent potential model degradation caused by an excessive number of unlabeled images, we randomly selecting 50 unlabeled images into our training datasets. All volume from this datasets are 3D and in different size. In a word, we train our model and other semi-supervised segmentation method based on 10 labeled images, 50 unlabeled images, and valid in 2 labeled images. For fair comparison, we only evaluate our model and other methods in test datasets. More details about data pre-processing are introduced in Sect. 2.1.

3.2   Implementation Details and Training Protocols

Throughout the entire experimental process, we implemented our code based on PyTorch library, while all model are trained on two NVIDIA 3090 GPUs. During the second model training phase, we use Adam optimizer with initial learning

Table 2. Training protocols.

Network initialization	Random
Batch size	2
Patch size($2^n d$ phase model)	$256 \times 256 \times 72$
Total epochs	500
Optimizer	Adam
Initial learning(lr)	$1e^{-3}$
Lr decay schedule	Cosinoidal decay
Loss function	KL divergence and Dice

rate of $1e^{-3}$ for 500 epochs and the learning rate are in cosinoidal decay. We mainly apply Dice loss and KL divergence to optimize the model parameters, more detail about our designed loss function in Sec. refloss. More environment settings and training protocols are in Table 1 and 2.

4   Results and Discussion

4.1   Quantitative Results on Test Set

To validate the effectiveness of our method, we conduct comparative experiments with the following state-of-the-art semi-supervised medical image segmentation methods, as shown in Table 3. It is noteworthy that all our experiments are evaluated on 50 test cases using metrics such as Dice coefficient (Dice), Intersection over Union (IOU), and Hausdorff Distance (HD). Following the provided calculation methods online, we also calculate the weighted averages of the above-mentioned metrics as the final evaluation indicators, which are formulated as $Score = 0.4 \times Dice + 0.3 \times IOU + 0.3 \times (1 - HD)$.

Table 3. Comparison with existing methods on MICCAI 2023 Challenge STS database

Method	Image Usage		Online Validation			
	Labeled	Unlabeled	Dice(%)	IOU(%)	HD(mm)	Score(%)
DAP	10	50	0.6631	0.7468	0.1874	0.7331
UA-MT	10	50	0.6864	0.7627	**0.1634**	0.7543
MC-Net	10	50	0.7664	0.8111	0.1870	0.7938
C-CPS (w/o CMS)	10	50	0.7634	0.8091	0.1956	0.7894
C-CPS (w/ CMS)	10	50	**0.7670**	**0.8146**	0.1642	**0.8019**

As seen in Table 3, our proposed method (C-CPS) are outperformed most of semi-supervised methods on 20% proportion of labeled images. Additionally, we

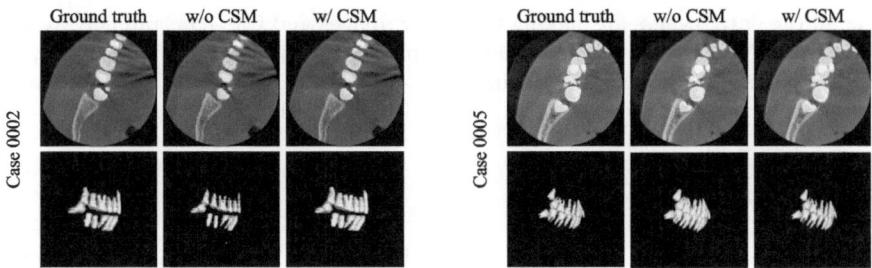

Fig. 3. Two segmentation results obtained without and with CMS.

also analyze the effectiveness of our Cycle Supervision Module (CSM) in the last two rows. Taken the experiments without CSM as basis experiment, CSM bring an improvement by 0.36% in Dice, 0.55% in IOU, and −3.14% in normalized HD.

4.2   Qualitative Results on Validation Set

Qualitative results of C-CPS with and without Cycle Supervision Module (CSM) can be seen in Fig. 3. Benefiting from cycle supervision module, results of our method are more approximate to the realistic shape with 50 cases annotated images.

4.3   Limitation and Future Work

In this paper, we generate pseudo PA-map based on the coarse segmentation of unlabeled images, however, such a strategy undoubtedly causing that PA-map contains some of noise. Although we apply connected components algorithm to select the largest one of pseudo PA-map, it is inevitably that model probably learning wrong information during cycle supervision.

5   Conclusion

In this paper, we propose a cascade semi-supervised method named C-CPS. Compared with solely apply generate pseudo labels with sharpen function, we go a step further by leveraging additional information from images without annotations. Building on the concept of cross-pseudo supervision, our proposed method demonstrates satisfactory performance, particularly in the context of imbalanced datasets.

Acknowledgements. The authors of this paper declare that the segmentation method they implemented for participation in the STS 2023 challenge has not used any pre-trained models nor additional datasets other than those provided by the organizers. The proposed solution is fully automatic without any manual intervention. We thank all the data owners for making the X-ray images and CT scans publicly available and Alibaba Cloud for hosting the challenge platform. This work is supported by Zhejiang Provincial Natural Science Foundation of China (LY22A010003), and National Natural Science Foundation of China (Grant No. 11801511).

References

1. Bai, W., Oktay, O., Sinclair, M., Suzuki, H., Rajchl, M., Tarroni, G., Glocker, B., King, A., Matthews, P.M., Rueckert, D.: Semi-supervised learning for network-based cardiac MR image segmentation. In: Descoteaux, M., Maier-Hein, L., Franz, A., Jannin, P., Collins, D.L., Duchesne, S. (eds.) MICCAI 2017. LNCS, vol. 10434, pp. 253–260. Springer, Cham (2017). https://doi.org/10.1007/978-3-319-66185-8_29
2. Chen, X., Yuan, Y., Zeng, G., Wang, J.: Semi-supervised semantic segmentation with cross pseudo supervision. In: Proceedings of the IEEE/CVF Conference on Computer Vision and Pattern Recognition, pp. 2613–2622 (2021)
3. Chen, Z., Zhang, R., Zhang, G., Ma, Z., Lei, T.: Digging into pseudo label: a low-budget approach for semi-supervised semantic segmentation. IEEE Access **8**, 41830–41837 (2020)
4. Dong, C., et al.: Segmentation of liver and spleen based on computational anatomy models. Comput. Biol. Med. **67**, 146–160 (2015)
5. Isensee, F., Jaeger, P.F., Kohl, S.A., Petersen, J., Maier-Hein, K.H.: nnu-net: a self-configuring method for deep learning-based biomedical image segmentation. Nat. Methods **18**(2), 203–211 (2021)
6. Li, S., Zhang, C., He, X.: Shape-aware semi-supervised 3D semantic segmentation for medical images. In: Martel, A.L., Abolmaesumi, P., Stoyanov, D., Mateus, D., Zuluaga, M.A., Zhou, S.K., Racoceanu, D., Joskowicz, L. (eds.) MICCAI 2020. LNCS, vol. 12261, pp. 552–561. Springer, Cham (2020). https://doi.org/10.1007/978-3-030-59710-8_54
7. Lu, L., Yin, M., Fu, L., Yang, F.: Uncertainty-aware pseudo-label and consistency for semi-supervised medical image segmentation. Biomed. Signal Process. Control **79**, 104203 (2023)
8. Mittal, S., Tatarchenko, M., Brox, T.: Semi-supervised semantic segmentation with high-and low-level consistency. IEEE Trans. Pattern Anal. Mach. Intell. **43**(4), 1369–1379 (2019)
9. Ouali, Y., Hudelot, C., Tami, M.: Semi-supervised semantic segmentation with cross-consistency training. In: Proceedings of the IEEE/CVF Conference on Computer Vision and Pattern Recognition, pp. 12674–12684 (2020)
10. Peng, J., Estrada, G., Pedersoli, M., Desrosiers, C.: Deep co-training for semi-supervised image segmentation. Pattern Recogn. **107**, 107269 (2020)
11. Sohn, K., et al.: Fixmatch: simplifying semi-supervised learning with consistency and confidence. Adv. Neural. Inf. Process. Syst. **33**, 596–608 (2020)
12. Wu, H., Prasad, S.: Semi-supervised deep learning using pseudo labels for hyperspectral image classification. IEEE Trans. Image Process. **27**(3), 1259–1270 (2017)
13. Wu, Y., Xu, M., Ge, Z., Cai, J., Zhang, L.: Semi-supervised Left Atrium Segmentation with Mutual Consistency Training. In: de Bruijne, M., Cattin, P.C., Cotin, S., Padoy, N., Speidel, S., Zheng, Y., Essert, C. (eds.) MICCAI 2021. LNCS, vol. 12902, pp. 297–306. Springer, Cham (2021). https://doi.org/10.1007/978-3-030-87196-3_28

14. Xu, Y., et al.: Dash: semi-supervised learning with dynamic thresholding. In: International Conference on Machine Learning, pp. 11525–11536. PMLR (2021)

15. Xu, Y., et al.: Cross-model pseudo-labeling for semi-supervised action recognition. In: Proceedings of the IEEE/CVF Conference on Computer Vision and Pattern Recognition, pp. 2959–2968 (2022)

16. Yu, L., Wang, S., Li, X., Fu, C.-W., Heng, P.-A.: Uncertainty-aware self-ensembling model for semi-supervised 3D left atrium segmentation. In: Shen, D., Liu, T., Peters, T.M., Staib, L.H., Essert, C., Zhou, S., Yap, P.-T., Khan, A. (eds.) MICCAI 2019. LNCS, vol. 11765, pp. 605–613. Springer, Cham (2019). https://doi.org/10.1007/978-3-030-32245-8_67

17. Zhang, Y., et al.: Multi-phase liver tumor segmentation with spatial aggregation and uncertain region inpainting. In: de Bruijne, M., Cattin, P.C., Cotin, S., Padoy, N., Speidel, S., Zheng, Y., Essert, C. (eds.) MICCAI 2021. LNCS, vol. 12901, pp. 68–77. Springer, Cham (2021). https://doi.org/10.1007/978-3-030-87193-2_7

18. Zheng, H., et al.: Semi-supervised segmentation of liver using adversarial learning with deep atlas prior. In: Shen, D., et al. (eds.) MICCAI 2019. LNCS, vol. 11769, pp. 148–156. Springer, Cham (2019). https://doi.org/10.1007/978-3-030-32226-7_17

19. Zhong, Y., Yuan, B., Wu, H., Yuan, Z., Peng, J., Wang, Y.X.: Pixel contrastive-consistent semi-supervised semantic segmentation. In: Proceedings of the IEEE/CVF International Conference on Computer Vision, pp. 7273–7282 (2021)

High-Precision Semi-supervised 3D Dental Segmentation Based on nnUNet

Bingyan Zhang[1]([✉])[ID] and Xuefei Zhu[2][ID]

[1] Dalian Maritime University, Dalian, China
m15566499051@163.com
[2] Sunwoda Electronic Co., Ltd., Shenzhen, China

Abstract. In the field of medical imaging, tooth segmentation based on 3D Cone-Beam Computed Tomography (CBCT) is recognized as a very challenging task. Precise segmentation of the teeth is crucial for dental diagnosis and treatment planning, providing dentists with detailed tooth structure information to facilitate personalized treatment planning and improve the success rate of clinical treatment. Based on nnUNet, we developed a tooth segmentation method suitable for 3D CBCT data. This innovative training process combines a semi-supervised learning method based on Kullback-Leibler divergence and a supervised learning strategy combined with dynamic convolution and introduces morphology-based preprocessing operations in data processing. In the MICCAI STS 2023 Challenge: STS-3D CBCT-based tooth segmentation task, our method achieved a Dice similarity coefficient of 0.9111 and 0.7261, an IoU of 0.9164 and 0.7855, and a 3D Hausdorff distance of 0.0453 and 0.2595 on the preliminary and rematch test data set.

Keywords: Semi-supervised learning · Tooth segmentation · MICCAI STS Challenge

1 Introduction

As a key issue in the field of medical image analysis, the automatic and accurate segmentation of teeth from 3D Cone Beam Computed Tomography (CBCT) images holds paramount significance for computer-assisted dental diagnosis, oral surgery planning, dental visual assistance systems, orthodontic treatment evaluation, and the identification of oral health biomarkers [5,6]. In related medical image segmentation competitions, nnUNet [8] frequently emerges as a core component of numerous top solutions, demonstrating exceptional performance. However, its substantial consumption of CPU memory and GPU resources correspondingly escalates the demand for computational resources. Enhancing accuracy without increasing computational resource consumption presents a challenge. Moreover, nnUNet mainly focuses on supervised learning, and while medical imaging data is abundant, data annotation requires significant human and material resources. Therefore, the industry faces the challenge of using unannotated data for model training to achieve high precision standards, thereby resolving the difficulties associated with manual annotation [1].

Y. Wang et al. (Eds.): STS 2023, LNCS 14623, pp. 180–191, 2025.
https://doi.org/10.1007/978-3-031-72396-4_16

In this paper, we have designed an improved nnUNet architecture that incorporates dynamic convolution techniques and proposed a pseudo-label semi-supervised learning method based on Kullback-Leibler divergence [11]. The aim is to achieve high precision semi-supervised 3D CBCT dental segmentation without increasing the computational resource burden and without adding to the workload of manual annotation.

The main contributions of this study are summarized as follows:

- During the model training process, a semi-supervised algorithm is utilized. A novel uncertainty correction module is proposed, enabling the framework to progressively learn from meaningful and reliable consensus regions across different scales. For the 12 labeled cases, supervised learning is conducted on the four outputs of the decoder using cross-entropy loss and dice loss. For the 500 unlabeled CT samples, KL-divergence loss is used as a measure of uncertainty between the average prediction and the predictions at four scales, and pseudo labels are computed accordingly.
- An improved nnUNet scheme incorporating dynamic convolution techniques is proposed. This strategy, while maintaining or even enhancing segmentation accuracy, effectively optimizes the use of computational resources, exhibiting higher efficiency particularly when processing medical images with diverse features.
- Before inputting into nnUNet, morphological operations are applied to 3D CBCT data, utilizing the morphological characteristics of teeth (size, shape, and relative position) to guide nnUNet for more accurate segmentation of teeth.

2   Method

2.1   Preprocessing

We employed a preprocessing step based on morphological prior knowledge to optimize the segmentation of 3D CBCT dental images. This preprocessing step aims to leverage the morphological characteristics of teeth to enhance the representation of dental structures in the images, thereby providing clearer and more accurate input data for subsequent nnUNet segmentation. Specifically, before processing, we first analyzed the typical morphological features of teeth in CBCT images, such as their size, shape, and relative position. These characteristics are crucial for determining appropriate morphological operations and parameter selections. Then, based on these features of the teeth, we chose opening and closing operations as the primary morphological operations. The opening operation helps remove small noise points in the image and smooth the edges of the teeth, while the closing operation helps fill small voids inside the teeth and connect adjacent dental structures.

Finally, for the opening and closing operations, we selected elliptical or circular structural elements that match the scale of the teeth. Teeth typically appear as small circular or elliptical areas in images, and we, therefore, chose circular

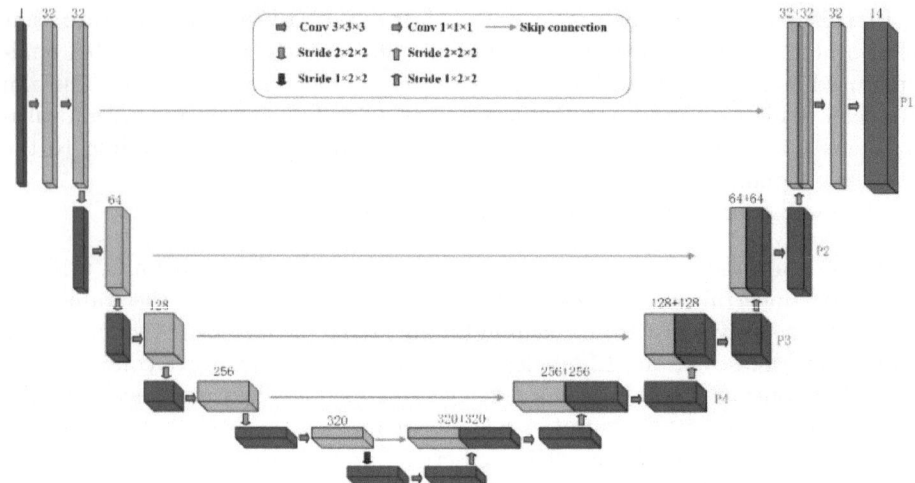

Fig. 1. Baseline network architecture. Four solution piers (P1-P4) are used for subsequent semi-supervised learning.

or elliptical structural elements of corresponding sizes. The size of the structural element is adjusted based on the average size of teeth in CBCT images. The average width of the tooth structures in the images is 10 pixels, so we chose a circular structural element with a diameter of 10 pixels. Additionally, we adjusted other parameters of the morphological operations, such as the number of iterations, to find the optimal balance that highlights the dental structures without overly altering the characteristics of the surrounding tissues.

2.2   Network Architecture

For 3D CBCT data, we utilized a 3D U-Net as our baseline model [10], as shown in Fig. 1. Within the baseline model, we enabled deep supervision, meaning that the four decoding heads P1-P4 will ultimately be used to construct pseudo labels and calculate the KL divergence.

To increase the model's complexity without adding to the network's depth or width, we integrated dynamic convolutions as a substitute for standard convolutions, as illustrated in Fig. 2. Dynamic convolutions do not employ a single convolution kernel per layer but rather dynamically aggregate multiple parallel convolution kernels based on input-dependent attention. As the kernels are small in size, combining multiple convolution kernels is not only computationally efficient but also provides a stronger representational capability due to the kernels being aggregated in a non-linear manner through attention [8].

In the dynamic convolution layer [2], the parameters of Avg pool, FC, ReLU, FC, conv1, conv2, and conv3 are fixed, while the parameters of softmax, $\pi 1$, $\pi 2$, $\pi 3$, and conv change dynamically with the input data. Compared to static convolution, dynamic convolution has a stronger capability for feature representation.

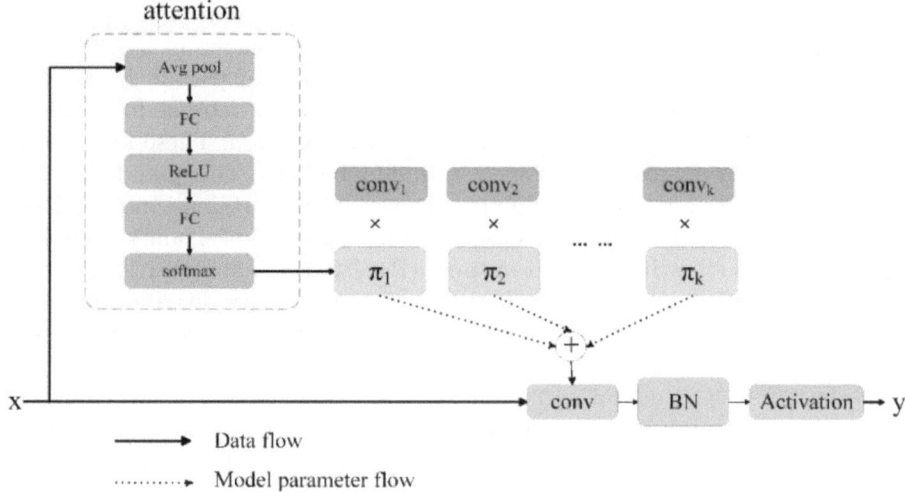

Fig. 2. Dynamic convolution layer, where π is the attention weight, which is not fixed but changes with input.

Dynamic convolution involves two additional computations: (a) the calculation of attention weights; and (b) the dynamic fusion of weights. Nevertheless, the computational load of these additional calculations is so minimal that it can be considered negligible compared to that of convolution. Unlike the usual integration of attention mechanisms, such as in SENet [7], which assigns attention to channels, dynamic convolution assigns attention to the convolution kernels. Since these kernels are relatively small, the process of kernel integration is computationally efficient [9].

2.3 Semi-supervised Learning

Description of Semi-supervised Learning of the Model. Given that there were only 12 labeled samples and 500 unlabeled samples, the training strategy of the model primarily revolved around this semi-supervised learning algorithm. We proposed a new uncertainty correction module, enabling the network framework to progressively learn from meaningful and reliable consensus areas of different scales [12].

Supervised Learning Part. First, training was conducted on the dataset of 12 labeled samples. The training adopted a standard supervised learning approach, using a 3D U-Net architecture combined with dynamic convolution, as shown in Fig. 2. This architecture has four different outputs (P1, P2, P3, and P4). Cross-entropy loss and dice loss were used to minimize the gap between the predictions and the true labels.

Semi-supervised Learning Part. Then, semi-supervised training was conducted on unlabeled data (500 unlabeled samples). As shown in Fig. 3, the following steps were applied to optimize the generation of pseudo labels: 1) A forward pass (inference) of the model was performed to obtain four different outputs (P1, P2, P3, and P4). 2) Pseudo Label Generation: These four outputs were added and averaged to generate a 'pseudo label' (P). This pseudo label was a temporary 'true label' for the unlabeled data. 3) Uncertainty and KL Divergence: The KL divergence loss was used as a measure of uncertainty, comparing the pseudo label (P) with the four outputs (P1, P2, P3, and P4). KL divergence is used to quantify the differences between two probability distributions. Here, it was employed to measure the similarity between the model's predictions and the generated pseudo labels.

In the 3D CBCT dental segmentation task, there are only two categories: teeth and background. In this context, the calculation process for KL divergence is as follows: first, obtain the four outputs (P1, P2, P3, and P4) and the averaged pseudo label (P); then, normalize all outputs and the pseudo label at each 3D voxel point to form valid probability distributions.

$$P_{teeth,i} + P_{background,i} = 1 \tag{1}$$

$$P'_{teeth,i} + P'_{background,i} = 1 \tag{2}$$

Next, the calculation of KL divergence is performed. For each voxel point P_j in the output of each decoder head, there are two probabilities: one is the probability that the voxel point $P_{teeth,j}$, j belongs to teeth, and the other is the probability that the voxel point $P_{background,j}$ belongs to the background. Similarly, the pseudo label also has two probabilities for each voxel point: $P_{teeth,i}$, $P_{background}$, and for that pixel point, the formula for calculating the KL divergence is as follows:

$$KL_{j,teeth} = P_{j,teeth} \log(\frac{P_{j,teeth} + \epsilon}{P_{teeth} + \epsilon}) + P_{j,background} \log(\frac{P_{j,background} + \epsilon}{P_{background} + \epsilon}) \tag{3}$$

where $KL_{j,teeth}$ represents the KL divergence corresponding to the output of the decoder head j; ϵ is a small positive number 1e-10; which is added to the logarithm function to avoid computing $\log(0)$.

Finally, the average KL divergence calculated for all voxel points gives the overall KL divergence for each decoder head. The four decoder heads vote based on the KL divergence and a set threshold. A pseudo label for an unlabeled sample is saved for subsequent training only when at least three out of the four outputs have a KL divergence lower than the set threshold.

Final Model Training. After filtering to obtain all high-quality pseudo labels through KL divergence, the corresponding samples are combined with the 12 samples to form a dataset. This dataset is then trained on the improved nnUNet architecture for 1000 epochs. The model obtained from this final training is used to make inferences on the test set.

3   Experiments

3.1   Dataset and Evaluation Measures

The MICCAI 2023 Challenges: STS - 3D CBCT Dental Segmentation Task dataset was curated by multiple medical groups, including the Hangzhou Dental Group, Hangzhou Qiantang Dental Hospital, University of Electronic Science and Technology of China, and Queen Mary University of London. The training set for the preliminary and semifinal rounds includes 12 labeled dental CT scans (approximately 2400 slices) and 600 unlabeled dental CT scans (approximately 100000 slices) [3,4]. The test set comprises 60 CT scans (approximately 12000 slices). The task objectives are as follows in the diagram below:

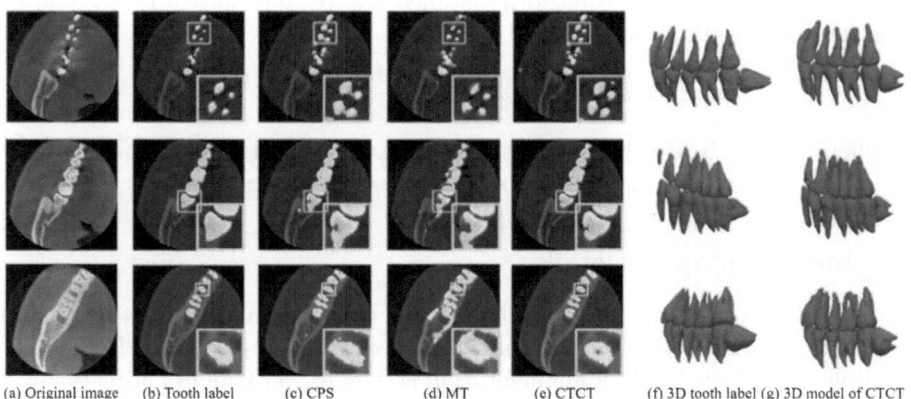

(a) Original image   (b) Tooth label   (c) CPS   (d) MT   (e) CTCT   (f) 3D tooth label (g) 3D model of CTCT

Fig. 3. Data set visualization example.

3.2   Evaluation Metrics

We perform dental segmentation on all images in the test set, generating corresponding binary masks. The predicted masks are compared with the baseline masks using Dice, Hausdorff distance, and IOU metrics.

The Dice Coefficient is used to evaluate the similarity between two sets, with the formula is calculated as follows:

$$Dice = \frac{2 * |A \cap B|}{|A| + |B|} \tag{4}$$

Table 1. Development environments and requirements.

System	Windows 10
CPU	AMD EPYC 7V13 26-Core Processor
RAM	96GB
GPU (number and type)	One NVDIA GeForce RTX 3090 24G
CUDA version	11.7
Programming language	Python 3.8
Deep learning framework	Pytorch (torch 2.0.0)

The intersection over union (IoU) formula is as follows:

$$IoU = \frac{|A \cap B|}{|A| + |B|} \tag{5}$$

The three-dimensional Hausdorff distance is a distance measure based on the voxel level, the formula is:

$$H(d) = min(|x1 - x2| + |y1 - y2| + |z1 - z2|) \tag{6}$$

where A and B are the predicted label of model and the true label respectively; $(x1, y1, z1)$ and $(x2, y2, z2)$ present the coordinates of A and B.

3.3   Implementation Details

Data Augmentation. During the training process, to enhance the generalization ability of the 3D Cone Beam Computed Tomography (3D CBCT) data, we applied a variety of data augmentation strategies: 1) Gamma adjustment to modify the brightness contrast of the images; 2) Introduction of random scaling within the range of [0.8, 1.2] to ensure the model can better handle dental images of various sizes; 3) Random contrast enhancement and Gaussian blur to simulate a range of challenges that images might encounter in the real world; 4) Considering slight differences in relative angles and positions during the scanning process, we also introduced minor random rotations and small translations.

Environment Configuration and Hyperparameters. Table 1 lists the environment configuration and requirements. Hyperparameter configuration and details are shown in Table 2.

Table 2. Training protocols.

Network Initialization	"He" normal initialization
Batch size	2
Total iterations	1000
Optimizer	SGD with nesterov momentum($\mu= 0.9$)
Initial learning rate (lr)	0.01
Lr decay schedule	PolyLRScheduler
Training time	30 h
Number of model parameters	30.86M
Number of flops	68.43G

Table 3. Evaluation metrics of the internal validation dataset: Dice coefficient, Intersection over Union (IoU), and three-dimensional Hausdorff distance.

Method	Dice coefficient(%)↑	IoU(%)↑	Hausdorff distance (%)↓
Our	0.7868	0.8254	0.1866

Table 4. Ablation experiments on different modules.

Preprocessing	CondConv	Unlabeled Data	Dice coefficient(%)↑	IoU(%)↑	Hausdorff distance (%)↓
			0.7256	0.7988	0.2054
✓			0.7416	0.8102	0.1977
✓	✓		0.7544	0.8129	0.1982
✓	✓	✓	0.7868	0.8254	0.1866

4 Results and Discussion

4.1 Quantitative Results on Validation Set

We employed a five-fold cross-validation locally, and the overall results averaged across the metrics on the five validation sets are as shown in Table 3. Our method achieved a Dice similarity coefficient of 0.7868, an IoU of 0.8254, and a three dimensional Hausdorff distance of 0.1866 on the five-fold validation sets.

We conducted ablation experiments on our internal five-fold validation set to analyze the impact of various improvements on model performance, as shown in Table 4. Our segmentation baseline, trained on a standard nnUNet, achieved a Dice coefficient of 0.7256, an IoU of 0.7988, and a three-dimensional Hausdorff distance of 0.2054 on the validation set. By adopting a morphological preprocessing approach, we reached a Dice coefficient of 0.7416, an IoU of 0.8102, and a three-dimensional Hausdorff distance of 0.1977 on the validation set. Building upon this, the use of an architecture combined with dynamic convolution achieved a Dice coefficient of 0.7544, an IoU of 0.8129, and a three-dimensional Hausdorff distance of 0.1982. By further adding unlabeled data, we ultimately

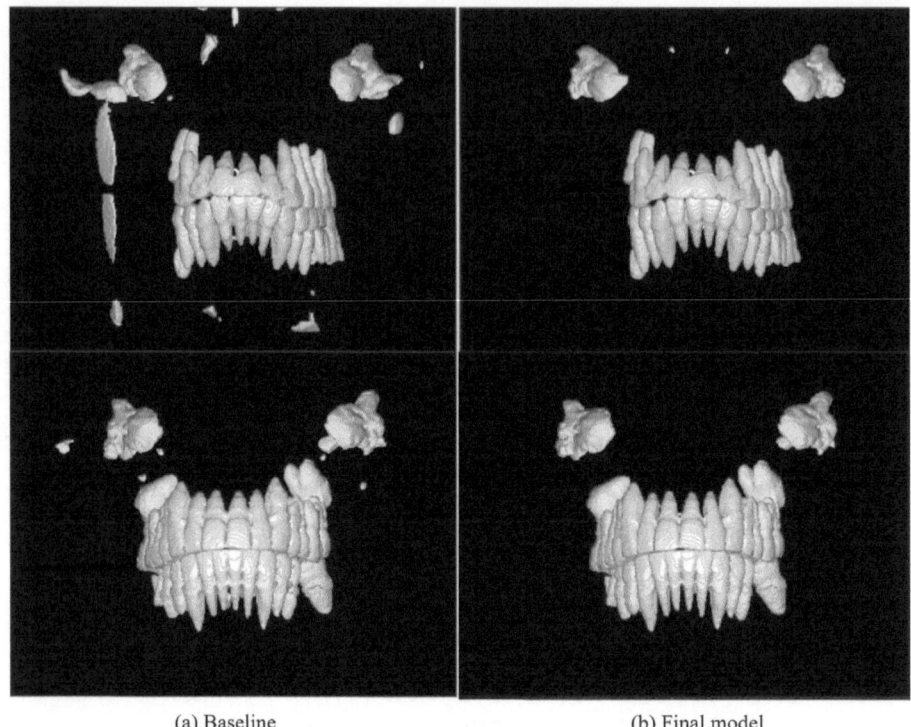

(a) Baseline   (b) Final model

Fig. 4. 3D visualization of Baseline versus Final Model segmentation results.

reached a Dice coefficient of 0.7868, an IoU of 0.8254, and a three-dimensional Hausdorff distance of 0.1866.

As shown in Fig. 4, from the 3D images in the figure, it can be seen that compared to the Baseline, our final model ignored most of the false positives and also achieved better visual effects.

4.2 Qualitative Results on Validation Set

We analyzed samples that were relatively well-predicted and those that were poorly predicted, as shown in Fig. 5 and 6 respectively. Figure 5 presents a well-segmented data sample, where it can be observed that well-segmented cases have clear dental boundaries, and the dental regions are localized. Figure 6 shows a poorly segmented data sample, where it can be observed that the dental structures on the horizontal plane are more complex. How to accurately identify and segment dental structures from CT images with other misleading elements is a challenge we need to address in the future.

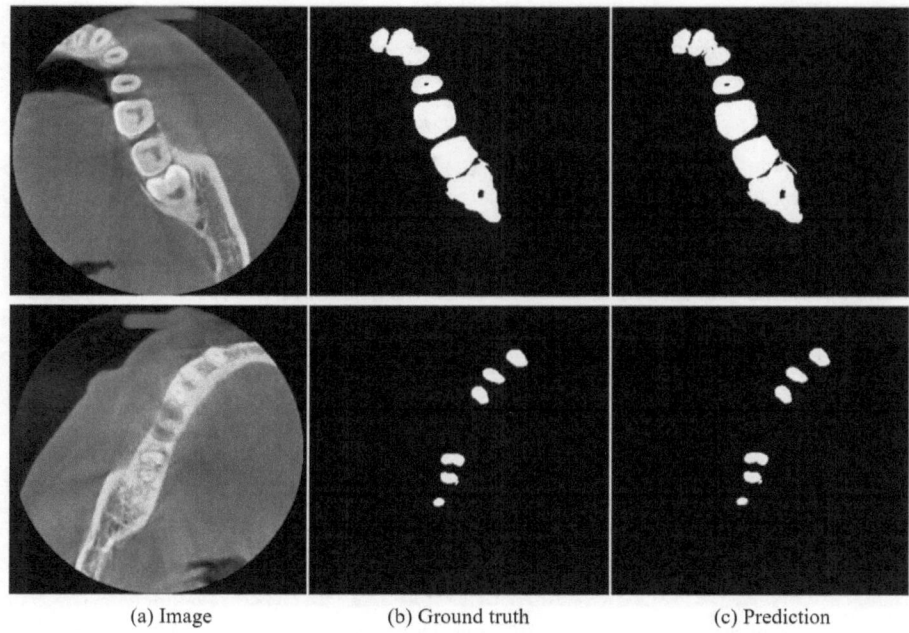

| (a) Image | (b) Ground truth | (c) Prediction |

Fig. 5. Good segmentation cases.

Table 5. Dice coefficient, Intersection over Union (IoU), and three-dimensional Hausdorff distance in the test data set of the preliminary and final.

Stage	Dice coefficient(%)↑	IoU(%)↑	Hausdorff distance (%)↓	Score (%)↑
Preliminary round	0.9111	0.9164	0.0453	0.9258
Final round	0.7261	0.7855	0.2595	0.7483

4.3   Results on Final Testing Set

The overall results are presented in Table 5. Our method achieved a score of 0.9258/0.7483 on the preliminary/semifinal test dataset of the MICCAI 2023 Challenges: STS - 3D CBCT Dental Segmentation Task.

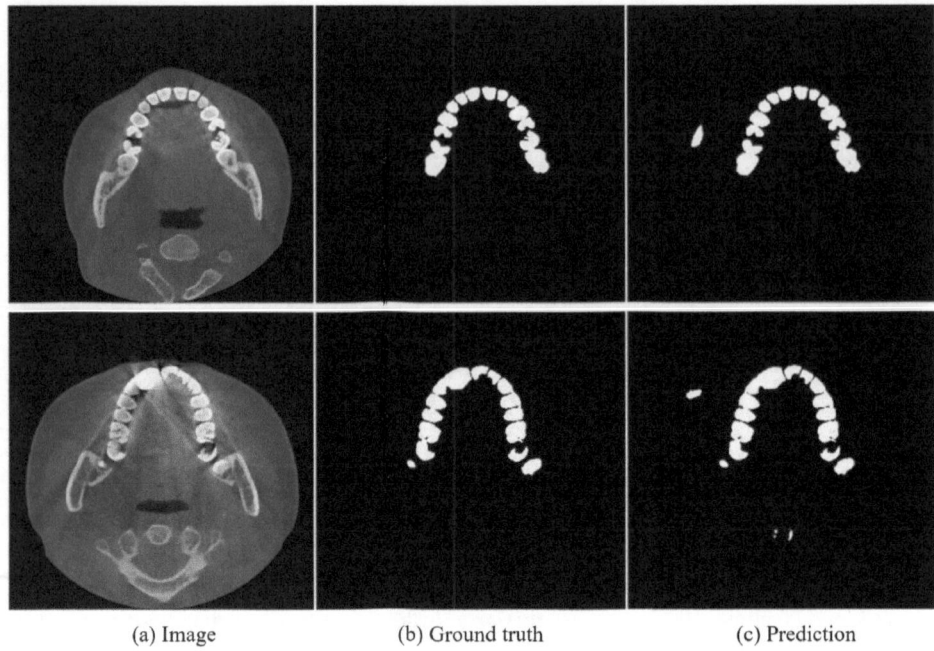

(a) Image   (b) Ground truth   (c) Prediction

Fig. 6. Failure segmentation cases.

5   Conclusion

In this paper, we developed a dental segmentation method for 3D CBCT data based on nnUNet. This innovative training process integrates a semi-supervised learning method based on Kullback-Leibler divergence and a supervised learning strategy combined with dynamic convolution, with morphological preprocessing operations introduced in data processing. Through quantitative evaluation, this method achieved a Dice coefficient of 0.7868, an IoU of 0.8254, and a three-dimensional Hausdorff distance of 0.1866 on the validation dataset. It also achieved Dice similarity coefficients of $0.9111/0.7261$, IOUs of $0.9164/0.7855$, and three-dimensional Hausdorff distances of $0.0453/0.2595$ on the preliminary/final test dataset of the MICCAI 2023 Challenges: STS - 3D CBCT Dental Segmentation Task.

Acknowledgements. The authors of this paper declare that the segmentation method they implemented for participation in the STS 2023 challenge has not used any pre-trained models nor additional datasets other than those provided by the organizers. The proposed solution is fully automatic without any manual intervention. We thank all the data owners for making the X-ray images and CT scans publicly available and Alibaba Cloud for hosting the challenge platform.

References

1. Chen, X., Yuan, Y., Zeng, G., Wang, J.: Semi-supervised semantic segmentation with cross pseudo supervision. In: Proceedings of the IEEE/CVF Conference on Computer Vision and Pattern Recognition, pp. 2613–2622 (2021)
2. Chen, Y., Dai, X., Liu, M., Chen, D., Yuan, L., Liu, Z.: Dynamic convolution: attention over convolution kernels. In: Proceedings of the IEEE/CVF Conference on Computer Vision and Pattern Recognition, pp. 11030–11039 (2020)
3. Cui, W., et al.: Ctooth+: a large-scale dental cone beam computed tomography dataset and benchmark for tooth volume segmentation. In: MICCAI Workshop on Data Augmentation, Labelling, and Imperfections, pp. 64–73. Springer, Cham (2022). https://doi.org/10.1007/978-3-031-17027-0_7
4. Cui, W., et al.: Ctooth: a fully annotated 3d dataset and benchmark for tooth volume segmentation on cone beam computed tomography images. In: International Conference on Intelligent Robotics and Applications, pp. 191–200. Springer (2022). https://doi.org/10.1007/978-3-031-13841-6_18
5. Cui, Z., et al.: A fully automatic ai system for tooth and alveolar bone segmentation from cone-beam ct images. Nat. Commun. **13**(1), 2096 (2022)
6. Cui, Z., Li, C., Wang, W.: Toothnet: automatic tooth instance segmentation and identification from cone beam ct images. In: Proceedings of the IEEE/CVF Conference on Computer Vision and Pattern Recognition, pp. 6368–6377 (2019)
7. Hu, J., Shen, L., Sun, G.: Squeeze-and-excitation networks. In: Proceedings of the IEEE Conference on Computer Vision and Pattern Recognition, pp. 7132–7141 (2018)
8. Isensee, F., Jaeger, P.F., Kohl, S.A., Petersen, J., Maier-Hein, K.H.: nnu-net: a self-configuring method for deep learning-based biomedical image segmentation. Nat. Methods **18**(2), 203–211 (2021)
9. Luo, X., Liao, W., Chen, J., Song, T., Chen, Y., Zhang, S., Chen, N., Wang, G., Zhang, S.: Efficient semi-supervised gross target volume of nasopharyngeal carcinoma segmentation via uncertainty rectified pyramid consistency. In: de Bruijne, M., Cattin, P.C., Cotin, S., Padoy, N., Speidel, S., Zheng, Y., Essert, C. (eds.) MICCAI 2021. LNCS, vol. 12902, pp. 318–329. Springer, Cham (2021). https://doi.org/10.1007/978-3-030-87196-3_30
10. Ronneberger, O., Fischer, P., Brox, T.: U-Net: convolutional networks for biomedical image segmentation. In: Navab, N., Hornegger, J., Wells, W.M., Frangi, A.F. (eds.) MICCAI 2015. LNCS, vol. 9351, pp. 234–241. Springer, Cham (2015). https://doi.org/10.1007/978-3-319-24574-4_28
11. Wang, P., Peng, J., Pedersoli, M., Zhou, Y., Zhang, C., Desrosiers, C.: Self-paced and self-consistent co-training for semi-supervised image segmentation. Med. Image Anal. **73**, 102146 (2021)
12. Yang, L., Qi, L., Feng, L., Zhang, W., Shi, Y.: Revisiting weak-to-strong consistency in semi-supervised semantic segmentation. In: Proceedings of the IEEE/CVF Conference on Computer Vision and Pattern Recognition, pp. 7236–7246 (2023)

Author Index

Y. Wang et al. (Eds.): STS 2023, LNCS 14623, pp. 193–194, 2025.
https://doi.org/10.1007/978-3-031-72396-4